Conspiracies

OF THE

Ruling Class

HOW TO BREAK THEIR GRIP FOREVER

LAWRENCE B. LINDSEY

Simon & Schuster

NEW YORK   LONDON   TORONTO   SYDNEY   NEW DELHI

Simon & Schuster
1230 Avenue of the Americas
New York, NY 10020

First Simon & Schuster hardcover edition March 2016

SIMON & SCHUSTER and colophon are registered trademarks of
Simon & Schuster, Inc.

For information about special discounts for bulk purchases,
please contact Simon & Schuster Special Sales at
1-866-506-1949 or business@simonandschuster.com.

The Simon & Schuster Speakers Bureau can bring authors
to your live event. For more information or to book an
event, contact the Simon & Schuster Speakers Bureau at
1-866-248-3049 or visit our website at www.simonspeakers.com.

Interior design by Ruth Lee-Mui

Manufactured in the United States of America

10 9 8 7 6 5 4 3 2 1

Library of Congress Cataloging-in-Publication Data has been applied for.

ISBN 978-1-5011-4423-3
ISBN 978-1-5011-4425-7 (ebook)

To Christine,

Who by reminding me that all Gifts involve a Purpose

Made this book, and much else, possible

Tyranny, like hell, is not easily conquered; yet we have this consolation with us, that the harder the conflict, the more glorious the triumph.

—Thomas Paine,
The American Crisis,
December 1776

CONTENTS

PART 3

Securing Our Liberty Once Again

Conspiracies

OF THE

Ruling Class

Prologue

The American public is angry. They feel the government has become too intrusive, that government has positioned itself as a true "nanny state" and has tried to make itself the source of everything people need, from food, to housing, to health care, to education, to happiness. They feel that government is taking more and more—more resources, more freedom, and more power—and has strayed from how it can best serve them. Public services are misplaced and ineffective. The country is in retreat in the world arena. Those in power seem to see government as a vehicle for themselves: an opportunity to make a personal mark in history and not as a means of helping Americans lead better lives and pursue their dreams.

The public is right to feel this way. We have been badly governed, particularly in the last quarter century, and the trend is one that is spiraling downward at an accelerating rate. This government has been expanding exponentially and has become bloated, unaccountable, out of touch, and replete with fraud, waste, and abuse.

My father used to tell me that when I pointed a finger at someone else, I was pointing three fingers back at me. So let me be up front as I point a finger at what I call the Ruling Class. I was part of the government that hasn't governed well. I served in policy positions in the White House under three presidents. I was a governor of the US Federal Reserve. I was even a professor at Harvard University, which often functions as a government in waiting. So it's hard for me to pretend that I am some powerless victim who has no responsibility for what's happened.

I did serve in government. And while I like to think that most of what I did there was well intentioned and produced some good results, I also saw plenty of things that weren't going as they should. I recognize that I was part of the problem.

I've also interspersed my three stints of government service with one stint in academia—reflecting on that service—and two in business: as managing director of one company and as the CEO of my own firm. Seeing it from the outside as well as the inside has given me a perspective on government that most people don't have—as well as new ideas for finding solutions.

When I was in government, it sure didn't seem like I was part of a Ruling Class. Most of the people I worked with—in both parties—viewed themselves as serving in government for only part of their lives and certainly not as their life's work. When one views oneself that way, you're hardly thinking the way a ruler would, and you certainly don't think of yourself as part of a permanent Ruling Class. We were there to get the job done and move on.

But there was always a core group of people who saw things differently: the experts in bureaucratic politics. They took pleasure in winning battles, not in creating a plan that would lead to an effective and efficient outcome. Saddest of all, they came to see themselves as "naturals" eminently qualified to be in charge: people who were good at fighting and winning political battles and beating enemies into submission. Serving in government was not the means to an end to create a better country but an end in itself. The purpose of their government service was to accumulate personal power and to exercise that power over others. They didn't have a noble cause, even though they always acted as though they did, but a hidden need to wield power and maintain control of their little domain.

You can tell who they are just from watching TV. They enjoy ridiculing their opponents. They tell you how smart they are whenever possible. Some of them like to belittle other people, setting them up as straw men just to knock them down. I will leave it to you to figure out what this says about them psychologically. Sometimes their personality is so *Ruling Class* that you don't even need to watch with the sound on to tell who they are. Just watch their body language: the way they hold their head, or the thrust of their jaw. They just *know* they are superior to you, though they may try to hide it by telling you how they are there to help you, as if you needed their help to run your own life.

I never took these people too seriously until they stopped being content with their own tiny fiefdoms and started turning their attention to the nation and people like me. Back in July 2012, President Barack Obama said, "If you've got a business—you didn't build that." Well, I did build a business. Senator Elizabeth Warren said, "There is nobody in this country who got rich on his own—nobody." Really? And back in October 2014, as she was unofficially kicking off her presidential campaign, former secretary of state Hillary Clinton said, "Don't let anybody tell you it's corporations and businesses that create jobs." Who did, then, the government? Personally, I've hired the people who work for me, and my efforts created those jobs, not the government.

This is not an isolated attitude, but quite widespread among those who now run Washington. These are politicians, appointees, and bureaucrats who had spent their lives ensconced in government or at institutions such as Harvard waiting for their chance to assume a position of political power. This is a class of like-minded people with similar backgrounds and résumés with a classic ruler's attitude: "You couldn't

accomplish that on your own. You needed me to do the hard work because I am smarter and better educated than you."

It seemed to me like such an alien way for a real leader to act. If you
were leading an organization, would you belittle the people in your organization who were the most successful? Wouldn't it make more sense
to thank and congratulate them for a job well done, to encourage them
to do even more in the future, and to empower them to achieve more
success? It would seem to be even more important in the case of a country with an economy that wasn't doing so well. A real leader would be a
cheerleader for accomplishment, not denigrate it.

So I began to think of these people as what they are: the Ruling
Class. They view their jobs not as leaders, who encourage the rest of us to
make the most of our talents, but as people who are superior—as though
they are the shepherds and we the sheep. They ridicule the successful
and do everything they can to make the population dependent on them.

Conspiracies of the Ruling Class is the story of how I came to understand the behavior of people with this mind-set. First, we will examine
the historical roots of the Ruling Class. Our Founding Fathers knew all
about them; they rebelled against their tyranny and set up a government
designed to make it hard for a Ruling Class to assume control. But after
a hundred years of trying, it seems that the Ruling Class have finally
achieved their goals. We might still have the power to dislodge them, but
with the way things are going, we might not have it for long.

Second, we examine the results of the efforts of the Ruling Class;
the fruit of their labor. If they really were as superior as they think they
are, we should live in a trouble-free country. The power and resources
at their disposal are enormous and, if well deployed, should produce a
quality result. But that is not the way it is. Because they are *rulers* and not
real *leaders*, they squander the power and wealth the country gives them,
and when they fail, they come back and ask for more.

Finally, we consider how we can break their grip on power. This will
not be an easy task. It will require a single-minded focus on restoring
liberty and trimming the power the Ruling Class have amassed. There

is a clear majority that supports the values upon which this country was founded, but they must be activated and united. Assuming we can prevail at the ballot box, there are structural changes we can make to get America back on track. Mainly, these changes involve undoing some of the many policies and positions the Ruling Class created to facilitate their hold on power.

We believe that we need to rekindle the vision of liberty that was the impetus for our founding in 1776. America is a *cause*, and not just a *country*. We need to be a beacon of hope and a model for the *right way* to govern in the twenty-first century.

PART 1

The Greatest
Threat to Liberty

CHAPTER 1

A History of Ruling in the Absence of Liberty

For most of human history, mankind has lived under the command of the Ruling Class. Sometimes those in charge did a good job, sometimes not, but the ever-present temptation for those with power to seek even more has always been there. As a result, most people who have ever lived have had very little control of even the most rudimentary aspects of their lives. Their occupations have been determined largely by what their parents did. Their marriages have either been arranged, or their choice in partners has been limited severely by their unchangeable social standing. Their day-to-day activities have not been a matter of choice but have instead been driven by necessity, custom, and the dictates of their overlords. More than 90 percent of the roughly hundred billion people who have ever been born[1] have lived out their lives in fear: fear of dying from starvation, illness, accident, war, or as helpless victims of a totalitarian ruler. Even today, only about a third of the world's population live in democratic countries, and, for most of these, the freedoms they experience are only a heavily watered-down version of what many take for granted in America.

History provides a few short-lived examples where mankind has experimented with individual freedom. More commonly, there has been a ruler or a ruling class that seizes power by offering citizens a better life, through free food, health care, or other services their government can supply, or a solution to real or imagined problems of the moment. These problems usually are manufactured issues involving either a vague, potential threat that can't really be detailed and solved easily (for example, "The crops may fail," or global warming), or issues of conflict with other groups (such as tribalism or racism). The reason the ruler needs to manufacture these problems is that the society needs to be focused only on what the ruler wants and not distracted by their lack of freedoms or individuality. This keeps the "great unwashed masses" in line, peaceful, and accepting of the current ruling class. These rulers' ascension depends ultimately on the assumed superiority of the ruling class to make all the rules the people must follow and on their subjects' acceptance of a society without freedoms.

This book is about a very real battle that will result in either the continuance of the United States as a global beacon of freedom and individual liberty for our children or the end of the American experiment that began almost 250 years ago. To begin, we look back to consider how civilization's early ruling classes rose to a position of prominence, and how they were able to maintain this standing, ruling for their own benefit at the expense of their people.

The Ruler Knows Best (or At Least He Thinks So)

Historically, giving up control of one's life to an all-powerful ruler began as a matter of necessity. Life was dangerous. Starvation was a constant threat. Defeat, death, and capture by another tribe or group were always possibilities. Humans learned early on that they had to stick together to survive. When the tribe went hunting large game, their success was based on teamwork. There might have been some discussion, but ultimately one person called the shots, and the others followed. Those who didn't fall in line risked endangering the entire group. This logic continued when one group came into contact with another: battles were fought—and won—with teamwork under the direction of a few. So, in terms of the effective use of force by the tribe—for food or for battle—it became useful for a few to emerge who gave orders to others.

With the agricultural revolution, the survival of the entire tribe became a matter of planting crops at the right time and hoping that the weather cooperated. "Specialists" emerged who improved the odds of success through early scientific advances, like tracking the movement of the moon and stars. Evidence suggests that large megalithic structures such as Stonehenge functioned to enable these enhanced powers of observation. Though their actual scientific knowledge was likely very basic by today's standards, these specialists were elevated within society because of their importance to the tribe's well-being and often became the religious leaders of the community. After all, no one knew why the seasons happened, just that they did, year after year, and it was left to the specialists, who could specify more accurately when spring would begin, to come up with an explanation.

Useful fictions such as "Who are we to question the will of the gods?" fit the need of the emerging Ruling Class very well. They could say that they possessed a specialized "skill set" not accessible to the common man, and thus held an exclusive position as the gods' mouthpiece to the people. This made them absolutely critical to the group's survival, at least in the narrative they promoted. Conveniently, the Ruling Class continued to refine their marketing message to the masses. If a spring brought unseasonably cold weather and lower crop yields, the story was always some variation of "You have angered the gods because . . ." Or even better, "You can appease the gods again by . . ." But never "I've made a mistake."

Now, pretend you're a member of the community that relies on this specialist to determine when to plant. He's been right most of the time. If you go against his dictates, you risk ruining the crop and starving to death. So, for lack of other options, you follow this specialist and his policies, because the downside is so catastrophic. Coincidence becomes causation, and over time, you and your family grow even more attentive to what the specialist says the gods want in the future, to the point that you're hanging on his every word. In Mesoamerica and many other early cultures, ritual human sacrifice was a regular practice mandated by high priests, the specialists of that time, to appease the gods society worshipped. Though extreme acts like this were barbaric, they were deemed necessary in order for society to continue, and thus became a way of life.

So, early in human history, individuals relinquished significant control of their lives as a matter of survival to the Ruling Class, who were cunning enough to take advantage of their helplessness. The early rulers flourished not because they were exceptionally knowledgeable or skilled but because, even when outnumbered, they were able to rule with elaborately crafted narratives that explained why they deserved a position of such prominence. Of course, they were crafty and capable, and did contribute to the refinement of early society, but they were focused mostly on advancing their own agenda of seizing and wielding power. This has always been the strategy of the Ruling Class, whether as the chief of a small tribe or an emperor ruling millions of people.

Common to all of these rulers are the three basic tenants of the Ruling Class. First, most people are incapable of managing their own lives. Second, only a government can succeed in maintaining order in society. Finally, the members of the Ruling Class possess an innate superiority that makes them worthy of their position and the power they hold over everyone else.

As society became more complex, the real leadership the ruler showed on the hunt or in battle was no longer crucial. So his narrative evolved as to why individual liberty had to be sacrificed. Opposition to the ruler's ways, the thinking goes, could weaken the group as a whole — just as it could on the hunt or in battle, even though the immediate threat was far more remote. So for example, if you don't marry according to society's standards as imposed by the Ruling Class, you risk disrupting the status quo and the well-being of the group. If you don't follow in your father's footsteps, then your town might not have a trained blacksmith or baker, and would thus be unable to meet its population's needs. If you act in a way that the ruler claims angered the gods, then the tribe might starve as punishment. The narrative maintained that if people didn't give up their resources or acquiesce to the rules, the order of the group would unravel, enemies would invade and pillage, or the gods would grow angry at their behavior and punish them with devastating natural disasters. The Ruling Class, time and again, promoted this structure under the guise of forming a well-balanced and successful society, when in reality, theirs was a system designed to keep lower subjects in line and easy to control, the way it had always been.

And if all else failed, hideous punishment awaited those who defied the narrative of the Ruling Class. Ancient rulers roasted whole families alive in metal ovens shaped like a bull. Crucifixion was developed as a slow, torturous death. Treason was so heinous a crime that painful death was not enough: the traitor was hanged, cut down alive, drawn and quartered, and forced to watch his own bowels burn in front of him as he bled to death. Heretics were burned at the stake, for it was believed that the flames would expunge not only their lives but also their evil thoughts.

Public Works Require a Strong Ruler

Just as the Ruling Class took advantage of their community's need for safety in a dangerous world, they created other areas of exploitation as society advanced and became more developed. By manning the helm of massive public works projects, the Ruling Class gained another rationale for increasing the power at their disposal. These involved both a pressing need for defense and also for control of water and food. Most of these endeavors were of mind-numbing size, especially considering the technological and logistical constraints of their time.

In Mesopotamia (a region containing modern Iraq), seasonal changes in the flow of the Tigris and Euphrates Rivers posed a significant problem for early civilization. To meet the food production needs of a rapidly expanding population, water had to be managed in order to maximize the amount of arable land.[2] The Ruling Class of the third millennium BC, seizing the opportunity to extend their influence, constructed extensive irrigation canals. Similarly, the massive reach of the Nile River and its regular flooding necessitated the implementation of similar systems in Egypt. These projects, while important to the development of the community, offered the Ruling Class an opportunity to solidify their positions.

In analyzing the essential feature of water in the building of these early civilizations, the German American historian Karl Wittfogel coined the term "hydraulic despotism."[3] Building and maintaining the irrigation system that sustained society required an immensely powerful ruler capable of marshaling most of the population into contributing their labor toward that collective goal. A large and powerful bureaucracy then emerged to make sure that this highly centralized rule was carried out. Other historians have refined Wittfogel's hypothesis since the time he wrote in the 1950s. The current view is that the control of water was not so much the origin of despotism (which existed in any case), but the key to the evolution of a bureaucratic state under the despot, because it created issues that could not be adjudicated by a single individual. As such, these water tyrannies were fundamental in moving from a single ruler toward an entire Ruling Class.

A similar bureaucracy formed to execute an even more massive project in China in the seventh century, although work had begun several hundred years before. The Grand Canal is the largest man-made waterway the world has ever seen.[4] It is 1,100 miles long and links Beijing with the two great river systems of China: the Yangtze River and the Yellow River. The commitment of men and national output to build this project was massive and involved a mobilization of resources that could be completed only by a great ruler with far-reaching power. To put the commitment into perspective, the Erie Canal of the 1820s was less than one-fifth as long but cost $7 million to complete at a time when the total federal budget was $19 million. Given the much lower gross domestic product (GDP) and poorer technology 2,500 years earlier, it is not hard to imagine that most of the surplus production of China was dedicated to building the canal.

The most massive public works project of all time, however, was not conducted to control water or food but for defense. Construction on the Great Wall of China began in the seventh century BC as a means of guarding against invasion by northern tribes.[5] It was built, rebuilt, and expanded many times. Each revision enlisted a massive number of laborers, all under the direction of the Ruling Class of that day, and many paid the ultimate price during this forced service. Historians estimate that as many as 400,000 people died during the building of the Great Wall. Criminals too were forced to work on the wall, and if they died before completing their sentence, their family had to provide a replacement. In one of the wall's later revisions during the Ming dynasty, other estimates say that as many as one-third of all adult males in China labored on the wall for the national good. This is a staggering burden on a society operating on barely-above-subsistence agriculture, and an enormous amount of power commanded by a small group of individuals.

Of course, many of the gargantuan projects of history were not only exceptionally costly but also served only to glorify the upper echelon of the Ruling Class. Egypt's pyramids are a prime example. The Great Pyramid of Giza took the efforts of 30,000 men over a twenty-year period, all for a glorified monument to the Pharaohs. They involved the moving and lifting of some 2.5 million cubic meters of stone.[6] In terms of excavation, they moved enough earth to build an irrigation ditch three feet deep, six feet wide, and a mile into the desert the entire length of the Nile River on both sides. Think of that with respect to lost agricultural output. In terms of stone laid, they could have built the equivalent of a Roman road (eighteen inches of stone deep and thirty feet wide) the entire length of the country.

The Mausoleum of the First Qin Emperor in China is similarly renowned.[7,8] Constructed over thirty-six years, this tomb contains an estimated eight thousand terra-cotta soldiers—weighing between three hundred and four hundred pounds each—built to protect the emperor in the afterlife. But all of this speaks to the perceived importance of the ruler compared with the needs of the people. Just the fired clay in those statues could have provided every family in Beijing forty gallon-size pots for cooking or for water. The great societies of the past emerged from the untold sacrifices of ordinary people, yet only the names of the Ruling Class who forced their subjects into such deprivations are remembered. These rulers did deliver some of the essentials of civilization, and that doubtless helped people tolerate the costs of being ruled. This tolerance for suffering was augmented by a narrative that this arrangement was how it was supposed to be; and that narrative was backed up by a combination of superstition and force. The notion of individual liberty rarely ever arose—and was quickly vanquished when it did.

The Best the Ancient World Had to Offer

There were some brief exceptions. The clearest example of the concept of liberty was espoused by the second-century Roman emperor Marcus Aurelius, who was considered unusual even in his own time and thus received the appellation "philosopher king." In particular, he advanced the philosophy of Stoicism, which advocated a belief in duty, self-restraint, and respect for others. In *Meditations*, a collection of his personal writings, he wrote of "a polity in which there is the same law for all, a polity administered with regard to equal rights and equal freedom of speech, and the idea of a kingly government which respects most of all the freedom of the governed."[9]

However, this was only a brief glimpse of liberty, and actual practice didn't always follow his enlightened theories. For example, the traits that Aurelius wrote about didn't apply to the rising Christian population; their persecution increased during his reign, as recurring military defeats required a scapegoat in order to maintain the narrative that justified his power. Even worse, most important tenets of Aurelius's philosophy were utterly rejected by his successors. Rome quickly returned to its old ways of totalitarian governing after his departure. Part of this might have been due to his own mistake when it came to planning for his succession. Niccolò Machiavelli, the Italian Renaissance political theorist, described

Aurelius as the last of the "five good emperors";[10] those five became emperor after being "adopted" by their predecessors. Hence, the practice of imperial succession was maintained, but the next emperor was selected based on merit rather than blood. This trend ended with Aurelius, who was succeeded by his biological son Commodus.*

Still, the Stoic philosophy provided a clear departure from the practice of most ancient governing structures. It placed a moral obligation on the ruler to create good governance, with at least a modicum of freedom for his subjects. British historian Edward Gibbon, in his epic *The History of the Decline and Fall of the Roman Empire*, called this "the period in the history of the world during which the condition of the human race was most happy and prosperous."[11] Gibbon was writing in the middle of the eighteenth century and clearly meant that this was a superior outcome up until and including his own time, so this is high praise. But Gibbon's view was that its prosperity arose because "The vast extent of the Roman Empire was governed by absolute power, under the guidance of virtue and wisdom."

The guidance of virtue and wisdom is undoubtedly better than the guidance of greed and narcissism, but that is a low bar for what government should aspire to be. Absolute power, even given to a well-intentioned ruler, is still quite different from a guarantee of liberty to citizens, even if it mimics some of its virtues in everyday life. And the practicalities of governing even in these less despotic ancient societies meant that the state and Ruling Class still held precedence over the individual.

Nowhere is this clearer than in another example held up as a model of tolerable early governance: ancient Greece. We credit the city-state of Athens as one of the first democracies, and indeed it was. Starting in the sixth century BC, reforms were initiated to expand political participation. By the fourth century, when there were perhaps 250,000 to 300,000

---

*In the movie *Gladiator* (2000), Marcus Aurelius was portrayed by Richard Harris. The story line is that his son, Commodus (Joaquin Phoenix) ensured his succession by eliminating his father's alleged preference, the general Maximus, played by Russell Crowe. The historical accuracy of this account is doubtful, but conceivable.

people in Attica, the territory that Athens controlled, roughly 100,000 were recognized as citizens, and of these, perhaps 30,000 could vote in the assembly. Votes were cast directly by these people rather than by representatives and had to be made in person. So it was a pure democracy, limited to certain members of the population—not a representative government such as the one we have today.

Although there was democracy, there was not what we would call liberty. It was what might be called a democratic dictatorship. Though individuals had a say through their vote, the assembly's power was unlimited. It could do as it pleased, reversing itself completely if it chose and thus upending what we today might call "the rule of law." Additionally, both civil and criminal trials involved a democratic process in which a subsection of the population (typically five hundred people) sat as a jury. There were no protections in place for the accused, who could be convicted based on a simple majority alone. Unlike in America, where jury decisions usually have to be unanimous, those on trial in Greece could be found guilty by a single vote. The trial took a single day; perjury and falsifying evidence might be found later and used to convict the perjurer, but the harm caused by verdicts could not be undone. So the Athenian government had power as great as any tyrant, the only difference being that power within the government was broadened to include more people in the Ruling Class. The individual was still totally subservient to the society as represented by the State.

The greatest example of this came with the trial of Socrates, whom the assembly charged with corrupting the young and with impiety, not believing in the state-accepted gods. Impiety in that day was punishable by death. How could an individual be free with such state-imposed standards on personal beliefs? The "corruption" the assembly spoke of was in reference to the Socratic method of teaching through questioning, the way that Socrates encouraged his students to question constantly the basis of their thinking. Society is usually terrified of ideas that contradict accepted belief, and that was Socrates's real crime. The concept of liberty in terms of thought and speech was seen as subservient to the democratic will, not a "right" that trumped it.

Socrates was found guilty by a vote of 280 to 220 in favor of conviction, a decision that was essentially a political verdict.[12] A narrow majority of the jury felt that Socrates was causing too much trouble for Athens, an attitude Socrates summarized by describing himself as a gadfly. He was an irritant to too many powerful people, often questioning their actions and motives. The lesson, which is still true today, is that questioning those who see themselves as "intellectually superior" might end up costing you dearly. The ability to do so, to question those in authority and those who claim some expertise, is an important cornerstone of liberty, one that was absent in even what is believed to be philosophically enlightened Greece.

The story of Socrates illustrates a confusion that many of the Ruling Class throughout history have seemed to suffer. Power does not mean that your beliefs are a source of absolute truth; your principles are still as fallible as anyone's. Admitting that your principles are fallible doesn't in turn mean that you need to change your mind, but it does suggest that your critics' opinions are worth hearing. If nothing else, opposition identifies weakness in your ideals worth correcting. This was lost on the different Ruling Classes that held power around the world, and meant that most people, for most of history, were trapped in a limited role, lacking the empowerment to change their circumstances.

The lesson of history is that liberty is a very radical idea, one that did not exist in any substantive form before our Founding Fathers declared independence from England and the Crown. These brave men demanded the right to live their lives free of Ruling Class interference. They demanded the right to question those entrusted with power; question their assumptions, question their motives, and to ensure as best as possible that they were acting in society's best interest and not merely their own. They created a constitution that for the first time in history provided a framework limiting the scope of the government rather than the rights of citizens. Most significant, the Founders realized the importance of these rights and were willing to die for them.

CHAPTER 2

Liberty: The Real
Meaning of 1776

When the Continental Congress met in Philadelphia to debate independence from Britain, they were well aware of the odds they faced. Britain had the most imposing military in the world, full of decorated career soldiers, while the American forces were hardly more than a ragtag collection of volunteers with one-year enlistments. Funding for this meager band was scarce, as was their military experience. At first, America's fighting force wasn't an army at all, but a collection of militias and armed civilians controlled by individual states, the financial backing of which was so weak that in 1781 Congress was forced to suspend all pay for the troops.[1]

Equally daunting were the historical odds. These men were well aware of mankind's overall submission to the Ruling Class, commenting famously in the Declaration of Independence, "and accordingly all experience hath shewn, that mankind are more disposed to suffer, while evils are sufferable, than to right themselves by abolishing the forms to which they are accustomed." They knew about Marcus Aurelius and his implementation of Stoic philosophy as a ruler and borrowed freely from his ideas on what government should be like. But they also realized that Aurelius's concept of governance had failed. They knew that Socrates had been sentenced to death by the Athenian assembly, and so they enshrined liberty—and not merely democracy—as a key right to which man was entitled. The "consent of the governed" that they penned did not mean that the opinion of 51 percent would negate the rights of the rest of the population. Instead, it indicated a generalized acceptance by the American citizenry of the legitimacy of a government that was there to act on their behalf.

To cope psychologically with the daunting nature of the task ahead, the Founders viewed what they were doing as a beginning and not a final result. As Americans, we celebrate the Fourth of July each year with fireworks and barbecues, remembering that day in 1776 when we won our independence from England and the signing of a document that proclaimed "Life, Liberty, and the pursuit of Happiness" as both a right and as an obligation of government in serving the needs of the people. But neither independence nor liberty was won on that day, and preserving both involves ongoing struggles.

At the time, British troops continued to occupy our cities, maraud through our countryside, and arrest our countrymen at will—and they continued to do so long after the Declaration was signed. The men who signed it had to flee for their lives from Philadelphia just fourteen months later, as the British took over what was then the budding heart of young America's revolutionary struggle in an occupation that would last until they moved their forces to New York in June 1778. In total, British armies harassed the colonists for seven years after they formally seceded from King George III.

Similarly, the signers of the Declaration knew that the liberty of which they wrote would be nothing more than a word to the roughly seven hundred thousand people enslaved in their new nation, around

20 percent of its population.[2] They realized that the phrase "All men are created equal" was laced with hypocrisy—the existence of slavery consumed a major part of their deliberations when drafting the Declaration. Many hoped at the time that this atrocity would die of its own accord, as it was becoming unprofitable; unfortunately, the invention of the cotton gin removed that possibility completely and necessitated the bloodiest war in American history. But emancipation didn't guarantee liberty any more than our initial independence guaranteed permanent security. Just as we are reminded that "Freedom is never free" each Veterans Day, securing liberty like the Founders envisioned is an ongoing battle, one for which people must be prepared to fight. Liberty requires eternal vigilance on the part of the governed to make sure that those in power do not overstep their bounds.

But even though it was just a beginning, our commemoration of July 4, 1776, is entirely justified. It marks the first time in the history of mankind that a governing document such as the Constitution declared formally that the purpose of government was to serve the people, not the other way around. Moreover, our Declaration stated that it was the obligation of the people to serve as a constant check on that government, and that if all else failed, it was their right to revise it to better suit their needs or even to throw it out altogether. This was the truly revolutionary idea declared on that day, not independence. History is full of acts of one people declaring freedom from another. But the Declaration was first in asserting boldly and directly that the *only* reason for government's existence was to preserve the liberty of its citizens.

The Philosophy of Liberty

Liberty can be best thought of as people having the ability to do as they please, free from arbitrary or oppressive rule. Governmental power almost always carries with it negative implications, limiting what one can say and do—for example, overreach of the type that would prevent a contract between two independent parties in mutual agreement. I might agree to work for you, but the terms of my employment are not up to the two of us and are instead decided by the government. I might own some land, but I cannot grow the crops I want or build what I want to build. As we shall see in coming chapters, these limitations can be quite extensive in their intrusion into personal life. Worse, this type of system lowers citizens to the position of supplicant, forcing them to continually seek permission from often-unqualified bureaucrats for the right to do something. Government "help" almost always comes with terms and conditions.

Liberty is the absence of this unnecessary clutter that government imposes on life and the hassle that comes with it. There is no regulatory overlord, one whose only purpose is to administrate needlessly over the actual producers in society. Getting a stamp of approval from a bureaucrat produces nothing. Liberty empowers individuals to use their time as they see fit.

The Scotsman Adam Smith described this consequence in his foundational work on economic liberty, *An Inquiry into the Nature and Causes of the Wealth of Nations*,[3] published in 1776. He notes that production soars when individuals are able to pursue their own interests: "As every individual, therefore, endeavors as much as he can both to employ his capital in the support of domestic industry, and so to direct that industry that its produce may be of greatest value; every individual necessarily labors to render the annual revenue of society as great as he can." As Smith, an economist, writes, the way to maximum output for society is by fostering individual economic success, not by jamming up the system with cumbersome and inept regulation, which he notes further by describing that the individual "neither intends to promote the public interest, nor knows how much he is promoting it . . . he intends only his own gain, and he is in this, as in many other cases, led by an invisible hand to promote an end which was no part of his intention."

Liberty is therefore the smart way to improve well-being. What matters is not how loudly a politician proclaims how much he or she wants to improve the country but how much individuals endeavor to produce on their own. There is no need for someone in the Ruling Class to plan this production. On the contrary, the more they interfere, the lower production is likely to be.

Smith broke with the Ruling Class on another matter as well. Until his work, a country's wealth was commonly measured by the size of the monarch's treasury or the amount of gold and silver in the government's coffers, as the Ruling Class confused their own wealth and prosperity with that of the nation. Smith, however, thought of it as the productive output of the country, or what he termed "the annual revenue of the society." In his mind, and in the minds of those who prize personal liberty, it is the well-being of the people, and not that of the Ruling Class, that matters.

But liberty is more than material well-being, though the latter stems from it. There's something to be said about the unquantifiable benefits that emerge when an individual is able to pursue his or her own agenda and not that of the state, even if it produces no additional income. Happiness is priceless and is impossible to attain in a society that under-values individual self-worth. Freedom to worship as one pleases or to speak out against mistreatment without fear of reprisal are just as necessary, yet overlooked when liberty is comprised. Without liberty, life loses its luster, becoming an endless series of sunrises and sunsets where one's actions are dictated by necessity, custom, or someone else.

Most of us understand these tenets of liberty. Yet included in its philosophy is an obligation that is not as readily apparent but equally important. The philosophical father of liberty was an Englishman named John Locke, whose two treatises on government—authored some ninety years before the Declaration—argue that "liberty is to be free from restraint and violence from others,"[4] and not just from the government. He continues: "All mankind . . . being all equal and independent, no one ought to harm another in his life, health, liberty, or possessions."[5] So along with liberty come self-restraint, tolerance, civility, and respect for the rights of others, even toward individuals with whom we disagree.

One hears echoes of Marcus Aurelius and Stoicism in this logic. It is our duty in enjoying liberty's benefits to extend the same opportunity to others. Just because it is within our means to do something doesn't mean that we should. Aurelius wrote of a kingly government that respects the rights of all. But what if we are all kings? Liberty provides the way for us to become masters of our own destinies. However, to accept that mastery, we must also accept that others are just as entitled to such a position.

Contrary to this fundamental principle of liberty, the Ruling Class often maintain that those who pursue liberty are inherently selfish, that they don't care about the good of their fellow man. This is partly a ruse to hide the fact that they, as self-justified rulers, are constantly demanding more from the people they rule—demands best summarized as more resources to advance their agenda and the expansion of their power and influence necessary to do so. But their claim is also untrue and demonstrates a willful misunderstanding of liberty's most basic precepts. People who truly value liberty want it not just for themselves but also for everyone in the community, because unless one lives in a society in which liberty is the order of things, one's own liberty isn't worth very much. Liberty is not about being Robinson Crusoe on a desert island; it is about individuals being free to make arrangements with others without the government stepping in and telling them what they can and cannot do. Locke and the Founding Fathers did not see liberty selfishly but as an arrangement that entailed mutual consent, in which all could come out ahead.

Although Smith's *Wealth of Nations* almost certainly hadn't been read by the Founders before they declared independence, they understood that government interference works to prevent the advancement that comes with liberty. For example, during the 1760s, the British forbade trade between colonies: if a businessman in New York wanted to sell a suit to a gentleman in Philadelphia, he couldn't. His potential customers would either have to look locally or, more likely, buy from Britain. This is, of course, why Britain imposed such regulation: it left the colonies dependent on the British. Similarly, bureaucrats today drench America with regulation because it's their only way of gaining control of certain processes. The philosophy of liberty thus undermines the whole rationale for there being a Ruling Class. If we are free to act without government's permission, then those who rule have lost their purpose; they can no longer engineer society into their image of perfection. True liberty in turn destroys the belief that people can't run their own lives without government intervention. With that in mind, we need to take a closer look at what the Founders actually said about liberty, for the ideas they advanced were not merely about separating from Britain but also about upending the political arrangements that had governed mankind for millennia.

The Meaning of the Declaration

Most of us are familiar with the Declaration's first few sentences. "We hold these truths to be self-evident, that all men are created equal, that they are endowed by their Creator with certain unalienable Rights, that among these are Life, Liberty, and the pursuit of Happiness." Most of us also have a sense of what those words mean. But today, reference to a "Creator" might seem a bit out of place to some, particularly in our largely secular society where many deny the existence of such a concept. This leaves an opening for critics of liberty to suggest that because of their seemingly traditional religious views, these were a bunch of old white men who weren't as enlightened as we are today.

To be clear, most Americans in 1776, like today, believed in God and viewed Him as their Creator. And this is a perfectly acceptable interpretation of the Founders' use of the phrase. But it is not the only interpretation. The three men who led the subcommittee to draft the Declaration—Thomas Jefferson, John Adams, and Benjamin Franklin—were fairly "free thinking" in their views, and products of the movement we now call the English Enlightenment. Although all three were members of at least one church (Franklin had joined most of the churches in Philadelphia earlier in his life, for business reasons), they also had close associations with Freemasonry and speculated openly about there being life on other planets. Adams had become a Unitarian and no longer believed in the divinity of Jesus Christ. These were men with views on religion that would be considered quite modern, even today.

An alternative reading, one that has merit for all Americans, is that with these lines, the Founders were concerned mostly with establishing liberty from a practical point of view as legitimate and innate. What Locke and other English Enlightenment thinkers pioneered was the idea of "natural law": literally the way things are in nature. From this follows the notion that our rights don't spring from some government but are instead part of the natural order of things. This is important because it meant that the government had no greater access to our fundamental rights as human beings than it did to the other characteristics that make us unique individuals.

After making this important distinction, our Founders went a step further, declaring that government has one purpose: "That to secure these rights, Governments are instituted among Men, deriving their just powers from the consent of the governed." This is a pretty radical idea, and one that represented a dramatic shift from the paradigm established worldwide since man emerged from the caves. As detailed in the last chapter, prior to 1776, ruling bodies existed for a lot of reasons—to fulfill the Ruling Class agenda, to control a lower caste of subjects so that the cunning and shameless could maintain power, or simply to glorify a select and privileged few—but never as a service to the common people. The Pharaohs built the pyramids by official decree. King Louis XIV of France, self-described modestly as the "Sun King," declared *"L'État, c'est moi"* ("I am the State"). That settles it, doesn't it? And for the great majority of human history, people had accepted that this was the way it was, that the Ruling Class were an insurmountable force easier to tolerate than change.

The writers of the Declaration formed a new moral narrative about why governments should exist: to secure the blessings of liberty.

Providing defense, dispensing justice, and building public works projects were only to secure the liberty and happiness of the people and not for other reasons.

Having provided a new sole justification for government, the Founders then took another big step—one that, at the time, crossed the line into treason. "That whenever any form of Government becomes destructive of these ends, it is the Right of the People to alter or abolish it, and to institute new Government." This was big stuff back in 1776, and it is still big stuff today. It means that defense, justice, and public works are not enough if these acts are for any other purpose than advancing the liberty of the people. Once government starts acting in its own self-interest rather than in the interest of securing these basic rights, then the time has come for action. Here the authors of the Declaration pivoted from idealism to practicality.

Abolishing one government and instituting another is, to put it mildly, a very messy process, so things had to get pretty bad before such extreme action was taken. "Prudence, indeed, will dictate that Governments long established should not be changed for light and transient Causes . . . But when a long Train of Abuses and Usurpations, pursuing invariably the same Object, evinces a design to reduce them under Absolute Despotism, it is their Right, it is their Duty, to throw off such Government and to provide new Guards for their future Security." It's important to understand that the Founders were promoting liberty and not anarchy. Instead of upending government for just about any perceived wrong, they advocated a more conservative process whereby drastic action such as rebellion was a last resort taken only after peaceful political participation yielded no change.

These men understood the gravity of their course, and that once they set out in the pursuit of liberty, there was no turning back. But where exactly did they draw the line? What explicitly was "a long Train of Abuses and Usurpations"? The most useful answer is the most practical one. None of the Founders started out as a revolutionary; particular events turned them that way.

The Personal Experiences of the Founders

When the Declaration was written in 1776, and the writers intoned the words "absolute despotism," they were exaggerating slightly. King George III was nothing like the Chinese emperor Qin Shi Huang, or the Roman emperor Gaius Caesar Caligula, or even France's Louis XIV. In fact, Britain and America were probably the freest places on earth, as most of the world still lived in virtual darkness. Slavery existed in most societies in the same form that had persisted for millennia: individuals were captured, usually in battle along with their families, and forced to serve the victors. Most of those who were not slaves toiled in some form of serfdom, tied to land that they generally did not own outright, subjected to arbitrary rules and punishments. Elections were virtually unheard of; the idea that ordinary people should have a say was considered preposterous. Although America maintained property requirements to vote, nearly half of the adult male population could still participate. Comparable circumstances didn't arise in England until the Reform Bills of the middle of the nineteenth century. The Reform Bill of 1832 expanded the franchise to about one fifth of adult males. It wasn't until the Reform Bill of 1867 that all male heads of household were allowed to vote. There was trial by jury, though this system was far from perfect.

What the Founders objected to was not so much the absolute standards of freedom but the logic used by King George III. If rights were not inalienable, then the government could take away one right today, and another one next year—and this process of slicing away liberty like salami would continue until there was nothing left. The "Constitution" of Great Britain, which was not written down in a formal document but based on precedent, was what is known today as a "living Constitution"—basically, those in power changed it to fit their needs as they went along. And if the purpose of government was not to protect the individual, then what was it? It was whatever the government of the time thought it should be. Perhaps it was the ruler's favorite cause; say, what he considered "social justice." Or maybe it was some "global emergency." Or maybe the ruler just wanted a monument to himself—what today we call "a legacy."

The Founders knew from recent experience that liberty is hard to win and easy to lose. England had a civil war in the 1640s and executed its king in the process. When that king's son was ultimately restored to the throne, the body of the leader of the revolt, Oliver Cromwell, was exhumed, cut into pieces, and then scattered across the land. A second rebellion soon followed, known as the Glorious Revolution, in which the king fled the throne. Only in its aftermath did the new king and queen sign the English Bill of Rights in 1689, which incorporated many of the same ideas our Founders were now asserting.

Our Founders also saw themselves as Englishmen and identified with the progress made during these two major English revolutions. Deprived of what they viewed as hard-won rights, they led an American revolution that took things a step further than their predecessors. While Englishmen such as John Locke viewed personal consent to government as the key to political legitimacy, the Founding Fathers put it into practice by declaring that it was the right and the duty of people to make sure that government protected their rights. To make these philosophical leaps, each man had a different experience that transformed him. Let's examine a few cases to get a sense of what these men considered the threshold at which drastic measures were warranted against a government with which they had become so familiar.

BENJAMIN FRANKLIN

Benjamin Franklin reached this threshold on January 29, 1774. Franklin had been assigned to London to represent the interests of the colonies before Parliament. In a sense, he was their lobbyist. He had been somewhat effective in offering compromises that defused the tensions between the British government and the American colonists. In 1765, he led the fight against the Stamp Act, which Britain used as a way of collecting revenue by requiring that each document, including all newspapers, bear a stamp to be valid and eligible for sale. His efforts led to its successful repeal. In 1773, Franklin forwarded private correspondence to Boston that proved that the appointed governor was lobbying the king to crack down hard on the city. He was called by the solicitor general to appear before the Privy Council, a select group that oversaw judicial matters, where he was made to stand for hours while being humiliated and berated publicly.[6] It was said that Franklin entered the Privy Council chambers as an Englishman and left as an American.

Franklin, one of seventeen children, was a quintessentially self-made man. Although his father wanted him to attend school, he could afford to do so for only two years. Most of what Franklin learned was self-taught through voracious reading. He became apprenticed to his older brother at age twelve, helping him publish a newspaper. He ran away to Philadelphia at age seventeen and became a fugitive as a result. Ultimately he set up his own publishing company and became quite wealthy by publishing *Poor Richard's Almanack* and the *Pennsylvania Gazette*. His lively writing and heavy use of satire made the latter popular, and it became the leading newspaper in all the colonies. His commercial success allowed Franklin to semiretire in his midforties and pursue other matters, including science and politics.[7]

Popularly known for his work with electricity and the invention of the lightning rod, Franklin also invented bifocal reading glasses, the Franklin stove, and the flexible urinary catheter. He was a pioneer in the study of population, known as demography, and was credited by the British economist Thomas Malthus for his thinking. Franklin predicted in the 1750s that America, with its abundant food supply and availability of land, had the fastest rate of population growth in the world and would overtake Britain within a century.[8] He turned out to be right. He also published works on astronomy and ocean currents, and as a result gained recognition at the prestigious University of St. Andrews in Scotland and Oxford University in England. What an amazing and diverse mind!

Imagine what it must have been like for Franklin in his early sixties, a self-made man who had turned very little into astonishing financial and intellectual success, to be publicly humiliated by a member of the Ruling Class—someone who had received his position largely through birth and who came nowhere near rivaling Franklin's talents or accomplishments. Worse yet, someone who used the power of his position not to engage in forthright discussion on merits, but to project himself as morally and personally superior! Franklin entered the Privy Council on that January morning believing that for all its faults, Britain had the best the world had to offer. He left and returned to America strongly convinced otherwise.

JOHN ADAMS

If Franklin was the practical Founder who gradually came around to protecting personal liberty, John Adams was the idealist whose beliefs were so strong that he placed them ahead of the practical fight for freedom and made enemies as a result. So for Adams, the defining moment was not one of personal humiliation but the reverse: one of personal sacrifice as a signal of his idealism.

It began with the Boston Massacre of 1770.[9] A group of British soldiers, taunted and pelted with snowballs, fired on what today we would call a street protest. A shot rang out. We can't say with certainty which side fired first, but the British soldiers responded by firing into the crowd, killing three. The soldiers were charged with murder and, given the passions of the time, had trouble finding a defense attorney. Adams, ever the idealist, stepped forward to defend the soldiers, and in doing so put his popularity and his leadership role in Massachusetts politics at risk. Not only did he defend these men, but also he did so successfully. Six of the eight were acquitted outright. The two found guilty, who could have received the death penalty, were instead convicted of manslaughter, escaping with only a branding of their tongues. Gruesome and quite painful, perhaps, but decidedly preferable to hanging. Adams believed that under a system of liberty, even an unpopular defendant who acted on the wrong side of the battle for liberty deserved a vigorous defense;

that public passions should not overwhelm the legal defense of the individual, as they had with Socrates.

Adams had been warned that his intervention on behalf of the British soldiers would cost him dearly. He retorted with two famous observations. First, "Facts are stubborn things; and whatever may be our wishes, our inclinations, or the dictates of our passion, they cannot alter the state of facts and evidence."[10] Think how revolutionary an idea this is, even today, when political correctness, not fact, governs the prosecution of police officers charged with crimes involving incidents not too dissimilar from what Adams confronted in his defense of the soldiers in the Boston Massacre.

Second, Adams noted something that is very crucial to the relative position of the prosecutor representing the state, and therefore the Ruling Class: "It is more important that innocence be protected than it is that guilt be punished, for guilt and crimes are so frequent in this world that they cannot all be punished. But if innocence itself is brought to the bar and condemned, perhaps to die, then the citizen will say, 'whether I do good or whether I do evil is immaterial, for innocence itself is no protection,' and if such an idea as that were to take hold in the mind of the citizen, that would be the end of security whatsoever."[11]

In Adams, we have a critic of one of the most universal practices of the Ruling Class: to make the laws so broad, so vague, and their enforcement so dominated by political correctness, that they mock the concept of the rule of law. The root of the problem is overreach: in an effort to regulate the maximum amount of human behavior, commonsense notions of right and wrong become subordinate to legalistic nuance. When the understanding and enforcement of rules and regulations become so complex, the public loses respect. Adams's key moment was his decision to defend the concept of justice and limit the power of government, even though he agreed politically with those on the other side. This would make him an even more passionate opponent of injustice when his political sympathies aligned with the victims of that injustice.

JOHN HANCOCK

While Franklin was self-made and Adams austere, the man whose name has become synonymous with a signature was born rich and increased his fortune throughout his life in flamboyant fashion. As president of the Continental Congress, John Hancock signed the Declaration first— a likely explanation for why his signature is so large, though the official story is that he signed so loudly so that the king and his ministers could read it without their spectacles.

As a well-to-do businessman, he had a natural incentive to cozy up to everyone in power, and was so until the British pushed too far. Hancock's business empire was built on trade, and perversely, government regulations helped make trade extremely profitable.[12] As far back as 1651, Britain began passing the Navigation Acts, which controlled trade with all of the colonies and limited the ships that could be used to those registered with the authorities. When government limits competition, profits soar for those who are already in the business, which is why businesspeople in regulated industries tend to be quite close with politicians, then and now. Today we might call John Hancock at this stage of his life a "crony capitalist."

When the Stamp Act was repealed, Parliament sought to replace the lost revenue with stricter customs enforcement, authorizing its representatives to get tougher, tightening the penalties for breaking the law, and giving a portion of the penalties to the law enforcement agencies. (Note the similarities to today's rampant civil asset forfeiture, a legal tool that allows the government to confiscate a person's assets without ever convicting them of a crime.) The colonists' response was to boycott British goods. Hancock had not made any friends with the king's agents in Boston by supporting the boycott, instead making himself a target. British authorities boarded his boat, named *Liberty*, found that it held only twenty-five cases of Madeira wine when it could have held more, and claimed that Hancock had smuggled seventy-five cases of wine ashore without paying duty. The evidence was scant, and Hancock fought the charges, but ultimately the British seized the *Liberty* and put it to use in antismuggling operations.[13]

They also filed a personal suit against Hancock for treble damages: he would have had to pay three times the total value of the wine (not just the forgone tax) that they alleged he had unloaded, even though the supposedly smuggled wine was never found. The trial was to be held in a vice-admiralty court with no jury and with limited ability to cross-examine witnesses. Hancock retained none other than John Adams for his defense, but ultimately the trial was never held; the authorities contented themselves with merely seizing his ship. One suspects that, as is often the case today, a deal was made. Nonetheless, it was enough for Hancock, who then became a leading patriot, to declare that the military occupation of Boston served "to enforce obedience to acts of Parliament, which neither God nor man ever empowered them to make."[14]

The men who signed the Declaration each had his own reason for believing that "evils were no longer sufferable" and that abuses of the Ruling Class were taking the country back to the dark days in which most of mankind had existed. They were not perfect men, nor did they view themselves as such. Adams knew he was unpopular. Franklin knew that in living life to the fullest, he had estranged much of his family. Hancock was at first the ultimate cynic about politics and came to understand the price that carried. Because they understood their own flaws, they appreciated that no one man should be a ruler, but that a system of mutual respect based on liberty was the only way to maximize human potential.

When the men gathered in Philadelphia to sign the Declaration, they pledged their lives, their fortunes, and their sacred honor to the cause. They meant it. Of the fifty-six who signed, nine died of wounds or hardships during the war. Five were captured and imprisoned under brutal conditions. Twelve had their homes burned to the ground.

Seventeen lost their entire fortunes. Several have tales that are absolutely harrowing.[15]

Abraham Clark of New Jersey saw both of his sons captured in the battle of New York and sent to the prison ship HMS *Jersey*, where thousands perished in hellish conditions. His eldest son was starved to death. He was offered their release if he recanted his signing of the Declaration. He did not. Francis Lewis of New York saw his home burned and his wife captured and badly abused; she later died from her mistreatment. Philip Livingston, another New York delegate, was one of the richest men in America. His fortune was confiscated, and he died a poor man, still working in the Continental Congress. John Hart of New Jersey tried to return home to see his wife on her deathbed. He was hunted by Hessian soldiers—German mercenaries who fought on the side of the British—and forced to live in caves to evade capture. When he finally made it to his home, he found that his wife was dead and that his thirteen children had been carried away. He never saw them again and died a broken man. Today we can scarcely imagine such indignities or such tremendous personal loss.

Once young America was on its feet and out from under Britain's rule, the Founders then had to turn their attention to securing what they had achieved, a mission formally stated as "securing the Blessings of Liberty for ourselves and our posterity."

It would not be an easy task. The Founders appreciated the lessons of history and saw the difficulty of enshrining liberty in any form of government. There always seemed to be a Ruling Class able to reassert power. But these men were willing to navigate such a treacherous route and pay such steep tolls because they knew liberty was worth it. They understood that those who valued personal power above all else would go to great lengths to secure it, and that because of an ever-lingering Ruling Class, the pursuit of liberty would be a long struggle met with intense opposition. They put their faith in the notion that the ambition for power could best be checked by others with similar ambitions, a novel thought at the time. Power gravitates toward hierarchy, so the Founders' goal was to flatten governmental power and distribute it broadly. With these aims in mind, we turn next to the framework they laid out for young America — the Constitution — to ensure that their original intentions would be protected long after they were gone.

CHAPTER 3

Locking Down Liberty
with a Constitution

One of the many key qualities that united our Founding Fathers was their strong mistrust of central authority. They had, after all, just risked their lives and the safety of their loved ones to rebel against a ruling system that was exactly that. In fact, the Founders' fear of allowing a similar Ruling Class to take hold in America was so great that the first version of our country's government, stipulated by the 1781 Articles of Confederation, lacked enough central authority to function. There was speculation on both sides of the Atlantic that it would only take a few years for the former colonies to return to their previous master out of necessity or to be reincorporated into the British Empire by force. And indeed, this early framework for America lasted until just 1789.

After this failed attempt, the Founders endeavored to create a government unlike any that had existed before, one that allowed for centralized power but was formally limited by the Constitution and also internally self-checking through a complex power-sharing arrangement. They had no idea whether it would work, but they did have a good understanding of human nature when it came to politics. Most of the Founders had spent time in the political arena. Moreover, the states they represented had experienced ongoing conflicts between their legislative bodies and executives. They were also students of history and were aware of the experiments in governance instituted by Greece and Rome, as well as Italian city-states such as Florence and Milan. So their brainchild, the Constitution, is a fusion of many ideas tempered by the lessons of history.

Importantly, the Constitution was penned to be accessible to the common man, and not just scholars and academics. It is written in plain English, is relatively concise, and is quite deliberate in what it says the government can and cannot do. And bear in mind that the original language as selected by the Founders really was supposed to be the rules by which the American government operated, and its transparency was intentional. The Founders were keenly aware of man's urge to rule, and wanted to make sure that the document that was to be the chief protector of individual liberty in the future was clear and easy to understand. And they succeeded: even as a governing document for a large and complex institution, the Constitution is a model of clarity.

Let's start at the beginning. After the preamble, its first words are "All legislative powers herein granted shall be vested in a Congress of the United States." Though it might seem simple, this short phrase contains two very powerful ideas.

First, Congress, and only Congress, has the power to come up with new laws. Not the executive branch, for all of the power given to the president, not the judiciary, for all its legal expertise, and certainly not some independent commission invested heavily in an agenda divergent from the American people's best interests. Legislative power lies with Congress, a body made up of elected representatives from everywhere in the country, each battling for his or her constituents' needs. This point seems straightforward and indisputable, at least as plainly as it's written in the Constitution.

Second, note the words "herein granted." They mean that Congress is limited to the set of powers specifically described in the Constitution. The Founders left no room for artistic license. And, indeed, what follows just a bit later in Article 1, Section 8, is a list of powers given to Congress. Dubbed "enumerated powers," these aren't numbered but are listed quite explicitly. The Founders had just risked everything to escape a government where most laws stemmed from the whims of one man, and they were well aware that those with power throughout history had nearly always abused it. In writing the Constitution, they therefore intended to control the power of the federal government by limiting the items it could legislate.

Third, in case these limitations were somehow unclear, Congress added a Bill of Rights: the original ten amendments to the Constitution. In the Ninth Amendment, they wrote, "The enumeration in the Constitution, of certain rights, shall not be construed to deny or disparage others retained by the people." Similarly, in the Tenth Amendment, "The powers not delegated to the United States by the Constitution, nor prohibited by it to the States, are reserved to the States respectively, or to the people."

Like the rest of the document, these words and the Founders' intentions are easy enough to understand, even today. The Ninth and Tenth Amendments go together, in a sense, because both are meant to limit the power of the federal government and preserve the power of the people, which is a nice summary of what the Constitution was supposed to do. The Ninth Amendment means that the rights of the people go beyond those listed in the Constitution. Note the difference here to the restrictive tone the Founders adopted when addressing the rights of the government. From this, the Tenth Amendment follows, as it means that if the Constitution doesn't say that the federal government, designated here as the United States, was given a certain power, then it doesn't have that power. Period. Instead, jurisdiction falls with either state governments or the people.

Consider the view of the Constitution's author, James Madison. He considered the Ninth and Tenth Amendments redundant of what came earlier, as it was his central intention that the Constitution be interpreted that way. To President George Washington, he wrote, "If a line can be drawn between the powers granted and the rights retained, it would seem to be the same thing, whether the latter be secured, by declaring that they shall not be abridged, or that the former shall not be extended."[1]

The Founders left little room for misinterpretation. The federal government is strictly limited in what it can do. Only Congress can legislate, and only on a specified set of issues. The rights of the government are restricted, while those of the people are not. Clearly, these were men who prized individual liberty, and they went to great lengths to protect it while engineering America's governing structure.

But the Founders weren't content with merely limiting what Congress could do through a list of permissible activities. They also wanted to make it hard for Congress to legislate within that set of particular laws. They wanted laws to have a broad consensus. The Athenian idea of a simple majority vote of the people was viewed as both unstable (as the population could easily change its mind) and, as we saw with Socrates, a threat to liberty.

So they split the legislature into two branches, the House of Representatives and the Senate, and passage of laws required approval from both. House members were elected on a short-term basis to represent the interests of the people. Alternatively, senators occupied much longer terms in which they primarily represented the interests of state government, and only indirectly those of the people in that state. This required reaching a broad consensus before legislation was passed, which we can analyze in two parts.

First, in order for a bill to be approved by the House, it had to be consistent with current public opinion. House members, elected every two years and apportioned based on population, were to serve as a close analog for America's citizenry, one up-to-date with its issues and interests. On the other hand, every two years, one-third of the Senate's members were to be reelected or vacate their seats at the end of their six-year terms, and so this branch of the law-making process was to reflect a longer public perspective, one weighted more by time and consideration.

Second, by giving each state two senators, the Founders prevented a few large states and their issues from dominating passed legislation. Just as important were the small states in the union and what mattered to them. The Founders further protected the little guys by mandating that senators be chosen by state legislators, and not by popular vote (though this process was changed in 1913 with the ratification of the seventeenth amendment). Of course, the state legislators were elected by the people, so they indirectly influenced who made it to the Senate, but senators were to operate primarily with the self-interest of their states in mind to protect them from overreach by the federal government.

The Founders then added the executive branch as a final check on the legislative process. The president was given the power to veto bills passed by Congress, a decision that could be overridden only by a two-thirds majority in both the House and the Senate. Institutionally, the president was meant to represent the interest of the country as a whole, while senators and representatives reflected the views of the states and the districts from which they came.

But even with the agreement of Congress and the president, the Founders felt there was still potential to violate individual rights. So they added a provision to ensure that personal liberty in America was constant in the face of new laws. They gave the people the right to free speech so that they could criticize the government and possibly force it to change. They forbade the establishment of a formal state religion but guaranteed the free exercise of religion to prevent the government from interfering with people's religious practices. They gave the right to bear arms, the need for which became apparent during the revolution, when the British tried to seize colonial munitions at Lexington and Concord, Massachusetts. They guaranteed the right to a trial by jury of our peers, protected us from cruel and unusual punishment, and guaranteed the protection of our property from government seizure, among other rights. So even a broad consensus at the center was not enough. Rights guaranteed that the people trumped even the combined views of Congress and the president.

Finally, the Founders believed that within the government, power should be decentralized. They not only limited what the federal government could do but also gave the states the power to act on their own. This would make it harder for self-interested parties to advance their own agendas, because they would have to gain support from each state. Moreover, to ensure political protection for the states on a national level, they gave state governments the power to decide how their electors for president would be chosen.

The end result was several tiers of defense against government becoming too big or too powerful. Passing laws was made difficult by requiring a broad consensus. Additional rights against government action were included in the Bill of Rights. States were granted powers and protections to make sure that they could act on their own. And there was one more protection: directly or indirectly, we the people got to choose our government.

Not all of the ideas the Founders had to secure liberty were perfect. We sometimes complain that it is difficult to get things done in Washington. This is a consequence of our Founders' very deliberate intentions, however. The passage of legislation was made cumbersome specifically to make it hard for the federal government to take away our liberties.

While legislative power was quite constrained by a complicated set of rules, executive power was straightforward. The idea was that presidential power should be broad in terms of implementation but narrow in terms of subject matter. The president was granted three powers: (1) to make sure that the laws were carried out faithfully (as well as the power to appoint people to do so); (2) to conduct foreign policy with remarkably little interference from Congress; and (3) the ability to report to Congress on things he felt needed doing—what we now call, as the Constitution did, the "State of the Union."

In this case, the rules for the president stressed operational efficiency. For example, the president was given the power of appointment, which required consent of the Senate in the cases of Cabinet officers, ambassadors, and judges. But the Constitution also provided that "the Congress may by Law vest the Appointment of such inferior Officers, as they think proper, in the President alone." In modern parlance, the president is the boss. He could hire and fire pretty much at will.

Not only that, but also the president had the power to hold the people who worked for him accountable: "[H]e may require the Opinion, in writing, of the principal Officer in each of the executive Departments, upon any Subject relating to the Duties of their respective Offices." Of course, if you worked for one of these principal officers, you had to answer to him or her, and in turn to the president. In the Constitution, the chain of command within the executive branch is deliberately simple.

The same holds true in terms of the military and foreign policy power of the president: "The President shall be Commander in Chief of the Army and Navy of the United States, and of the Militia of the several States, when called into the actual Service of the United States." So again, he was the boss. Now Congress had the power, and the responsibility, to fund the military, and it could exercise control in that way, and the Constitution limited such appropriations to a term of two years to ensure review. But in between appropriations, the president could direct the armed forces. He also had the power to make treaties, but he had to get the approval of two-thirds of the Senate to do so.

But on legislative matters, the president was limited to recommending actions, not enacting them: "[The president] shall from time to time give to the Congress Information of the State of the Union, and recommend to their Consideration such Measures as he shall judge necessary and expedient." This was the means by which the president could infuse the details of policy implementation learned in carrying out his or her executive duties. The president was not supposed to enact new laws, amend existing laws, or even interpret legislation in a broad way. Instead, the president was limited to reporting to Congress what he believed to be the most important ideas to make the country run more efficiently. There was to be no end run around the legislative process, even if the president believed he had some special knowledge or expertise on how to do things.

The Constitution is therefore a mixture of the cumbersome and the expeditious. Passing new legislation is a difficult process that requires the agreement of many with differing viewpoints, particularly when the law might infringe on the rights of the people. But the president is able to carry out new laws that were enacted and to conduct foreign policy without a lot of time wasted, especially when such actions are critical to the safety of Americans. This mixture of efficiency and restraint is probably what has allowed the government, based on the Constitution, to function as long as it has.

The framers of the Constitution did not think they did a perfect job. As such, they provided a means to improve the Constitution when it became unworkable or failed to meet the needs of a changing society. Importantly, they specified only one way to bring about such significant changes in America's governance—one that entrusted all power to elected representatives, and by extension, the people. The Founders were very deliberate in crafting the process for changing the rules of the game, so that any would-be Ruling Class could not seize power easily. In a sense, then, the Constitution is a living document, but it is supposed to live and grow by a process set down within the document itself and not according to the whims of those who might hold power at a particular point in time.

The Ruling Class have never wanted to deal with such an unwieldy process when it comes to imposing their will. At first, Britain thought the Constitution might collapse of its own accord and waited for such a fortuitous event. After all, the belief that a country of farmers and tradesman could govern themselves was totally alien. But they were wrong; the Constitution proved more durable than expected. Then Britain tried invasion in 1812, but was repelled as the country came together despite regional differences.* Over time, a domestic Ruling Class emerged, who also tried their best to gain power. These were the successors of the old

---

*The War of 1812 was simply an extension of the Napoleonic Wars, from the British point of view, but America declared war because Britain was blocking its trade with France and kidnapping its sailors and forcing them to serve in the British Navy.

aristocracy, but theirs was an aristocracy based on what they perceived as innate superiority. They still held to the core Ruling Class principle that people could not manage their own lives and that only the government could, and naturally they felt that they were the ones to run that government. Their battle to make America safe for the Ruling Class was a long one. It involved some rethinking and rebranding, and what we've ended up with is a de facto Ruling Class that call themselves "progressive." We turn next to the story of how that happened.

CHAPTER 4

The Ruling Class
Rethink and Rebrand

In the beginning of mankind's history, the acceptance of a strong ruler reflected an instinctive need for safety in a dangerous world. This expanded into more regulation as society became more complex, based on the same assumption that a ruler needed to set down rules in order to maintain social stability. But the English revolutions of the seventeenth century suggested that this instinct needed to be buttressed by a more formal philosophy, since the right of the ruler to do this on his own whim became suspect. A period we call the Age of Enlightenment, driven by the scientific revolution, was dawning, and reason—or at least logical argumentation—was rapidly gaining popularity, while "Because I said so" was losing its credibility as a justification for rulers to get their way in the evolving world. In 1794, Thomas Paine, an American political activist, published *The Age of Reason: Being an Investigation of True and Fabulous Theology*, which became a bestseller in the new United States.

Paine inspired many free thinkers by advocating for reason in the place of revelation, challenging the political power of the religious ruling class.

But the Ruling Class were crafty, and realized a need to reinvent themselves to provide a more elaborate rationalization for why they should remain in control. Titles such as "ruler" and "sovereign" had to go. In earlier times, these had their place in manipulating the common man to develop a sense of deference, but individuals were now beginning to see themselves as having self-worth—separate from some tribe or empire, in which their potential and role were severely limited. The well-being of society was no longer linked to the well-being of the ruler. The notion of a "social contract" emerged, leading people to think that maybe rulers were meant to serve a greater purpose than themselves; that perhaps those in power were obligated to protect the welfare of those they ruled. John Locke and the Founders did this by making the contract one in which the government's purpose was to protect the liberty of the people. If rulers did not want to lose their subjects, as King George III did, they would have to find a way of defining the social contract differently. As we shall see, they found a new concept of the social contract that justified their role amply. Indeed, this new ruse for the Ruling Class would serve them so well that it can be found even among our current political leaders. The basis of this social contract was that the people still needed them to take care of them.

The modern-day Ruling Class have survived by changing their image time and again, rebranding themselves to take advantage of real or imagined problems; convincing others by whatever means necessary that only they can rule effectively. Perhaps their greatest skill is using the media to convince the gullible of whatever is needed to retain power.

However, the truth is that the Ruling Class have only one abiding belief: they are superior beings placed on earth to be its rulers. Common people are incapable of managing their own affairs. While those who prize liberty seek to minimize government's role and influence, the contemporary Ruling Class see an overly involved government as absolutely essential, just as their forebears believed that without their firm hand gripping the proverbial leash, society would fall apart. Of course, the Ruling Class view themselves as the natural controllers of the levers of power, though they mask just how powerful their position is by painting themselves as humble public servants there to protect the Common Man and his interests from the baser instincts of other, less noble souls. Although there is some diversity in their philosophy, the modern Ruling Class have developed their preferred label "progressive" to suggest that they are a self-christened guiding light toward progress. This designation unites their party line of helping the less fortunate, opposing outdated and selfish notions such as unfettered economic liberty, and leading society to a better future. But *progressive* is just another modern brand name for this ancient group; the impulses of the Ruling Class remain the same.

This long process of rebranding began with the writings of Thomas Hobbes during the first of the revolutions of seventeenth-century Britain. Hobbes's mission was to provide a justification for a Ruler that comported with the Age of Enlightenment's concept of Reason. Hobbes, a philosopher, wrote about a quarter century before Locke, and the two men form opposite bookends regarding the purpose of government and the extent of its role in society. One of Hobbes's most famous works, titled *Leviathan or The Matter, Forme and Power of a Common Wealth Ecclesiasticall and Civil*,[1] or simply *Leviathan*, summarizes his political theory. *Leviathan* is named after an extremely powerful monster in the Bible's book of Job. This is what Hobbes thought government should be: an entity given absolute power. Hobbes believed that men were incapable of pursuing anything but their own self-interest, and that this inherent drive would create anarchy—a "war of all against all"—as individuals struck out furiously in their own selfish directions. "In such condition, there is no place for industry, because the fruit thereof is uncertain," he wrote.

Here Hobbes defines industry broadly, fitting closely what we call today an economy. There would be no farming, or what he termed, "culture of the earth," and, of course, "no navigation, nor use of commodities that may be imported by sea, no commodious building, no instruments of moving and removing such things as require much force, no knowledge of the face of the earth; no account of time, no arts, no letters, no society, and which is worst of all, continual fear and danger of violent death." Hobbes characterized life in this miserable state as "solitary, poor, nasty, brutish, and short." *

Hobbes carried his view to its logical alternative. Self-interest could not be allowed to lead to anarchy. The only solution, in his eyes, was to instate a ruler with absolute power to restrain the desires of man and create a state of peace in which they could function. He wrote that "for their own preservation and of a more contented life," men needed a "visible power to keep them in awe, and tie them by fear of punishment" to proper behavior. Note that in this worldview, man is simply not capable of civility in his community because he lacks what Locke and the Founding Fathers saw as key: a respect for the rights and liberty of others as a way of protecting one's own rights and liberty.

Hobbes's Leviathan was all-powerful, and his powers could not be changed or reduced. He was the author of all laws, as well as judge, jury, and executioner. He could, "[reward] with riches and honour" and "[punish] with corporal or pecuniary punishment, or with ignominy, every subject according to the law he hath formerly made." In Hobbes's world, questioning the almighty state or allowing for judgments other than that of the sovereign could not be permitted, because it would introduce individual self-interest back into the equation. To prevent this kind of threat to the state—and ultimately societal stability—thought too

---

*Further examination of the work of Adam Smith offers a convincing rebuttal. Smith would point out that Hobbes's "war of all against all" was actually competition to deliver better products at lower prices, and that this competition was the key to economic progress. As discussed in chapter 2, Smith believed that individual self-interest was an indispensable motivator of man's productivity. Self-interest checked by competition actually allows man to specialize, making life richer, more pleasant, gentler, and longer, Smith argued. But Smith's work came later, and in the meantime, Hobbes's argument was gaining traction.

had to be controlled.* In return, the sovereign was bound by a "social contract" to govern "well," though Hobbes did not define *well*, nor did he allow the sovereign's subjects a say in the matter.

But Hobbes's idea had some practical flaws aside from not defining what good government was supposed to look like. The biggest was succession. In Hobbes's conception of the world, the sovereign's successor didn't have to be a son or a blood relative but would be someone the sovereign picked. Since the Leviathan had all the power, who else was going to do it? Yet even if one supposes that the original despot did a great job and looked after his or her subjects, how could one be certain that the person he or she picked was up to the task? And what if the original despot went mad or simply declined in old age? The job of being an absolute ruler was a tough one for any individual. A wide variety of events could shock the whole system, and dealing with that array of possibilities required more skills than one person could reasonably possess.

Leviathan Becomes the Party

The Ruling Class notion of the "perfect" Leviathan changed in the nineteenth century. The basic idea that a country needed an absolute dictatorship so that individual self-interest did not take over was kept. The key of using the full power of the government to advance the nation's interest remained. But the problem of succession was solved, and the definition of governing *well* was clarified. The new Leviathan was the *party*. It determined who succeeded whom in office, and governing well was identified as ruling in the interest of the proletariat, or working class.

Like the despots of old, the party never had to consult the proletariat about what it thought its interests really were. There was no need, and it would serve no purpose, because the proletariat wouldn't have an

---

*"[T]he sovereign may judge what opinions and doctrines are averse, who shall be allowed to speak to multitudes, and who shall examine the doctrines of all books before they are published" (from *Leviathan*, chapter 18).

answer anyway! The word "proletariat" is actually a somewhat derogatory term of Roman origin referring to people who didn't own property, could not support their families if called away to battle, and therefore had only one purpose for the state: procreation, to provide the next generation of the working class. That shows what Marxists really thought of the people in whose name they claimed to be governing. Average citizens were not competent to run the affairs of the government or their own lives in the absence of an all-powerful government. That is why they needed a Ruling Class with absolute power in the form of the party to rule for them, to actually be the dictators in the dictatorship of the proletariat. So just as in ancient Rome, the proletariat really did not have any say. Those decisions were made by the new "upper class": the inner circle of the Communist Party.

This new Ruling Class coined the term "democratic centralism," effectively voting at the center, to describe how decisions were to be made. Marxist or Communist governments tend to be governed by a small elite, and this was formalized into a group called a politburo or a central committee. These are typically people who run and manage various parts of the state apparatus. Power and expertise were brought together in a small group that actually ran things. When one of their number no longer met their needs, he was purged and replaced with another. This solved the succession problem.

Hobbes justified Leviathan based on society's best interest, and as such, was not taking sides among groups in the population. Sometimes he might side with one group, sometimes another, all based on whatever served the best interest of all. This new view was that the ruler was there explicitly to take sides on a systematic basis. The role of the party was to advance the interests of the proletariat, not the society as a whole. This liberated the Ruling Class from any obligation of "fairness."

In a democratic model, this would allow the Ruling Class Leviathan to offer itself tactically to *whoever* the party thought could help provide it with a majority. Karl Marx, coauthor of *The Communist Manifesto*, did not perceive this to be a problem. The proletariat made up the vast majority of the population and so the party was by definition ruling in the interest of the majority.

Rebranding for America

None of this would work in America. The core impulse of some to believe that they had a unique insight into how to make life better was kept. And, of course, this was joined with these rulers' view that they needed to have the power to make good things happen. But the mode of gaining power, and in whose interests the government was to be run, were entirely different.

The great majority of the American people did not think of themselves as being part of the proletariat—or, really, part of any particular social class. In the agricultural sector, most people were independent farmers who owned their own land. In urban areas, a substantial middle class existed consisting of shopkeepers and skilled individuals who either owned their own small businesses or were specialized employees of a larger firm. All had "capital" of some form: land, financial wherewithal, or skills. And even in the late nineteenth and early twentieth centuries, most people had some schooling.

Power was not to be gained through a revolution but at the ballot box. So people had to be persuaded that you were going to act in their interest. In America, this was complicated by a long tradition of individualism and self-reliance. Therefore, a much more complex form of marketing was needed; a whole new branding of the Ruling Class ideology.

First, demanding bluntly, "Give me power to run your life," doesn't work. Instead, one must focus on the insecurities of the voter. "Give me power so I can protect you from someone else" works much better. So the new focus was not on being the ruler but on saving you from *another* potential ruler who was far more dangerous. In late-nineteenth-century and early-twentieth-century America, this alternative Ruling Class were the titans of industry, often called the robber barons. And there was more than a grain of truth to the argument.

Most people saw these men—men like J. P. Morgan, Jay Gould, Andrew Carnegie, and John D. Rockefeller—as bringing overall economic gain: widespread access to electricity, cheap transportation by rail, and car ownership were the most obvious signs. The agglomeration of industry was actually reducing costs—and prices were falling, allowing more individuals to acquire more things. But in the process, a lot of those small business owners and skilled workers who worked for businesses that failed became resentful. In addition, the existence of these monopolies or near monopolies made people nervous that they would become dependent on someone who could exert power and raise prices at will. Protecting people from these fears meant that the Ruling Class needed new powers: the ability to break up these economic powerhouses even though they had not done something that traditionally had been illegal. It required that the government could divide and reorganize these businesses simply because they were too big and could monopolize economic power.

Second, with all this industrialization, one could persuade voters that there really was something that the Ruling Class could offer: a deeper understanding of the way the world worked. Most people had finished the eighth grade, and, increasingly, people were graduating from what we now call high school. This had long been enough to be able to run one's own life with competence in reading, writing, and arithmetic. But whole new lines of thought were emerging in science and the way the economy functioned. This provided an opening. The Ruling Class began to promote itself as either being "expert" or inclined to hire experts to run things. A trend called "credentialism" began to emerge. People who had gone to school and studied something enough to have earned a "credential" were held up as folks worthy of deference. The old notion of "common sense"—that every man with real-world experience could claim, became discredited. We needed a society run by experts, not by ordinary folks relying on their everyday life experiences to provide them with common sense.

Third, a government that was out to protect you and was run by experts who knew better needed not be a government that had to be fair and impartial. In fact, the whole rationale was to take sides: to protect the people against powerful interests and to guide society in the way that experts thought would lead to a better tomorrow.

So the next thing one needed to provide voters was a "vision." It was not enough for America to be the land of the free and the home of the brave; it could be something more, something grander. What exactly was the vision? Well, that was fluid. It worked out to whatever produced the most votes. But it came under the overall rubric of "progress" and aspirants to rule coalesced around a common theme: that they were progressive. What exactly is progress? It depended on the ruler of the day; he defined progress based in part on his own judgment but also based on what he thought would best garner political support. One thing that becomes obvious when looking at the American progressive Ruling Class of the last century is its flexibility. As we shall see in chapter 6, early progressives held very little in common in terms of policy with their modern counterparts. The only common thread was a belief that with enough power, they could make America a better place.

The Rise of Paternalism

But during this process, an old theme still dominated: the notion that progressives really did know how to run people's lives better than the people did themselves. This came under the broad rubric of social engineering; that manipulating society and the choices people make was key to human and social progress. One example of this phenomenon was Margaret Sanger, founder of Planned Parenthood. There is no doubt that the bulk of Sanger's work was dedicated to improving the status of women as mothers. She genuinely believed in the goal that women, not the state, should have control of their own reproductive choices. But that didn't mean she thought that birth control should not be used as a part of social engineering.

In a 1921 pamphlet, *The Morality of Birth Control*, Sanger argued that society was composed of three groups when it came to reproduction. The first group she called "educated and informed," as they limited the size of their families. The second group was "intelligent and responsible," who wanted to limit their families but lacked the knowledge and means. The third group was "irresponsible and reckless," as religion and other views stopped them from regulating their own reproduction. Sanger said, "There is no doubt in the minds of all thinking people that the procreation of this group should be stopped."[2]

Her reasoning was straightforward if harsh: "For if they are not able to support and care for themselves, they should certainly not be allowed to bring offspring into this world for others to look after. We do not believe that filling the earth with misery, poverty, and disease is moral. And it is our desire and intention to carry on our crusade until the perpetuation of such conditions has ceased." Here Sanger's paternalism extended well beyond simply "informing" people to a desire to actually control their lives. This brought her uncomfortably close to sentiments shared by believers in eugenics, though she diverged from them in her belief in persuasion rather than coercion. Still, it is hard to disagree that she had a strong view of her own moral and intellectual superiority.

Sanger also favored a very restrictive immigration policy on the same grounds. In 1939, she began a program with the unfortunate name "the Negro Project,"[3] aimed at working to introduce birth control into the black community. Her goal was to solve a problem as she defined it: that having too many children ended up miring people in poverty. But her story nonetheless points out the difference between people who believe in progressive social engineering and people who stress the value of liberty. It comes down, as it always had, to who knows best, a phenomenon known as "paternalism."

To win an election, a candidate does not tell the individual whose vote they are seeking that they know better than he or she does how to run their life. No, you posit, as Sanger did, that there is some group out there that we both know needs their lives run for them because they are doing a poor job of it. The people listening to her doubtless felt themselves "educated and informed." They certainly knew that many of their neighbors were "intelligent and responsible," but they also undoubtedly knew a third group of people in another part of town who were "irresponsible and reckless." It is the rhetorical equivalent of telling voters that if they like their doctor and health plan, they can keep it, but that we need to do something about those people who don't. There is always someone out there who needs help—or that we can believe needs help. Of course, this type of reasoning quickly becomes a slippery slope. Once a social engineer is given the power to control decisions in order to achieve some "better" world, there is no limitation on what he or she can or might do. Paternalism can spread quite far and quite fast.

Social Engineering and Self-Interest

We all make mistakes, and those mistakes can be taken as an indication that we do not know what is in our own best interest. We might eat too much and exercise too little. We might even engage in behaviors that we know are extremely detrimental to our health, like smoking cigarettes. But most important, these are our mistakes to make. It is up to us, and not the government, to determine what our *self*-interest is.

But when we opt for our own self-interest, we might be choosing something that the Ruling Class views as against their interest or society's interest. When we do not take care of ourselves, we might be running up health care costs, and if the Ruling Class claims it is responsible for those, it might try cracking down on our individual behavior. In his classic work *Nineteen Eighty-Four*,[4] George Orwell describes an extreme case of a government-run society in which this principle is applied. Through the two-way television installed in every apartment, Big Brother, the leader of the totalitarian state, conducts morning exercise routines in which people are expected to participate, or they might get a visit from the Thought Police inquiring why they are not behaving as they should. Winston Smith, the hero in the novel, disliked this part of the day, as he suffered from a hernia, which the state did not prioritize

as needing repair. Big Brother knew best. So Smith did his morning cal-
isthenics. This is a type of government behavior straight out of Hobbes's
Leviathan.

Though his writings represent exaggerated examples, Orwell understood quite well how living under a controlling government might be in
real life, even one that was elected democratically. He contracted tuber-
culosis in 1947 and was prescribed the antibiotic streptomycin. Trouble
was, England's newly established public health system, the National
Health Service, rigidly rationed access to such medications, as they were
imported and viewed as too expensive. Approval for his prescription went
all the way to Aneurin Bevan, the national minister of health. Fortunately for Orwell, he and Bevan knew each other, as Orwell had written
for the Labour Party organ, the *Tribune,* of which Bevan was a director.
As a result, Orwell had access to someone who could make an exception
for him and provide access to the drug he needed, an option that most
people did not have. He later returned the favor and helped out Bevan's
faction of the Labour Party in its battle against more pro-Soviet elements
by writing supporting articles and serving as a behind-the-scenes political strategist. As Orwell observed in another of his classics, *Animal Farm,*
"All animals are equal, but some animals are more equal than others."[5]

The case of Orwell and the streptomycin highlights a different
problem the Ruling Class have with the concept of each person making decisions in his or her own interest. If people are allowed to decide
for themselves what constitutes their own self-interest, then different
people will make different choices. And if different people make different choices, that will lead to different results. And that will lead to
greater inequality and unfairness. Someone has to work to prevent such
an unequal outcome, and that is yet another marketing message as to
why the Ruling Class are needed: so they can promulgate the myth to
make everything more fair and equal.

Why couldn't Orwell be allowed to import his own antibiotics?
Frankly, not everyone who needed them could afford them. So allowing
someone to import the drug for his or her own use would be unfair to

everyone else who might need it. The British National Health Service could not afford to pay for everyone to have streptomycin, as Britain was nearly bankrupt in the aftermath of World War II. It would be hard to raise more money; the top tax rate on labor income was 83 percent, and on capital income, 98 percent. To prevent money from leaving the country, England instituted strict rules on obtaining foreign currency, and individuals traveling abroad were limited to taking £50—about $240 at the time—with them. Having people buy their own drugs abroad was not only unfair, but also it would have violated the nation's economic interest. There might be "special circumstances" which is why the minister of health could make exceptions, as in Orwell's case. That is another imagined reason why we need a Ruling Class: to decide when exceptions to the rules need to be made in society's best interest.

Today defenders of Ruling Class ideals would say that they have no intention of limiting individual choices the way it happened in Britain. We are much wealthier and can afford far more. Of course, that is true. But that does not mean we can let everyone on a government-sponsored plan buy every drug they might want or every medical procedure they might desire. Ultimately the government must ration what it delivers somehow. So Ruling Class control has to be a part of any kind of government-run health care system.

So if the Ruling Class are responsible for health care, why might they not control things that affect our health? In 2013, New York City banned the sale of soft drinks and other sweetened beverages in servings larger than sixteen ounces. First, let's agree that these drinks are not healthy and that they contain lots of empty calories, and so to avoid argument, let's agree that the idea was well intended. But even if there is no road to hell paved by good intentions, there certainly is a road to bureaucratic complications. What about fruit juice? Orange juice, which has roughly as many calories as Coca-Cola, is okay, but only if it is pure fruit juice; cranberry juice is not. Unsweetened grapefruit juice is okay, but not the sweetened variety, even if it contains fewer calories than orange juice. Most fruit smoothies fail. Drinks that are at least 50 percent milk are okay, even the high-calorie ones. For example, Starbucks's pumpkin spice lattes and Dunkin' Donuts's macchiatos are exempt. Alcoholic beverages are exempt. Hope that all makes sense to you!

Also, the rules apply only to vendors regulated by the city's health department. This means it does not apply to food stores. The customer can still buy those large two-liter bottles at the supermarket, or even at 7-Eleven, where you can still buy a Big Gulp. But, you can't buy one from a street vendor or at McDonald's. And finally, if you really want to get that supersized thirty-two-ounce cup of Coke when you do go to McDonald's, there is nothing to prevent you from ordering two sixteen-ounce drinks, or from refilling the first one you buy.

So what is the point? With this rule, with all of its exceptions, can the Ruling Class really say that they are looking out for the well-being of others; or is this just a way of making life more difficult for the rest of us, and thereby to exert their own power and authority? Thomas Jefferson identified these enemies of liberty and the possibility that they might take control when he said, "if we can but prevent the government from wasting the labours of the people, under the pretence of taking care of them, they must become happy." [6]

Rebranded, but the Same Old Ruling Class

It would seem that everything has changed in terms of human governance since our earliest days in tribal societies. We have gone from hereditary rulers to democratic elections. But in many ways, things have not changed. There are still people out there who believe they know best and need power to make sure that their superior vision is carried out.

The Ruling Class have rebranded themselves from the beneficiaries of a despot who inherited his position to a new kind of despot who rules for the benefit of his society. The rulers moved to rule in the interests of the proletariat, then an amorphous group of people who believed in progress and a better society. This led back to the Ruling Class running our lives because we did not know how to run them ourselves.

Throughout, rulers deluded themselves as having a special and unique claim to ruling. They are convinced of their own superiority and their superior idealism. They say to themselves that they are not there because they think governing others is a great job, and they're certainly not doing it because they find it fun to boss others around. *Others* might want to rule the world for their own selfish ends, but not *them*. They are doing it for their fellow man. Bertrand Russell, a twentieth-century British philosopher, logician, and social critic, identified this trait in the Ruling Class almost a century ago: "Much that passes as idealism is disguised hatred or disguised love of power."[7]

The contemporary member of the Ruling Class talks about other ideals, such as "social justice." That vision defines a "just" world, but only within a limited perspective that serves his or her goals best. Today the words "social justice" are usually used to manipulate people into accepting a Ruling Class message that supports their current theme. There is little objective truth in that message, just an attempt at manipulation using emotion. Sometimes achieving that particular vision of social justice involves taking money from one person and giving it to another, or using the funds for some governmental function that is "just." So if justice is needed, and only the Ruling Class know what that is, then they must control the government in order to be able to tax and spend their way to a "just" society. A member of the Ruling Class must harbor no doubts about the rightness of his or her cause to justify having and using so much power over others.

Note that this Ruling Class view will be presented to the public as idealistic, but it certainly is not altruistic. The member of the Ruling Class is not taking some of the money he or she earned; instead, they are using the taxing power of the government to take the money; and then as they are the rulers, deciding what to do with it. Far from being altruistic, it is hard to think of anything more selfish than someone expecting others to pay for the things they want in life, even if what they claim to want is a "just" society. It takes an unusual type of "idealist" to think that the way to achieve one's "ideals" is by spending someone else's money. This requires a further belief from the Ruling Class: that they have an intellectual or knowledge advantage that allows them to know how to spend your money better than you do.

Throughout history the Ruling Class have justified themselves on three core beliefs. First, that man cannot run his own individual affairs. Second, the government is best suited to run his life instead. Third, that there are unique traits that qualify someone to be in charge of the government, which by their definition are the traits of the Ruling Class. How they argued each of these points has varied with the times. There has been a tremendous amount of rebranding, particularly on that last point. Today a member of the Ruling Class cannot claim it to be his birthright, as did kings of old. A Hobbesian divine despotism might be the ideal to a ruler, but it too is not practical. Nor can one claim to be simply carrying out the wishes of the proletariat that does not even have the capability of knowing what it wants. Having the right credential helps, as this provides a qualification, at least on paper. But ultimately the ruler must believe in himself or herself as a first step to making others into believers. This requires a sense of natural superiority that is the subject to which we now turn.

CHAPTER 5

The Progressive Superiority Complex

Today it is widely believed among Ruling Class members that they occupy an intellectually superior upper echelon of society and that this entitles them to the lofty positions they claim at the helm of our government. Many in the Ruling Class of old felt they had a divine right to power—that their position was not only deserved, but that God put them on earth to rule the masses. This rationale is actually not far from how the modern-day Ruling Class see themselves. Did you ever meet a progressive who didn't think that he cared more about other people than most, or that she was smarter and better informed than the average citizen?

There is a great deal of both popular and more scholarly literature on the subject. The main conclusion from the bulk of these studies, written by people who share the values of the Ruling Class and often fancy themselves as part of it, is that those who believe in a powerful and activist government, progressives or liberals, are smarter than a group they term conservatives.

Consider for example a recent article in *Psychology Today* entitled "Why Liberals Are More Intelligent Than Conservatives."[1] Not surprisingly, the article acknowledges openly that liberals are the Ruling Class, but says that it *should* be that way: "Liberals *do* control the media, or the show business, or the academia, among other institutions, because, apart from a few areas in life (such as business) where countervailing circumstances may prevail, *liberals control all institutions.* They control the institutions because liberals are on average more intelligent than conservatives and thus they are more likely to attain the highest status in any area of (evolutionarily novel) modern life."

Note the use of the phrase "evolutionarily novel." The article suggests strongly that liberals represent a more advanced evolutionary state because of their willingness to help genetically unrelated individuals. Noting that this type of behavior has been absent from *all* recorded human cultures, the author posits that liberals are more intelligent than those (for example, conservatives) that they lump in with our ancestors. (The term they use is "evolutionarily familiar.") To bolster this claim, they cite research that shows that the childhood IQs of liberals average 106, while those of conservatives average just 95.

Now, before exploring the "science" in this area, consider for a moment the audacity of this study (and it is by no means unique). Progressives take great umbrage at the notion of IQ differences based on race or gender. Consider what happened to Larry Summers as president of Harvard. He gave a speech that noted that the variance, but not the mean, of male IQ was greater than female IQ. That means that when you look at really smart people, or really dumb people, the majority are male. The statistics back him up. However, he made the mistake of noting that this might explain why there are a disproportionate number of males at the top of the science profession. Oops. The faculty senate denounced him, and ultimately he was booted out as president. So publicly talking about one group being smarter is generally not acceptable among the Ruling Class unless it is saying that liberals are smarter than conservatives.

But the article does not stop there. Consider the assertion that liberals are more evolved. More evolved by what mechanism exactly? Has Darwinian natural selection favored them? Have they been around for more generations so that the evolutionary clock has had a longer time to "improve" their rating on the evolutionary scale? What does this say about them in terms of social evolution, as in their ability to interact with others? Next time you're in a group, try telling those around you that you are "more evolved" than they are and see what happens.

Finally, their most outrageous claim is that their alleged intellectual superiority justifies their control of most societal institutions. This is a group that (at the moment at least) tends to stress "diversity" in terms of the race, ethnicity, sexual orientation, and gender of people in the workplace, especially of those in charge. But ideological diversity is not on the list. Why? Maybe there just aren't enough smart conservatives around. How about some affirmative action based on ideology? Shouldn't that be especially useful at institutions that pride themselves on free intellectual inquiry, such as colleges and universities? Perhaps not. Maybe a liberal arts education should be just that: liberal, untainted by any conservative thoughts.

Of course objective qualifications should dominate decisions. But there can be a good case for an emphasis on diversity if one is seeking a wide variety of different perspectives. Nowhere would that be more the case than in an academic setting, where the whole purpose of the institution is the free exchange of ideas. Yet academia today is one of the most ideologically monolithic institutions in American society.

A 2012 survey by the UCLA Higher Education Research Institute[2] found that 63 percent of professors considered themselves "liberal" or "far left." Just 12 percent identified as being on the political right, and they were outnumbered by the far-left group alone. On a bell curve, this made self-identified liberals the middle of the road on campuses.

Moreover, faculties had moved further left during the previous three years, with the left gaining 7 points and the right dropping 4. Maybe liberal superiority is so great in evolutionary terms that it doesn't even take a generation—it happens in just three years.

Put aside the arrogance and the hypocrisy. A closer look at the *Psychology Today* article suggests that the science might not actually say what progressives claim, and depends very much on how one distinguishes liberals and conservatives. As the article says, "[O]ne may reasonably define liberalism (as opposed to conservatism) in the contemporary United States as *the genuine concern for the welfare of genetically unrelated others and the willingness to contribute larger proportions of private resources for the welfare of such others.*" This, of course, is the crux of what progressives think separates them from everyone else, and, most importantly, what they feel makes them morally superior. It is the most commonly used deception today and, as such, has become the most common marketing message among progressives. It is why they believe they're entitled to control our government to a degree that was specifically guarded against by our Founding Fathers—to forcefully redistribute large proportions of *private* resources from one part of the population to another.

It's important to recognize that the private resources that liberals seek to distribute include others' wealth, not their own. In fact, when one examines the willingness to contribute personal assets across ideologies, the story is quite different from the narrative that many self-proclaimed liberals tell to gain power.

Progressives Are Neither Morally Nor Intellectually Superior

During his tenure at Syracuse University in 2006, Arthur Brooks, current head of the American Enterprise Institute, a Washington think tank, published a book titled *Who Really Cares—America's Charity Divide: Who Gives, Who Doesn't, and Why It Matters*.[3] It contains some rather interesting facts about acts of private charity. First, although liberal families' incomes averaged 6 percent higher than those of conservative families, conservative-headed households gave, on average, 30 percent more to charity. And their greater generosity extended beyond material wealth: conservatives spent more time volunteering and donated more frequently at blood banks. (Talk about caring for genetically unrelated individuals!)

Financial data based on state voting trends in the 2004 election paint the same picture.[4] Residents of states that voted for Democrat John Kerry gave smaller percentages of their incomes to charity compared with states that voted for George W. Bush. Moreover, Bush carried twenty-four of the twenty-five states where charitable giving was above average. And in the ten most conservative states, where Bush support topped 60 percent of the vote, an average of 3.5 percent of personal income was donated to charity. Residents of the bluest states, in which Bush garnered less than 40 percent, donated just 1.9 percent.

These results are no doubt puzzling to the progressive self-image and, particularly, its progressive marketing message, but another statistic presented by Brooks offers a likely explanation. Those who reject the idea that "government is responsible for reducing income inequality" gave an average of *four times more* than people who accepted that proposition. This, combined with the other data, suggests that the real difference between liberals and conservatives is not that conservatives are inherently selfish cavemen, as their opponents would try to convince the public, but rather that they believe the obligation to help genetically unrelated individuals is a personal one, and not society's burden. In other words, conservatives are more willing to contribute *their own* resources, while liberals or progressives care most about marshaling the resources of others.

So the real distinction between liberals and conservatives is not about a difference in genuine caring for their fellow man, but a view about power. Conservatives realize that it is a threat to personal liberty to tell someone what to do with his or her money, and that allowing the government so extensive a reach sets a dangerous precedent. Progressives, in permitting the government to operate this way, fall into two camps: they are either naively idealistic, believing the government and its agents to be truly capable of objective use of such great power; or they are deliberately manipulative, amassing support through a high-minded narrative that directly contradicts their true views. This explanation fits both the data and the characterization of the progressive Ruling Class that we have used in this book, and it's important to remember that in most instances, progressives want to be the ones to redistribute the money! This is not so much an act of selflessness as an act of self-interest in maintaining the self-delusions of the Ruling Class.

Other studies buttress this point and suggest that if you define political viewpoints in terms of controlling versus trusting others to manage their own affairs, the IQ trend liberals tout so proudly reverses. Markus Kemmelmeier, a professor of social psychology at the University of Nevada, examined this issue with six questions: the first three designed to assess conservative viewpoints on social issues, and the latter three on economic issues and government power over the economy. Kemmelmeier found that while those who espoused conservative social views did have lower IQs, those who supported conservative economic views—for example, citizens against government interference in the economy— had higher IQs than their progressive counterparts.

Kemmelmeier, who was a supporter of the idea of progressive Ruling Class superiority, said he found the results "surprising," and indeed they are if you're a progressive whose entire self-image centers on your status as an enlightened being. These data, however, are quite understandable if you actually think about human nature and the characteristics of the people involved. Smart people naturally trust their own judgment over those of bureaucrats. They believe in their ability to make better business decisions than those with less experience and involvement, and realize the insanity in allowing a clumsy, overburdened office in Washington any significant say in their personal affairs. The intelligence of those who respect the danger of state control is not surprising at all.

Noah Carl published a similar result in the journal *Intelligence* in

2014 during his doctoral work at Oxford. First stating that social science research "has consistently shown that intelligence is positively correlated with socially liberal beliefs and negatively correlated with religious beliefs,"[5] Carl then compared IQ by party preference, finding that Republicans consistently had higher IQs than Democrats. Furthermore, IQ difference increased as party allegiance grew stronger. Strong Republicans had a 5.5-point IQ advantage over strong Democrats. In Carl's view, the IQ advantage held by those who believe in liberty was so great that it overwhelmed the supposed Republican "disadvantage," as that party also attracts people with strong religious beliefs, who have been found to have lower mean IQs. In sum, the widespread Ruling Class view that they are smarter is just not true.

What is one to make of this? Aside from the obvious conclusion that the Ruling Class have a self-aggrandizing view of their own superiority—which happens to be false—not much. There are a variety of possible explanations for the differences. First, as noted above, smarter people are more inclined to believe in their own ability to make smart judgments—better judgments than a Ruling Class bureaucrat might make. None of this, however, makes that a "correct" decision. If you believe in liberty, then you respect the right of all people to judge their own self-interest.

But even if you take the progressive view of a Darwinian world, there might be a good evolutionary reason for people who don't think of themselves as being particularly smart in terms of IQ to favor religious or traditional values. Consider again the notion in *Psychology Today* that liberals are more evolved than others. Is their "more evolved" view actually going to turn out to be a wise evolutionary point or simply another of nature's evolutionary dead ends? Only time will tell. Smarter people might be more willing to gamble on their own abilities, but whether the gamble will pay off is another issue that will be decided only by the passage of time. People lacking self-confidence might therefore find the risk-averse strategy of doing what has worked for thousands of years (and so adopted by religious or traditional values) to be the smarter approach for them. Those who believe in liberty realize they must respect that.

In fact, really smart people, especially those who are worried about human evolution and our species' future fate, should prefer diversity in behavioral choice. If smart people typically want to think for themselves and engage in an evolutionarily risky behavior, fine. But that is far from saying that everyone should take the same risks. It might well turn out to be that *not* taking risks is the better way to go. So people who feel that way, regardless of their measured IQ, should be allowed to do so—and it might even enhance the evolutionary survival of the species.

This goes right to the fallacy of the progressive view of social engineering. They must be in charge to push the rest of us to their "more evolved" vision of the world. There is no evidence that it will be "better" for mankind's evolution. Genetic diversity would suggest just the opposite. Individuals making what they think are the right personal choices for themselves not only provide more diversity than the lock-step conformity demanded by the Ruling Class, but also they are using their own talents to enhance the evolutionary survival of their traits. It takes a real arrogance to think you know how to run someone's life better than he or she does. And it is even more arrogant to assume that your view is also better from an evolutionary standpoint.

Ruling Class Cohesion

This leaves unanswered an explanation for the point made in *Psychology Today*: "Liberals *do* control the media, or the show business, or the academia, among other institutions, because, apart from a few areas in life (such as business) where countervailing circumstances may prevail, *liberals control all institutions.*" The article argues that this is because liberals are smarter than conservatives. But the data show that (only if one assumes the facts are relevant) this is the case only if conservatives are defined in a particular way, and that one's stance on personal liberty is what matters. So why do progressives control these institutions, and what are the "countervailing circumstances" that reduce their dominance in other arenas, such as business?

Using the logic of *Psychology Today*, but fitting it to the facts, a possible explanation for progressive authority emerges—one that answers the question of how the Ruling Class continually attains these positions, even with lower IQs than those who espouse liberty. Perhaps control does not depend on intelligence but rather on the progressive sense of class cohesion that is markedly absent in conservatives and people dedicated to liberty. As any nonliberal who has spent time at a college campus will tell you, the Ruling Class make it quite clear that anyone not on their team is unwelcome. And while "diversity" in many forms is valued even to the point of taking affirmative steps to hire people from distinct racial and ethnic groups, there is no affirmative action program to promote intellectual or philosophical diversity.

This behavior reflects a certain level of social intelligence, something not measured by IQ tests, described as group cohesion. After all, they believe that their progressive movement has a moral right and even an obligation to run things in order to save mankind. This belief system is not only a set of views on the world but also a justification for one's own place at the top of that world order. While it's a worldview that is as much an article of faith as the catechism of any belief system, it carries much more importance. One is not talking about the afterlife, but power right here on earth. So, challenges to this basic set of beliefs, the thinking goes, must be dealt with harshly, as one would deal with any heresy.

One can see this obsession with conformity in terms of current behavior on college campuses, where demands for control of speech are now reaching shrill levels. Campuses are supposed to be bastions of free speech. But the closeted progressives who inhabit those places and who see themselves as the future Ruling Class can't allow it. They want no challenge to their belief system, one that justifies themselves and their future role as Rulers. This suppression of criticism is even more vital for those working on projects in which major advancements in the power of the Ruling Class are at stake, such as climate change research and the development of education programs. So free speech is suppressed instead. Students demand "safe spaces" where only language they deem permissible is allowed. Peer pressure to conform to campus groupthink on the issues of the day is rigorously enforced.

This pressure grows as one moves up the ranks of the Ruling Class. Consider Professor Jagadish Shukla of George Mason University. Shukla was one of the many "lead authors" of the 2007 United Nations Intergovernmental Panel on Climate Change (IPCC) report. In 2015, he and nineteen of his colleagues signed a letter to President Obama and Attorney General Loretta Lynch that supported using the Racketeer Influenced and Corrupt Organizations Act (RICO) to investigate those who disagreed with him. From the letter: "We appreciate that you are making aggressive and imaginative use of the limited tools available to you in the face of a recalcitrant Congress. One additional tool—recently proposed by Senator Sheldon Whitehouse (D-RI)—is a RICO (Racketeer Influenced and Corrupt Organizations Act) investigation of corporations and other organizations that have knowingly deceived the American people about the risks of climate change, as a means to forestall America's response to climate change. We strongly endorse Senator Whitehouse's call for a RICO investigation."[6]

So here are a United States senator and academics who helped author a United Nations report recommending that the government use one of the harshest laws on the books—one meant to go after the *Mafia*— to silence the people who disagree with them. These are certainly not people who believe in liberty or in First Amendment guarantees of free speech. The point here is *not* to take sides in the climate change debate but to point out just how strongly members of the Ruling Class will react in suppressing opposing views. These are men and women who really do share Hobbes's philosophy as expressed in *Leviathan*.

It turns out that Professor Shukla's intense interest in prosecuting those who disagree with him is driven not just idealistically. He set up a nonprofit shell corporation, Institute of Global Environment & Society, to collect funds for his climate change work, making his wife "business manager" of the organization. This nonprofit paid the professor and his wife $350,000 to $400,000 per year on top of his $250,000 annual salary from George Mason. To a defender of liberty, there is nothing illegal or even immoral about Professor Shukla and his wife earning whatever they can. What might be of concern is that Professor Shukla does not care to extend the same ability to enjoy the blessings of liberty that he enjoys to others.

This analysis might also explain "those countervailing factors" about why liberals fare so poorly in business. Business thrives by selling products or services that people want. It does not have the luxury afforded to government or academia of letting office politics drive its behavior; if someone is good for the business, it is vital that that person rise to the top. To choose someone else who is less talented costs the business money. So, for their own survival, business institutions are forced to focus on the individual talents of the people they employ and not on their ideology. That might not always work perfectly in practice, as all organizations are subject to office politics, but their influence in promoting people is far less in an institution dedicated to the bottom line.

In conclusion, defenders of liberty and the members of the Ruling Class have very different views about society, freedom, and the appropriate role for government. The key moral basis for the progressive worldview might not be so much that they care about other people more but that they want to control the resources that society uses to take care of the needy. And their claims to intellectual superiority are not borne out by the facts, either. But these facts don't dent progressive self-confidence. Their key challenge isn't internal, but external: the barriers to their rule stated in the Constitution. We now turn to how progressives have massively increased government control of our daily lives and have come to control much of the government and most other societal institutions. In the process, they also have reduced the individual constitutional protections that the Founding Fathers created.

CHAPTER 6

The Progressive Attack
on the Constitution

If you've read this far, you're well aware that our United States is vastly different from the nation our Founding Fathers created and from the ideal they intended America to be. A modern Ruling Class with a belief system not far from that of their tyrannical ancestors have infiltrated our country. Their progressive ideology clearly dominates our society. The constitutional separation of powers crafted so deliberately by our Founders has been replaced by independent commissions creating federal rules, a process totally lacking the original legislative processes' safeguards. The *Federal Register*, which contains the list of all new rules from these agencies, amounted to more than seventy-seven thousand pages in 2014.[1] The courts have now become the dominant decision makers in the realm of social legislation, replacing the American citizenry. And the Founders' extensive restriction of the federal government's power has become an anachronism, as ever more creative interpretations of existing laws effectively make government power unlimited. All of this happened without the Constitution ever having been amended.

We look now to the story of how the Ruling Class took hold—how they've chipped away at our Founders' protection of liberty to warp our society into something unrecognizable. It's vitally important that we understand their rise in America if we are to prevent a complete progressive takeover and if we are ever to take our country back. The rebranding described in chapter 4 began in earnest in the early twentieth century. It changed our self-perception from a nation where common sense was a valid yardstick from which to develop an opinion to a country where credentialed experts were hailed as necessary because society had become too complex for the common man to understand. The progressives have tried to convince us that the Constitution is no longer relevant or applicable in today's world, having been authored by dead white men. As a result of rebranding themselves, the progressive Ruling Class also rebranded the country from one with self-government that was limited in its scope to one where an expert government required ever increasing amounts of power. The story of how this has happened gives us a great insight into the thinking of those who now rule us.

In 1913, a quintessential example of the Ruling Class's beliefs and philosophy rose to the presidency: Woodrow Wilson. He proudly labeled himself as progressive and cultivated the virtues that progressives still view as important today: moral and intellectual superiority. Wilson was keenly interested in improving the lot of mankind and saw government as the way to do it. Most important to the Ruling Class, he created an intellectual basis for getting around the pesky old restrictions of the Constitution, with a concept he termed the "Living Constitution."

In 1908, as president of Princeton University, Wilson wrote, "Living political constitutions must be Darwinian in structure and in practice."[2] During his 1912 presidential campaign, as governor of New Jersey, he developed this notion further, arguing, "Society is a living organism and must obey the laws of life, not of mechanics; it must develop. All that progressives ask or desire is permission—in an era when 'development,'

'evolution,' is the scientific word—to interpret the Constitution according to the Darwinian principle; all they ask is recognition of the fact that
a nation is a living thing and not a machine."[3]

Two key words in these writings bear close examination: "Darwinian" and "progressives." As noted in chapter 5, both are central concepts
to the Ruling Class's view of the world. The Ruling Class embraces the
idea that humanity makes forward progress through a process of natural selection—both genetic and in terms of social practice. "Superior"
wins out over "inferior" in life's struggle toward perfection. From this,
it follows that old ideas such as "liberty" should be discarded when they
were no longer useful to progressive thought—as should the basic arrangements of the Constitution, of which Wilson was no fan. Instead,
he favored the British parliamentary system and was an opponent of the
separation of powers. "I ask you to put this question to yourselves: Should
we not draw the executive and legislature closer together? Should we
not, on the one hand, give the individual leaders of opinion in Congress
a better chance to have an intimate party in determining who should be
president, and the president, on the other hand, a better chance to approve himself a statesman, and his advisers capable men of affairs, in the
guidance of Congress?"[4]

Wilson's purpose, of course, was that power be more concentrated,
which was exactly what the Founding Fathers wanted to avoid and why
they had created the idea of dividing powers. They had designed the
Constitution to slow things down; to require a broad consensus in the
country before new legislation was passed. Wilson and the progressives
wanted to speed things up. They favored this Darwinian concept because the "winner"—or the superior side—gets all the power in such a
system and is unfettered by others. Of course, as a practical matter, Wilson thought this would make it easier to push through progressive ideas
over the opposition of the more conservative "losers."

Wilson's ideas of social Darwinism and progressivism and the triumph of winners over losers had long been an interest of his. In 1901, as
a Princeton professor, he wrote an article for the *Atlantic Monthly* (now

known as the *Atlantic*), an archetypal Ruling Class magazine targeted at those who consider themselves "thought leaders." It was titled "The Reconstruction of the Southern States." Wilson writes:

> An extraordinary and very perilous state of affairs had been created in the South by the sudden and absolute emancipation of the negroes [*sic*], and it was not strange that the southern legislatures should deem it necessary to take extraordinary steps to guard against the manifest and pressing dangers which it entailed. Here was a vast "laboring, landless, homeless class," once slaves, now free; unpracticed in liberty, unschooled in self-control; never sobered by the discipline of self-support, never established in any habit of prudence; excited by a freedom they did not understand, exalted by false hopes; bewildered and without leaders, and yet insolent and aggressive; sick of work, covetous of pleasure—a host of dusky children untimely put out of school. . . . They were a danger to themselves as well as those whom they had once served.[5]

Self-described progressives like Wilson had a very clear idea of "progress": their own views. And his was not one that included a lot of liberty for others. In his first term, he pushed through rule changes that enforced racial segregation in the federal civil service, one of the few governmental avenues for advancement prior to his coming to office. The postmaster general established full segregation in his offices, with the Treasury and the Department of the Navy to follow. To make segregation in hiring easier, all applicants for jobs were required to submit a personal photo for the first time. After the House passed a bill making interracial marriage a felony in the District of Columbia, Wilson replied to a group of black leaders protesting the legislation, "The purpose of these measures was to reduce the friction. It is as far as possible from being a movement against the Negroes. I sincerely believe it to be in their interest."[6] This was a typical Ruling Class paternalist response, reminiscent of Wilson's contemporary, Margaret Sanger.

But Wilson's Darwinian views did not stop there. After winning re-election in 1916 with the campaign slogan "He kept us out of the war," he entered World War I shortly after beginning his second term. Wilson then began a swift crackdown on his political foes in opposition to the war. He established the Committee on Public Information (CPI) to both conduct a prowar propaganda effort and to censor any writings against it. The Sedition Act of 1918 extended the previous year's Espionage Act to make it a crime—punishable by twenty years in prison—to speak or write against the government, the war, or the sale of bonds to finance the war. One of his opponents in the 1912 campaign, Socialist Eugene V. Debs, went to prison under the act. The postmaster general was authorized not to deliver any mail that opposed government policy. A total of 1,500 prosecutions were carried out under these laws. President Wilson also passed amendments to the Immigration Act of 1917 that led to the deportation of legal immigrants who were not yet citizens who spoke against the war effort. His attorney general, Mitchell Palmer, a candidate for the Democratic nomination for president in 1920, called for a peacetime extension of the Sedition Act.

But Wilson remains a hero of the Ruling Class progressive movement for his success at shifting power away from elected leaders and toward nonelected decision makers. This was his way of dismantling one of the key obstacles the Constitution laid in the progressive's path: that only Congress could legislate. In his first term, he initiated and signed four major bills: the Federal Reserve Act, which set up the Federal Reserve System; the Federal Trade Commission Act, which established the FTC; the Clayton Antitrust Act, which expanded the role of the Justice Department in approving mergers and acquisitions; and the Federal Farm Loan Act, which established the Federal Farm Loan Board and Federal Land Banks.

This was a vast expansion of the bureaucracy that established a set of rule-making bodies inside the executive branch. Portions of economic policy could now be determined without Congress ever getting involved. The importance of this as a *constitutional coup* cannot be overstated.

Only twenty years before his election, the Supreme Court had ruled in *Field v. Clark*, "That Congress cannot delegate legislative power to the president is a principle universally recognized as vital to the integrity and maintenance of the system of government ordained by the Constitution." This view predated even the Constitution. In 1690 John Locke argued, "[Legislators] can have no power to transfer their authority of making laws, and place it in other hands."[7]

The argument by Wilson and progressives goes back to the "Living Constitution" based on the supposedly Darwinian idea that society and laws must adapt. In this line of reasoning, society was becoming more complicated. Technology and economic complexity were growing. Old and inferior institutions such as Congress could not possibly cope with these ideas. Instead, these special panels composed of experts were required to write the rules by which society was to function.

Note that this went beyond what the Constitution actually prescribed as the way that executive branch functionaries should deliver suggested rule changes to the Congress. The president was to pass ideas that were "necessary and expedient" on to Congress for their consideration. The presidential experts could, of course, actually design those ideas and even write the draft legislation. Congress would then have the chance to consider the idea on its merits. But this would, of course, require building a broader consensus. It was so much easier to simply empower executive agencies to write the rules, removing the American people and their opinions from the equation entirely.

Wilson is also a hero among progressives for one more of his actions. He called a special session of Congress shortly after being sworn in to reinstitute the income tax, which had been abolished after the Civil War. The promise when introduced was that the rates would never be above 15 percent and would apply only to the rich. When first passed, the standard rate was 6 percent, and only 400,000 taxpayers paid taxes.[8] By 1918, the top rate was 77 percent, and 4.4 million people paid income tax. Even after the end of the World War I, high taxes and a broad net of taxpayers were maintained. By reestablishing the tax, Wilson had opened up a new and seemingly unlimited source of resources for the Ruling Class to use.

Today there is some debate about how progressives should deal with Wilson's legacy, particularly his views on race. Given his personal nature and faith in his own judgment, it seems likely that Wilson's motivation was more driven by his love of social engineering than by explicit racism. This is a core progressive value, almost their raison d'être. Consider again their three core beliefs: ordinary people can't manage their own affairs; government is the natural way to help them; and the morally (and intellectually) superior progressives are the natural ones to run the government to accomplish those tasks.

Moreover, his almost unprecedented (in America) suppression of civil liberties and development of an internal propaganda operation adhered to the progressive Darwinian view that the efficiency and power of government should take precedence over individual liberties in the pursuit of the government's mission. That the ends justify the means is a natural outgrowth of Wilson's progressive Darwinism. Those actions of Wilson that today lack the political correctness the Ruling Class touts so proudly actually fit in quite well with their long-term structure. Wilson should be thought of as a natural hero to their cause.

Broadening Government's Power

Although Woodrow Wilson expanded the reach of unelected officials in rule making, he didn't expand the scope of federal government power. The bills he passed were either explicitly authorized by the Constitution (such as the income tax, through the Sixteenth Amendment) or within the scope of the enumerated powers given to Congress. But that list of enumerated powers was still rather constraining on the Ruling Class's ambitions to extend their rule. They really couldn't get around these limitations directly, so they turned to the enumerated powers to see if they couldn't "stretch" them a bit to broaden their authority. In the Commerce Clause (found in Article 1, Section 8, of the Constitution), they found an appropriate target. It gives Congress the power "[t]o regulate Commerce with foreign Nations, and among the several States, and with the Indian tribes."

Again, a plain reading of that would mean, as it was intended, that when goods cross a political boundary, such as between states or with foreign countries, that Congress could set the rules governing that trade. It did not mean that the federal government could step in when a farmer traded a horse with his neighbor, or when a merchant bought or sold goods in the town square. What the framers of the Constitution were concerned about was that one state might erect barriers to goods coming in from another state. They wanted a free market for goods and services within the country, and that led to the explicit wording "regulate Commerce . . . among the several States."

For roughly the first century and a half of the country's existence, the courts had followed this interpretation, as indicated by the Supreme Court's 1824 ruling in *Gibbons v. Ogden*. New York attempted to give a monopoly on all steamboat traffic within the state to inventor Robert Fulton and his colleague Aaron Ogden. Ogden argued that this included all traffic within New York's borders up to the New Jersey state line, which was in the middle of the Hudson River. This would mean that any person or any object would have to take an Ogden-Fulton ship up to the line and then transfer to another ship to enter New Jersey, or else New Jersey would simply have to allow the Ogden-Fulton ship all the way across. Of course, such routes would be impractical, and the monopoly was struck down.

So the ability to regulate interstate commerce took on a very practical meaning. The federal government could intercede to regulate commerce between the states in order to promote it when state actions were designed in a way to work against it. But the court was very leery about giving power to Congress to regulate interstate commerce even in a way that was clearly well intended. In 1918 in *Hammer v. Dagenhart*, the Supreme Court struck down a congressional statute that prohibited the interstate transport of goods that had been produced by child labor.

Disregarding Congress's reason for the statute, the court wrote, "It must never be forgotten that the Nation is made up of States to which are entrusted the powers of local government. And to them and to the people the powers not expressly delegated to the National Government are reserved." Effectively, the court was saying that the states could regulate child labor within their borders, but should they decide to allow it, the goods produced were fully legal interstate commerce. The court was not arguing with the outcome, it was simply arguing with how it came about. It had yet to make the progressive leap that the *ends justify the means*.

Then along came the Great Depression. In 1932 Franklin Delano Roosevelt was elected president to combat it. Roosevelt's background was one to the manor born: destined to rule. His ancestors were among the first Dutch settlers.[9] He attended the exclusive Groton School, where 90 percent of the students came from families in the *Social Register*, and, like nearly all of his classmates, he went on to Harvard. FDR had been secretary of the navy under Wilson and ran for vice president in 1920.[10] But the 1932 campaign showed he really had no specific plan. The Democratic platform on which he campaigned called for immediate and drastic reductions in public expenditure, abolishing useless commissions and offices, consolidating departments and bureaus, and for a "sound currency" to be maintained at all costs. After beating President Herbert Hoover, he turned down the incumbent's invitation to form a transitional government to set policy, confiding to reporters, "It's not my baby."[11]

By the time he took office four months after his election,* a severe banking crisis had developed. Roosevelt turned to experts for advice, a group he called a "brain trust." What followed was a massive array of programs that did the opposite of what he campaigned on. Spending was increased drastically, new bureaus and commissions were formed to oversee most of national economic life, and the dollar was devalued. Roosevelt wanted to do still more but came up against the Constitution.

---

*From 1793, George Washington's second term, until FDR's second term in 1937, Inauguration Day was held in March instead of January.

The Supreme Court resisted many of these programs because they violated the Constitution, at least the way it had been read since the country's founding 150 years before. In 1937, after winning a landslide reelection, Roosevelt threatened to pack the court with judges of his liking by expanding the number of justices from nine to fifteen. Even his own vice president, John Nance Gardner, considered this a bridge too far in upstaging the way the Constitution worked. But it had its desired effect: Associate Justice Owen Roberts changed his vote on a key piece of legislation (a federal minimum wage and working hours law in *West Coast Hotel Co. v. Parrish*) that the court then upheld 5 to 4, an event dubbed "the switch in time that saved nine."

The aftermath of the switch was much larger than the direct outcome of the case, and it triggered a breathtaking reversal of the reading of the Constitution. The most far-reaching change centered on the reading of the Commerce Clause, and with it, our judicial system went from placing extreme emphasis on ensuring that the legal decision-making process adhered strictly to constitutional principles to accepting a slight bending of the rules depending on the outcome of the case. Consider the decision in *Wickard v. Filburn* from 1942. In 1938, Congress had passed the Agricultural Adjustment Act, which attempted to prop up farm prices by limiting the amount of crops each farmer could produce. Mr. Filburn was a family farmer who exceeded his quota and was fined for doing so. He argued that all of his production was consumed on his own farm, used for things such as feeding his horses. And there was no evidence to contradict Filburn's claim. It was clear that his above-quota production wasn't being sold to neighboring states; even the end result of this surplus—his horse's droppings—was used to fertilize his fields.

Yet this new court held against Filburn, deciding that even though his farm's extra products stayed within its boundaries, they were still subject to regulation because of their potential effect on the surrounding interstate commerce. For example, if Filburn had not grown extra wheat, he would have been forced to buy it elsewhere:

It can hardly be denied that a factor of such volume and variability as home-consumed wheat would have a substantial influence on price and market conditions. . . . Home-grown wheat in this sense competes with wheat in commerce. The stimulation of commerce is a use of the regulatory function quite as definitely as prohibitions or restrictions thereon. This record leaves us in no doubt that Congress may properly have considered that wheat consumed on the farm where grown, if wholly outside the scheme of regulation, would have a substantial effect in defeating and obstructing its purpose to stimulate trade therein at increased prices.

This case set the dangerous precedent that even goods produced and consumed in one's home fell under the umbrella of interstate commerce and thus were within the regulatory reach of the government. A quick look at the history of the court's decisions in this area shows regulation of farm ponds, drainage ditches, and, most recently, the home production of medical marijuana in *Gonzales v. Raich*.

In 1996, California voters passed Proposition 215, the Compassionate Use Act, legalizing the possession and home growth of medical marijuana for patients with their physician's recommendation. Angel Raich was one such patient, a very sick woman who was using marijuana per her doctor's direction to treat chronic pain from a neurological condition. Though Raich's treatment was allowed in California, it violated several federal laws, including the Controlled Substances Act, and so her home was raided and her plants seized. During her trial, Raich's doctor testified that without marijuana, her quality of life would be nonexistent because of excruciating, persistent pain. Nonetheless, the court ruled against Raich, citing the 1942 decision against Filburn:

More concretely, one concern prompting inclusion of wheat grown for home consumption in the 1938 Act was that rising market prices could draw such wheat into the interstate market, resulting in lower market prices. The parallel concern making it appropriate to include marijuana grown for home consumption in the [Controlled Substances Act] is the likelihood that the high demand in the interstate market will draw such marijuana into that market. In both cases, the regulation is squarely within Congress's commerce power because production of the commodity meant for home consumption, be it wheat or marijuana, has a substantial effect on supply and demand in the national market for that commodity.

Not only are Americans unprotected from federal power under this interpretation of the Commerce Clause, neither are the states. Even as late as 1976, the courts still recognized state power apart from the federal government (again, as the Founders intended). In *National League of Cities v. Usery* they held that state and local employees were not to be regulated by federal wages and hours legislation. After all, if a state could not regulate its own employment practices with its own workers, "there would be little left of the States' separate and independent existence"—the end of the Tenth Amendment.

But that view lasted for only another nine years. In 1985, in *Garcia v. San Antonio Transportation Authority*, the court overturned its decision, subjecting states and cities to federal labor regulation. The court held that states and cities have redress through the electoral process: they elect Congress and the president, and if they don't like a law that applies to them, they should tell it to the people they elect. Note how contradictory this opinion is to James Madison's and the Ninth and Tenth Amendments. The court ruled that the Tenth Amendment "is a truism" that confers no additional restrictions on the powers of the federal government. That was a huge reversal of what the framers of the Constitution had in mind.

The direction the Supreme Court is leading our country is alarming indeed, one that's creating an America that is fertile ground for the Ruling Class and their ambitions. Our Founders' obvious intent to protect individual liberty by explicitly limiting the powers of the federal government is being overturned rapidly. Most troubling of all, these modifications to our way of life are not occurring through constitutional amendment but through a complete rereading of the Constitution by a group of people appointed for life. Worse, as the events of 1937 showed, the court had already proved susceptible to intense political pressure from the president. The "switch in time" might have saved nine, but it did not save our liberty—at least not in any way our Founders would have defined the term.

More Power to the Unelected

The reversal of the reading of the Commerce Clause triggered by President Roosevelt was a great victory for the Ruling Class. Also under FDR, the Wilsonian practice of expanding the power of the unelected gained pace. New bureaucracies were created, and the rule-making power of the executive branch became omnipresent, a change well summarized by a brief look at one man's career. James M. Landis was quite explicit in his view that government needed experts to run its affairs and that elected officials were just not capable of such a task. Although Congress and its jurisdiction as directed by the Constitution might have been appropriate for the days before widespread industrialization, it was outmoded as a rule-making body by the complicated nature of twentieth-century American society.

Landis served in numerous senior positions in a career that spanned four decades, from the 1930s through the 1960s. While dean of Harvard Law School in 1938, he wrote that the need for panels of experts to make decisions "springs from the inadequacy of a simple tripartite form of government to deal with modern problems."[12] Landis's answer was to make sure government "vests the necessary powers with the administrative authority it creates, not too greatly concerned with the extent to which such action does violence to the traditional tripartite theory of governmental organization." In other words, the powers of the "administrative authority" are key and should be exercised without too much worry for archaic details like the Constitution and its separation of powers.

Landis's view mirrors that of the progressive Ruling Class as a whole: that the Constitution as originally written is an antiquated document out of touch with the reality of modern-day America. Wilson too hinted at this, but his solution was a merger of the executive and legislative branches to expedite the passage of laws. Landis's answer was significantly more expeditious: since the elected representatives in Congress and the president were not really experts, why not divert some of their legislative powers to the "administrative authority" of unelected bureaucrats?

Of course, Landis spent most of his life as one of those unelected bureaucrats—a prototypical member of the Ruling Class who had never had to trouble himself with actually interacting with the voters and winning an election. His pedigree was unparalleled; he got his undergraduate degree from Princeton and his law degree from Harvard, after which he clerked for the Supreme Court before returning to Harvard to teach law. On President Roosevelt's request, he joined the Federal Trade Commission (FTC; 1933–34), and afterward he became a member of and finally chairman of the recently created Securities and Exchange Commission (SEC; 1934–37). Nevertheless, he still kept a finger in government, most notably as director of the Office of Civilian Defense during World War II. After the war, Landis chaired the Civil Aeronautics Board. In 1960 he was a special advisor to President Elect John F. Kennedy on how to organize and enhance the power of the chairmen of the various regulatory boards.

Despite (or maybe because of) all of this power over the rest of us, Landis neglected to file income tax returns from 1956 to 1960. In 1963, he pled guilty and was sentenced to just one month in jail—a sentence that was, of course, far lighter than common citizens might have expected for similar dereliction—for his many years of service to the Ruling Class.

Landis's philosophy pervaded America, even affecting the way our judicial system operates. For example, in the 1989 case *Mistretta v. United States*, the Supreme Court upheld a delegation of power to a Federal Sentencing Commission to set guidelines for federal sentencing procedures. The court's opinion stated: "[O]ur jurisprudence has been driven by a practical understanding that in our increasingly complex society, replete with ever changing and more technical problems, Congress simply cannot do its job absent an ability to delegate power under broad general directives." It is far from clear what is so technical about deciding what the sentence should be for a particular crime. It is also a bit amazing that the Supreme Court didn't even think that trial courts were capable of such determinations. They had to be left to a commission of "experts."

The main issue is that experts care little about individual rights. They have a job to do; a mission to carry out. And the progressive judges of the Supreme Court seemed to be reluctant to stand in their way. On May 3, 1942, five months after the Japanese surprise attack on Pearl Harbor catapulted American into World War II, another "expert," General John DeWitt, head of the Western Defense Command, ordered all individuals of Japanese descent, regardless of their citizenship, to report to detention centers. One Fred Korematsu, a US citizen born in Oakland, California, refused and was arrested, his appeal ultimately heard by the Supreme Court.

The court acknowledged that no evidence had been presented that Korematsu was a security risk; his "guilt" was based solely on his ethnicity. In an eerily Orwellian opinion, the justices wrote, "[W]e cannot reject as unfounded the judgment of the military authorities and of Congress that there were disloyal members of that population, whose number and strength could not be precisely and quickly ascertained." In fact, there were no cases of sabotage—zero—so saying that the number could not be ascertained quickly was a bit of a stretch. The fact is not that the experts were unable to discern the degree of disloyalty, it's that there was *no* indication of *any* disloyalty. According to the majority opinion, "[E]xclusion of those of Japanese origin was deemed necessary because of the presence of an unascertained number of disloyal members of the group, most of whom we have no doubt were loyal to this country. It was because we could not reject the finding of the military authorities that it was impossible to bring about an immediate segregation of the disloyal from the loyal that we sustained the validity of the curfew orders as applying to the whole group." In other words, the absence of evidence was the reason the court ruled in the government's favor. Imagine: a whole group could now be punished in the absence of any criminal activity, just because some "expert" thought there was a chance that one member of that group might engage in criminal activity in the future.

This decision was handed down entirely by the progressive members of the Supreme Court; the "conservative" justices dissented. In fact, the decision against Korematsu was written by Roosevelt's first appointee to the Supreme Court, Justice Hugo Black, who is considered one of the court's most liberal jurists, even today. On the other hand, the sole Republican justice, Owen Roberts, wrote, "[I]t is the case of convicting a citizen as a punishment for not submitting to imprisonment in a concentration camp, based on his ancestry, and solely because of his ancestry, without evidence or inquiry concerning his loyalty and good disposition toward the United States. If this be a correct statement of the facts disclosed by this record, and facts of which we take judicial notice, I need hardly labor the conclusion that Constitutional rights have been violated." Another dissenter, Justice Frank Murphy, described the case for what it was: racism. It was the first time that word had been used in an opinion from the Supreme Court. He noted in the midst of World War II that this action represented, "the abhorrent and despicable treatment of minority groups by the dictatorial tyrannies which this nation is now pledged to destroy."

But this government of experts went even further to make sure it got its way. In arguing the case for the government, Solicitor General Charles Fahy deliberately withheld from the court a report from the Office of Naval Intelligence the fact that there was no evidence that Japanese Americans were spies or were sending intelligence to Japanese submarines. In fact, Korematsu's conviction was voided three decades after the fact because of the evidence that the Roosevelt administration had misled the Supreme Court. This does not embarrass the defenders of the Ruling Class. Upon Fahy's death in 1979, one of the *Washington Post's* liberal columnists, Meg Greenfield, heralded him, saying, "Of those who have devoted their lives to public service, none gave more and asked less in return than Charles Fahy." Lying on behalf of the Ruling Class is in some ways a selfless act for an individual, but it is quite selfish and destructive in terms of advancing one's class interest.

So what does one make of the progressive ideology? What does one conclude from this long pattern of progressive attitudes, from Wilson's crude and sweeping description of emancipated slaves, or the willingness of progressive judges to put a group into concentration camps simply because of their ethnicity, or the readiness of a selfless public servant like Charles Fahy to lie to the Supreme Court as solicitor general to facilitate their imprisonment?

It would be a mistake to conclude that progressives or the Ruling Class are racists. It would be wrong to conclude that they like stamping on individual liberties. But it would also be wrong to conclude that progressive ideology is *anti*racist or *for* individual liberties. History shows clearly that neither characterization always holds; it depends on the needs of the Ruling Class at that moment. As an enduring philosophy on policy, progressives more generally have a fixed ideology toward their one true objective: power. Their core philosophy is that they know best and that this gives them the right to rule. This philosophy has become cemented in the progressive ideology and carries on to the present day.

Obama and the Progressive Legacy

Consider President Barack Obama, a fitting heir to the progressive legacy. He has the same type of academic pedigree as Wilson and Landis. He attended Columbia as an undergraduate and Harvard Law School, where he was chosen to be president of the *Harvard Law Review* by its editors. Strangely, Obama was selected without ever having written an article beforehand or during his tenure. He also exemplified the self-image of Ruling Class progressives as he promised in the 2008 presidential campaign to bring messianic change to the country. As he declared in his standard stump speech, "We are the ones we've been waiting for!"[13] Aside from some confusion regarding the pronouns, one could not imagine a better rallying cry for any Ruling Class.

One case that sums up the attitude of progressive "pragmatism" when it comes to the use of power was President Obama's attempt to appoint members of the National Labor Relations Board (NLRB) without Senate confirmation. The Constitution does allow the president to fill vacancies in Senate-confirmed positions when the Senate is in recess. President Obama claimed the Senate was in recess because it was holding pro forma sessions only every three days; those are meetings where no business is being conducted, and few if any members are present. This was not a recess from the Senate's point of view, but it was good enough for the president to try to fill the NLRB. He needed his members on the board to advance his prounion agenda, but the Senate had blocked their confirmations. Ultimately the Supreme Court found against Obama unanimously, declaring that "the Senate is in Session when it says it is." This, of course, is both clearly common sense as well as what our Founders intended. Imagine if the president could declare single-handedly that the Senate was not in session!

But the story does not end there. The practice that Obama was challenging was begun by Democratic Senate leader Harry Reid in 2007 in order to block recess appointments by then president George W. Bush. Obama, then a senator from Illinois, supported Reid's position. But that was when he was a senator. When he became president, things had changed. In his view, the rules that he thought appropriate when he was not president should not apply to him when he was president. Even more shocking perhaps was that Senator Reid now backed up Obama even though Reid was still the majority leader and therefore the one who was holding the pro forma sessions! Reid declared, "President Obama did the right thing when he made these appointments on behalf of American workers."[14] This reflects the progressive mind-set: the laws don't matter, the Constitution doesn't matter, and how they acted in the past doesn't matter. All that matters is pushing through what they want right now.

President Obama made this explicit in his 2014 State of the Union address, where he declared, "[W]herever and whenever I can take steps without legislation . . . that's what I'm going to do."[15] What has happened is a huge increase in a government run by executive order, not by legislation. The Friday before Thanksgiving 2015, with Congress leaving town and the media and public focused on the upcoming holiday, the Office of Information and Regulatory Affairs (OIRA) released its fall 2015 regulatory agenda. It included some 2,000 regulations introduced by federal agencies—of which 144 were considered "economically significant," in that they imposed economic costs of at least $100 million. This surpassed the old record of 136, which was achieved in the spring 2015 regulatory package, announced just before the Memorial Day weekend. They mandate higher energy-use standards for household appliances, increasing their prices, new food-labeling requirements designating the "right" portions to be consumed at any one sitting (Does that include Thanksgiving dinner?), and mandated paid sick leave for people who are hired as contractors rather than as employees. None of these was authorized by the Congress.

But it is the "big stuff" that rightly draws the most attention. Consider the implementation of the Affordable Care Act, better known as Obamacare. The president campaigned on the issue and received a mandate to pass legislation. However, he never submitted a formal proposal to Congress. Instead, he chose to let the House and the Senate, both of which had large Democratic majorities, craft the legislation. Although he taught constitutional law as an adjunct professor, he conveniently forgot that one of the reasons for bicameral legislatures is that they are there to take "two looks" at a law—that is actually what "bicameral" means. And not for the first time, the House and Senate disagreed. By the end of 2009, the House had completed legislation, but the Senate had not. The president's signature initiative was stalled.

So the day before Christmas recess, Majority Leader Harry Reid called the chairmen of the major committees having jurisdiction to his office to hammer out a bill to move things forward. They worked into the wee hours, essentially stapling together the work that each committee had produced thus far, and penciling (literally) special provisions into the margin. Some of these were side deals to buy key senators' votes, such as the "Cornhusker kickback" to get the vote of Nebraska senator Ben Nelson, which required the federal government to pick up the entire cost of Medicaid expansion in his state, and the "Louisiana Purchase," which was designed to get the vote of Senator Mary Landrieu, who sold her vote for $300 million in assistance to Louisiana. What emerged was not a cohesive or workable package, but it was a bill. And if the Senate could pass anything, it could then go to a conference with the House, and a whole new bill could be written through bicameral negotiations.

It being the day before Christmas vacation, with everyone wanting to get home, Reid needed a sixty-vote supermajority to suspend the rules of the Senate that required providing adequate time for debate. There were exactly sixty Democrats, and, not surprisingly, he got their votes. Many of them stood on the Senate floor and declared that they did not like the bill that they were about to approve, but that it would advance the process of legislation. House Democrat Louise Slaughter of New York commented, "[The] Senate bill isn't health reform." [16] It wasn't.

Everyone went home for Christmas expecting to come back in the New Year and have a conference committee write a whole new bill, which would then be passed essentially the same way as the first time. But there was a problem: Senator Edward Kennedy had died in August, and on January 19, 2010, a special election was held in Massachusetts to fill his seat. The Republican, Scott Brown, made opposition to Obamacare a key issue and won in this heavily Democratic state. The trouble was, the Democrats were now down to fifty-nine votes and so they would not be able to suspend the rules on debate to get Obamacare through a second time, after it was rewritten by the conference committee.

Democrats had two choices. The first was to go to the Republicans and pass a compromise bill. That was a no-go. The other was to have the House pass the exact same bill as the one the Senate had passed the day before Christmas. You remember: the one that had been written in Harry Reid's office in the wee hours the night before, which no one considered coherent. If the bill was exactly the same, there was no need for a second Senate vote. They chose this second option.

This itself wasn't easy. The House didn't like the Senate bill. One particularly sticky provision dealt with abortion. Prolife House Democrats, essential to the bill's passage, demanded that no funds in Obamacare be used to fund abortion. But they couldn't amend the bill to do so, as that would require a whole new bill be passed by the Senate. So in order to secure the votes of these prolife Democrats, the president signed an executive order saying that no federal funds could be used for abortions. This, despite the fact that Obama campaigned on a strong prochoice agenda.

But that left one more pesky matter. A key provision of the bill — a fine for people who did not buy health insurance — was studiously not called a "tax" because members of Congress did not want to be labeled as having voted for a tax increase. This was key to enforcing the individual mandate that required people to either buy an Obamacare plan, purchase another plan, or pay a fine. It was not located in the revenue portions of the bill, which would make it a tax. And it was not a tax according to the Constitution, which allows only excise taxes (when you purchase a specific item), import duties (when you purchase something from abroad), and income taxes, based on income. The fine or fee was paid for *not* buying something, had no relation to imports, and was not based on income. Still, the administration had to reverse itself (and logic) and say that it *was* a tax in order to win Supreme Court approval. You see, it would not be constitutional for the federal government to fine or make people pay a fee for something they did *not* do. Just imagine if that were possible: we could be fined for just about anything! So they had to reverse themselves 180 degrees and declare it a "tax" that would be constitutional under Article 1's grant of taxing authority.

It should surprise no one that a massive bill written in the middle of the night was unlikely to work well once it was implemented. And it did not. So how does one handle this failure, especially when the president can't go back to Congress to change the law to make it workable without acute political embarrassment? Easy! The president changes the law by executive order without going to Congress. It started right before the law was supposed to take effect on January 1, 2014. In December, as the "rollout" of the plan was proceeding disastrously and 6.2 million people were suddenly going to lose coverage, President Obama simply changed the start date to January 1, 2015, formally directing the Treasury Department not to enforce the law until that date. Most interesting, Republican senators Mike Lee and Ted Cruz introduced legislation to do precisely what the president had done by executive order. That way it could be done the way the Constitution intended. President Obama said he would *veto* such legislation if it passed. In other words, he would veto a bill that did what he wanted, because he wanted to assert that it was his right to do so without Congress. This was turning the Constitution on its head.

As of this writing, the president has unilaterally made thirty-four changes in the Obamacare statute that contradict the language of the Affordable Care Act. Some of them have been targeted at "advertising" the virtues of Obamacare at the expense of coverage. For example, on February 15, 2013, they prematurely closed the federal high-risk pool, designed to cover individuals with preexisting conditions that would cost a lot to insure—blocking coverage to forty thousand people—citing a lack of funds. Those funds had existed in a fund set up by Kathleen Sebelius, the secretary of the Department of Health and Human Services, but they were used by the administration to advertise Obamacare enrollment.

Incompetence drove some of the changes, including the delay cited above. But they didn't end there. In March 2013, the administration postponed the start of the Small Business Health Options Program Marketplace, saying that they wouldn't be ready to meet the 2014 deadline set by the law. That was followed up three months later with a delay beyond what the law mandated for the employer mandate for all employers, again because of incompetence—they couldn't implement it. That was followed later in the year by a forty-five-day delay in implementing the individual mandate. In December 2013, after unions complained, they simply exempted their plans from a reinsurance fee that will now have to be picked up by other plans. In March 2014 they decided to ignore the law's mandate of $200 billion in savings over ten years from cuts in Medicare Advantage plans to help pay for Obamacare and simply canceled the cuts the law required. And in March 2015, they decided that the hundreds of thousands of taxpayers who received too large a subsidy to purchase their Obamacare plans would not have to repay the excess.

The merits of these myriad changes can be debated. What cannot be debated is that the president and the administration are unilaterally changing the law that Congress passed and the president signed. The concept of there being a rule of law has no meaning when it comes to Obamacare. It is simply too politically embarrassing. An unworkable law, written in the wee hours of the morning the day before Christmas break, and rammed through for reasons of political expediency is simply not working. That is no surprise. But to cover this up, the administration simply ignores the law and even threatens to veto changes that are enacted in the way that the Constitution and the rule of law mandate.

The key, again, is that the *ends justify the means*. The progressive Ruling Class believe so firmly in the rightness of their cause that they are willing to transform our constitutional government and the protections it offers America's citizens to fit their own needs. The Constitution is to be made a "living" document—that means whatever the Ruling Class say it means and not what the actual words are. Of course, this actually makes the Constitution "dead," not living. Treating people based on race, despite the assurances of the Fourteenth Amendment enacted after the long and bloody Civil War, is just fine if it makes progressive social engineering possible. In the progressive view, power should be moved from the elected representatives to "experts" in the bureaucracy. And if worst comes to worst, laws should be ignored completely in order to implement policy.

How have they done? Are the progressive Ruling Class really justified in their assertion that they know how to run society better than ordinary individuals? So far the choice between liberty and a progressive Ruling Class has been described in theoretical and ideological terms. But progressives claim they are producing superior results. We are supposed to sacrifice some of our liberty and give them more control of our lives in order to achieve this. So ultimately the case for the Ruling Class is an empirical one. If the power and resources at their disposal have produced what they promised, then it might all make sense. If not, then the arguments of the progressive Ruling Class come down to nothing more than a pursuit of power for its own sake. The next section turns to precisely that point. Has the progressive usurpation of power and resources actually done what they thought it would? Have they delivered on their promises? Or is the end result just a power grab?

PART 2

Mismanagement of Government by a Self-Interested Ruling Class

CHAPTER 7

The Ruling Class Have Failed
in Reducing Inequality

Part 1 of this book detailed the predominant behavioral pattern of the Ruling Class: they identify a problem and implement a solution that invariably increases their own power or the amount of resources they are able to access. Often their solution runs up against the rules laid out by our Founders in the Constitution, so the Ruling Class simply change the rules. But with all of the power they've assumed, one would think that they would at least be able to solve any problem they wanted. If that were only so, America today would be a virtual paradise on earth! The problem is, all of that power and all of those resources usually don't end up solving anything. Most of the time they make things worse! Part 2 of this book considers some of the more significant failures of the Ruling Class in America. Their dismal record is so consistent that one wonders whether they care about the issues they talk about or use them just as a means to gain power.

One of the Ruling Class's greatest reasons for claiming they need more of the American public's resources and more latitude to operate is to tackle the unequal distribution of income in the United States. After all, one of the main tenets of their narrative is that they are in power to help the common man as a champion for the individuals who have gotten a raw deal from society. There is no question that the gap between the rich and the poor has broadened in our country recently. But, this has occurred despite the Ruling Class's continual marshaling of both resources and rhetoric to supposedly combat the problem. It turns out that their supposed fight against inequality is an epic case of Ruling Class failure.

Let's start with some facts. The US Census Bureau releases several statistics to measure inequality. Three of these indices, known as the Gini index, the mean logarithmic deviation of income (mean log deviation for short), and the Theil index,[1] illustrate the degree of inequality on a scale from 0 to 1, with 0 denoting perfect equality and 1 indicating perfect inequality—a hypothetical scenario in which one person holds all the resources. Consider what has happened in America since the Great Society and the War on Poverty began during the Johnson administration. These initiatives included a number of programs, such as Medicaid, Food Stamps, the Job Corps, and Head Start, designed to redistribute income as a means of alleviating poverty.

These programs have expanded massively in the last half century. For example, Food Stamps began with a $75 million appropriation and covered a half million people in 1965.[2] By 2014, the program had grown to provide aid to forty-six million people, costing $74 billion—almost a thousand times as much. Despite these efforts, the Gini index has risen from 0.386 to 0.480, the mean log deviation has climbed even more, from 0.356 to 0.611, and the Theil index has increased from 0.273 to 0.419. By these two industry standards, inequality has increased dramatically in the last half century.

The following table dissects these increases by administration. To be clear, none of these presidents was elected by promoting inequality; all favored a more equal country. Some presidents paid more attention to the matter rhetorically than others, but more resources were devoted to achieving fairness during each term. Nonetheless, each administration failed to make a significant impact on inequality.

Table 1. Neither Party Has Reduced Income Inequality

Presidency		Change in Gini Index	Change in Mean Log Deviation	Change in Theil Index
1968		0.386	0.356	0.273
Richard Nixon Gerald Ford	8 years	+0.012	+0.005	−0.002
Jimmy Carter	4 years	+0.005	+0.014	+0.003
Ronald Reagan	8 years	+0.023	+0.026	+0.040
George H. W. Bush	4 years	+0.007	+0.015	+0.009
Bill Clinton	8 years	+0.029	+0.074	+0.081
George W. Bush	8 years	+0.004	+0.051	−0.006
Barack Obama	6 years	+0.014	+0.070	+0.021
2014		0.480	0.611	0.419

Source: Carmen DeNavas-Walt and Bernadette D. Proctor, *Income and Poverty in the United States: 2014—Current Population Reports* (Washington, DC: US Census Bureau, 2015).

Most striking, the presidents best known for criticizing their predecessors for inequality increases during their tenure saw even greater rises in inequality during *their* administrations. For example, President Clinton frequently condemned President Reagan's "tax cuts for the rich," labeling the 1980s "the decade of greed." Yet the Gini index increased more under Clinton than under Reagan, and the mean log deviation rose nearly three times as much with Clinton in the White House than during Reagan's terms. Further, the Theil index increased twice as much under Clinton than under Reagan.

President Obama was probably the most outspoken of all our presidents against rising inequality before taking office. He frequently criticized Bush's tax policy as a "giveaway to the rich," and undertook a huge liberalization of the government's programs to aid the poor. But all three inequality indices rose more under Obama than Bush. By the Gini index measure, inequality increased more than three times as much in his first six years as president than it did in all eight years of the Bush 43 administration. By the mean log deviation, inequality increased 40 percent more under Obama than under Bush 43. And, by the Theil index, inequality actually decreased under Bush!

At a minimum, this highlights the difference between Ruling Class (particularly Ruling Class progressive) rhetoric and their actual delivery on promises to fight inequality. Words about fighting inequality still travel, and most progressive voters actually believe Ruling Class politicians when they promise to fight inequality. They shouldn't: the facts simply don't support the claims. If anything, inequality increases fastest under those presidents who campaigned on caring the most. So believing yet another politician about inequality is like a fourth marriage: the triumph of hope over experience. But Ruling Class progressives count on "hope" and not on facts; if they reported the facts on their performance, they would never win an election. In this, they are no different from the high priest of old saying, "We need more human sacrifices," after the crops failed. It is simply a way of hiding their failure by creating a hope that things will work out better the next time.

Unfortunately for the American people, all of those sweet words on fighting inequality were backed up by tax dollars. Either the resources to make good on promises to fight inequality were paid for by the work of current taxpayers, or they will be paid—with interest—by future taxpayers when the debt used to finance these programs comes due. So it is important to consider the dollars spent trying to reduce inequality. Some are used in programs to help the poor by increasing the services available to them. However, this is relatively minor compared with the money that is simply given to individuals by the government to spend on their own. Because it is given to people directly, that money is counted as part of their income. It should therefore reduce inequality directly.

These funds are known by the term "transfer payments," as they are taken from the taxpayer, funneled through a bureaucracy, and "transferred" in the form of benefits paid to various recipients.[3] In 1968, the year that Nixon was first elected, government transfer payments totaled $53 billion, or 7.2 percent of total personal income. By 2014, transfer payments had climbed to $2.5 trillion and composed 16.9 percent of personal income—a nearly 10-point gain. Imagine: in the name of reducing inequality, the government was taking more than a sixth of all the income that people earned, and yet inequality was still rising!

Looking at the figures in terms of sheer dollars, a similar pattern emerges. Accounting for inflation, transfer payments rose by 691 percent over these forty-six years, growing 2.8 times as fast as overall income (figure 1). In 2014, our government spent $1.45 trillion dollars *more* on transfer payments than it would have if transfer payments composed the same share of personal income as in 1968. There are about forty-seven million people living in poverty, so if the government divided that extra $1.45 trillion among the impoverished, each person would get $30,000. A single mother of two would receive a check for $90,000! The amazingly disgraceful tragedy is that despite moving around all this money, America still has forty-seven million people in poverty!

Figure 1. Real Wages vs. Real Transfer Payments 1965–2014

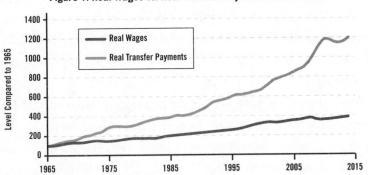

Source: US Bureau of Economic Analysis; data normalized so that 1965 = 100.

It is also important to compare those transfer payments with what is paid to people to work, save, invest, and run a business. The profits retained by all American corporations to grow their businesses amounted to $699 billion in 2014, hardly more than a quarter as much as transfer payments.[4] Also in 2014, interest and dividends paid to each US household for all of their saving and investing totaled $2.2 trillion—still not as much as transfers. Spending on America's entire national defense that year came to $748 billion, or one-third as much as transfer payments. For every dollar paid in wages to America's 144 million private sector workers, 38 cents were given out as transfers.

That's a lot of money, by anyone's standard. Again, the greatest tragedy is that we are nowhere close to abolishing poverty here in the United States despite all of the effort and resources expended. Incredibly, the progressive Ruling Class continue to try to convince us to give them *more* money to redistribute! At times, it seems like Ruling Class policies are on a never-ending treadmill. More money leads to failure of even greater magnitude, which triggers even more impassioned calls for more money. But the Ruling Class don't seem to mind failure, as long as it leads to them making a case for still more money and more power.

Under President Obama, transfer payments increased by $560 billion, basically moving the total from less than $2 trillion to $2.5 trillion. In 2008, the year before he took office, private sector wages and salaries were $5.4 trillion; these rose by $1.1 trillion by Obama's seventh year in office. That means that for every dollar in increased wages to private sector workers, there were 51 extra cents paid in transfer payments. So the rate at which transfer payments were outpacing wage growth was accelerating.

More than 45 million people received food stamps in mid-2015,[5] an increase of 46 percent since the end of 2008. As of September 2015, nearly 71.6 million individuals were enrolled in Medicaid, which offers medical assistance to the poor, and the Children's Health Insurance Program (CHIP), a similar program for children. Enrollment in Medicaid and CHIP has increased by 13.3 million since October 2013.[6] The number of persons receiving some form of "means tested" assistance (aid because of low income) rose by over 13 million in President Obama's first term to over 35 percent of the country's total population.[7]

Again, the most amazing fact is that despite all this effort, inequality still rose, and along with it, poverty. In 2008, the year of the deepest recession in three-quarters of a century, 13.2 percent of Americans were living in poverty. In 2014, after five years of economic expansion, the poverty rate had risen to 14.8 percent, an increase of 6.8 million people. Even with the help of an improving economic picture, extra spending to combat poverty was still ineffective.

Now, the Ruling Class might well claim that this failure was not their fault, even though it occurred on their watch. Many point fingers at the Bush administration. Some would argue that the state of inequality would have been so much worse if they hadn't done what they did, despite the inefficiency of their programs. Perhaps, but there is also a case to be made that what the Ruling Class did, particularly in the last few years, was so poorly designed that the effort was doomed from the start. The programs that were enacted and the money that was transferred may have been well intentioned, but was, in the long run, totally counterproductive to the goals of reducing poverty and increasing the incomes of the middle class.

Common sense would say that if you give people money but tell them that you'll take away that money if they go out and earn more on their own, then of course they will be less incentivized to work. The Ruling Class will tell us that common sense doesn't apply in these areas, but consider what happened to the workers-per-household figure between 2008 and 2014. For the first time during any presidency, the number of two-earner households declined (as of 2014).[8] By comparison, two-earner couples grew by 5 million under Reagan, 4.3 million under Clinton, 1.3 million under Bush 41, and 1.2 million under Bush 43.

Although the number of single-earner households rose by 2.6 million during the Obama presidency, households with no earners increased by almost 5 million. Stated differently, the number of households in

America grew by about 7.4 million under President Obama, but two-thirds of that growth was in families with no one working! It's easy to see what that would do to the poverty rate and the level of income inequality. Households without workers take in, through transfers, less than a quarter of what those in two-earner households make, and less than half of what households with a single earner make. Fewer people working means that more people will be poor, even if the government tries to make up some of the income gap lost by their not working. And when the number of people at the bottom grows, it is mathematically inevitable that inequality will increase.

Even center-left researchers have written about the disincentive effects of working under the new, more generous rules regarding entitlements to federal benefits. For example, the Urban Institute, a Washington-based think tank that focuses on issues related to inequality, found that a single parent's additional earnings—money made by working more hours or by getting promoted or getting a raise—were capped at 20 percent to 50 percent of their base income.[9] The government's take of this extra income (including both higher taxes and lower benefits) was therefore between 50 percent and 80 percent of any extra effort the single parent put forth. A study by the Hamilton Project, a Hillary Clinton think tank, found that the same was true for middle-income families with children when the second parent was thinking about going back to work.[10] Economists often call this the "marginal tax rate," or the share of extra income earned that the government keeps. We know that when higher-income people's tax rates go above 50 percent, they do not work harder, *and* they make extra efforts to avoid paying taxes. This doesn't mean that they're lazy; when the government takes most of what you're going to earn by working longer or harder or smarter, most people just aren't going to do it. It should surprise no one that with those kinds of tax levels, the number of two-earner couples reversed a decades-long increase, and the number of no-earner households skyrocketed.

Taxing the successful and redistributing their income to the poor is a noble idea, but it just does not work. The Marxist ideal "From each according to his ability, to each according to his needs" has proved to be a failure; if not, the Berlin Wall would still be standing. What the evidence shows is that we are now at the stage where we are at or near those limits. Further taxing and redistribution are already showing signs of making the "pie" smaller and turning us into a zero-sum society, where the only way one person gets ahead is at the expense of another.

I've debated this issue with many members of the current Ruling Class. Some have argued that "ordinary" people are incapable of understanding their marginal tax rate and, therefore, won't change their work habits as a result of something they do not know. In my experience, people *do* know precisely how much more their take-home pay goes up if they work extra overtime. People might not think in terms like "marginal tax rate," but they sure understand their own pay stub! Others of my Ruling Class friends (the number of which will surely dwindle following this book's publication) do not believe that people really change their work habits because they earn more or less money. Members of the Ruling Class are not motivated as much by money as by power and prestige, and so they believe that others are the same. They seek jobs that are "fulfilling" and that have an exciting "career path" but might pay less than other jobs. So they ascribe similar motives to others. But while most Americans like their jobs, their primary motivation for working is to pay the rent, put food on the table, and maybe, with what's left over, enjoy some of the finer things in life. Take-home pay is very important to them.

The Ruling Class demand for more resources so more transfers can be made also entails imposing higher taxes on the "rich." Surely, the Ruling Class argues, if we—the rulers—take more money from the rich and give it to the poor, we will have a more equal society. Turns out that might not be the case. Interesting work by the Brookings Institution (a center-left think tank in Washington) examined this idea and found that taxing the rich more in order to fund increased transfers to the poor resulted in what the authors describe as an "exceedingly modest" effect[11]—notable results, considering the political leanings of the researchers, one of whom was President Obama's director of the Office of Management and Budget.

The study undertook a two-step increase in taxes and transfers. First, the top income tax rate was theoretically increased from 39.6 percent to 50 percent, raising tax collections, on average, by $6,464 for households in the 95th percentile to the 99th percentile of income; by $111,000 for taxpayers in the top percentile; and by $569,000 for taxpayers in the top one-tenth percentile. Altogether, the government would take in $95.6 billion, assuming that taxpayers did not change their working behavior. Despite this extra money, the Gini index on *after-tax* income fell by a trivial 0.003. To put that into perspective, the decline reversed only one-fifth of the increase in the Gini index during President Obama's first six years in office.

The second step in the study was to take the extra $95.6 billion and mail each household in the bottom 20 percent a check for $2,650. Of course, that would be the most efficient redistribution possible, and the authors assumed no cost for the bureaucracy to administer the program or any change in work habits from the extra money. (Bold assumptions to make, indeed.) These extra transfer payments lowered the Gini index by an additional 0.011. Therefore, the combined increase in higher taxes and more transfers would theoretically reduce inequality by just enough to cover the increase during Obama's presidency, reversing only about one-seventh of the inequality rise since the Great Society began.

The authors also incorporated a modest behavioral response from the greater tax rates, assuming that the rich would work less and report less income because of the higher taxes. Of course, these effects themselves lower inequality sharply, as they mean that the rich are becoming less rich. In the most extreme case, government could tax 100 percent of personal income: while there would be no take-home pay, there would also be no inequality. But the authors noted a catch: "The highest-income households reduce their pretax income, which would amplify the reduction in income inequality, but *that leaves less revenue to redistribute.*"

Under these more realistic assumptions, the authors reported a Gini index reduction of 0.009, one-third lower than what was found originally.

The study's conclusion says it well: "That such a sizable increase in the top personal income tax rate leads to a strikingly limited reduction in overall income inequality speaks to the limitations of this particular approach in addressing the broader challenge." Based on these results, a tax-and-transfer program is not the answer to inequality. Further, such a program would shrink the economy, as those who make more work, save, and invest less and start fewer businesses.

So a fair question to ask is, why do members of the progressive Ruling Class insist on such plans? Maybe the real goal is not to solve a problem but to accumulate more power. Under any of these tax-and-transfer schemes, the amount of resources flowing through the government increases substantially. Importantly, these are spent at the discretion of the Ruling Class. Although the authors of this report assume that the money is simply handed out equally to the bottom 20 percent of households, in practice, that is not how it works. As mentioned previously, the Ruling Class actually redistribute twenty-five times this amount now and still have yet to see any meaningful reduction in inequality. Instead, the money is spent inefficiently on programs that satisfy particular interests in the political coalition that supports the Ruling Class. In fact, actually solving inequality would be one less reason for the Ruling Class to give themselves more resources. The key to Ruling Class control is to increase the resources and power they control, but keep the problem unsolved. No doubt some progressives actually believe they are doing the right thing and not just accumulating power, but this requires a willful ignorance about the performance of their programs in the past. It is this apparent indifference to their past failures that is why so many people in our country are angry today and why returning to our roots as a nation that prizes liberty is needed to break the Ruling Class's stranglehold on power.

CHAPTER 8

The Ruling Class
Have Mismanaged
America's Finances

Power is supposed to come with obligations, among which is steward-ship. When you're in charge, you have a responsibility not to loot the organization that you are running. Another is to turn over the organization that you manage to your successor in at least as good con-dition as you found it when you assumed control. Not doing so places your organization on the path to ruin. But that is exactly the path the US government is on today. This didn't happen by accident. The Ruling Class made changes to the way our country develops its budget to bias the system toward an expanding government. These rules hide the real cost of government programs, thus making them easier to get approved. Then, when the government runs into trouble, it is forced to either "cut" programs that have become entrenched, raise taxes, or borrow money to cover costs.

The dollar figures have become truly mind-boggling. Many in

Washington speak of the "-illion" illusion. When a number is presented on the nightly news, it always sounds big, whether it's a million, billion, or trillion. This allows politicians to make changes and lead attacks on programs measured in *millions* to make it look like they're actively tackling their constituents' problems, while avoiding the long-term gross mismanagement of finance that is measured in the *trillions*. This mismanagement is helped by the fact that elected officials no longer have control over most of the budget. As noted in part 1, one of the goals of the Ruling Class is to move power away from Congress, which is elected by the people, and toward the unelected. More and more spending programs are funded through automatic renewal each year without additional oversight from Congress, which puts most of our government on autopilot and removes any accountability from the process. More than seventy cents of every dollar the government spends happens without a vote. So a problem measured in trillions can be managed directly only by elected representatives who have control of spending measured in the billions.

Let's put the problem in perspective. The gross public debt of the federal government is about $18.1 trillion.[1] That amounts to about $56,000 for every US citizen, or $224,000 for a family of four. That gross debt is almost double all of the mortgages families have on their homes and is larger than the entire US economy. But while mortgages have houses as collateral, the US debt has technically only future tax collections standing ready to supposedly pay back the lender. Now, lenders have never really thought of this as a problem. They've always assumed that either the government will raise taxes, or more likely, that it will simply issue new debt to pay back the lenders when the bonds come due.

Our big problem is that this faith in the future on the part of lenders might be about to end. Let's begin by considering who has been lending Uncle Sam all this money. To a large extent, it's other parts of the US government (figure 2). Federal Reserve banks, the institutions that stand behind the money in circulation, have lent $2.4 trillion directly to the Treasury.[2,3] The government also guarantees an additional $2.1 trillion of debt held by the Fed, most of which has been purchased in just the last few years. Another $5 trillion is lent to the Treasury by other agencies of the federal government, such as the Social Security Trust Fund. This is money that is supposed to pay future beneficiaries; so when those beneficiaries are eventually paid, someone else is going to have to buy that debt from Social Security so that retirees can be provided for in the future. Of the remaining $11 trillion, more than half is owned by foreign governments, particularly foreign central banks (the equivalent of the Fed). The rest is owned by Americans, either directly or through pension funds and other intermediaries.

Figure 2. Who Owns America's Debt?

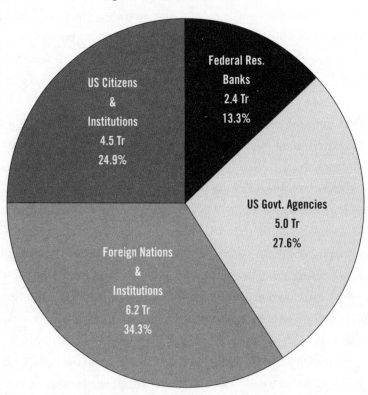

Source: *Treasury Bulletin*, US Department of the Treasury, Bureau of the Fiscal Service, December 2015.

What will happen as the Ruling Class continue to issue debt? Those same entities that bought our debt in the past will eventually stop doing so. For example, the Social Security Trust Fund and other government agencies will soon turn into net sellers of debt. The Federal Reserve has stopped expanding its quantitative easing program, which led to its purchasing more than $3.5 trillion of debt in the past few years, so it won't be a buyer. In theory, it plans to sell those bonds back into the market. Foreign central banks stopped being net buyers of debt in 2014. China, the largest buyer, became a net seller in 2015. So a new government agency or foreign central bank is going to have to step forward and start buying our debt. To be willing to do so, they are almost certainly going to demand greater compensation—higher interest payments—painting our country's financial future in a bleak light.

Even worse, the debt machine is likely to go into overdrive very soon—in fact, the next president is likely to face a real problem. Rather than deal in "trillions," let's consider the debt relative to the size of the overall economy, or as a percent of GDP. In 2015 the government collected 17.7 percent of GDP in taxes and spent 20.4 percent of GDP.[4] That means it had to borrow 2.7 percent of GDP, or a bit over $400 billion. Remember, this is just to run our country for one year!

But spending is about to skyrocket under the next president, no matter who he or she will be, in areas that are largely uncontrollable.[5] For example, spending on Social Security and health care is expected to rise from 10 percent of GDP in 2015 to 11.8 percent of GDP in 2025. Interest on our government's debt is expected to rise from 1.3 percent of GDP to 2.9 percent. That means an additional 3.4 percent of GDP in terms of spending. So if we keep taxes and the rest of the government growing as fast as the economy, government borrowing will more than double relative to the size of the economy: from 2.7 percent to 5.8 percent.

If we were to try to keep the borrowing rate the same by raising taxes, all federal tax rates would have to be increased by 20 percent. The top tax bracket would have to rise from 39.6 percent to 47.5 percent. The

corporate tax rate, already the highest in the world, would have to go
from 35 percent to 42 percent, and the Social Security payroll tax rate
would rise from 15.3 percent to 18.3 percent. And, for the math to work,
all of those extra taxes must be assumed to have no effect on people's
willingness to work, save, invest, and start new businesses, so as not to
slow the growth rate of the economy.

This is just the beginning. The Congressional Budget Office predicts
that by 2040, Social Security and health care will rise to 14.4 percent
of GDP, and interest payments will soar to 9.3 percent of GDP.[6] That
is 12.4 percent more GDP than today. To pay for this with higher taxes
would require all tax rates to rise by 70 percent. That would mean that
the top tax rate would go from 39.6 percent to 67 percent. The 28 percent
bracket—where many middle-class Americans find themselves—would
rise to 47.6 percent. The Social Security payroll tax would go to 26 percent, and the corporate tax rate to 59 percent. And again, all of this would
have to happen without any deviation from our current growth path.

But the Ruling Class aren't talking about this issue. Worse, they have
been allowed to get away with it, probably because most people think that
this problem won't matter for a long time from now. But 2040 really isn't
all that far away, and this is something we all need to be concerned with
now. Half of all people who are sixty years old today will still be alive and
needing Social Security and help with health care costs. Today's millennials will be in their peak earning years—and subject to those tax rates. And
they will be trying to make ends meet in an economy where the incentives
to create jobs and start businesses will have been essentially eliminated.

What are the Ruling Class's plans to manage this situation? The
truth is, they have no plans. Under current law, the Social Security system will go on a pure "cash in, cash out" basis in 2034—so that the only
money that Social Security can pay beneficiaries is from the taxes that
workers will be paying into the system at the time. This won't be enough
to cover promised benefits, so eighteen years from now, all Social Security recipients will have about a 23 percent reduction in their monthly
checks. Most members of the Ruling Class assume that those in charge

at that time won't let that happen. But they are doing nothing to stop it now; these future problems are someone else's to worry about, not theirs. They have no problem making promises on future issues about which they have no way to deliver. Many people have been paying into Social Security with the expectation that they will be taken care of in their retirement, and they voted for the Ruling Class, based on empty promises. But the money won't be there, and the Ruling Class that created this problem will be long gone. They're making empty promises today to gain immediate support, knowing that they'll never be held accountable in the future—a tactic that has always been common among rulers.

Are future Social Security recipients going to be cut off when they are likely to be too old to work? Maybe they were wrong to be duped by the Ruling Class promises, but they have been planning their lives on the basis that those benefits would be paid. So we should think of these promises as a debt that has to be paid, just like all other debt accumulated by the Ruling Class.

And by the estimate of the Social Security Board of Trustees—three of six are members of the Obama Cabinet, by the way—our long-term Social Security obligation represents a significant debt indeed, yet one that is constantly excluded when figuring our government's debt. (This is true also of many other similarly burdensome government programs that necessitate massive future funding.) Economists use the term "present value," the current capital value of a future income or outlay, to describe such a situation. Based on our country's economic statistics, the Trustees approximate the present value of our country's Social Security obligation seventy-five years into the future at roughly 100 percent of our current GDP, or about $17.5 trillion. (Looking past seventy-five years, the amount will be at least as large as that.)*

---

*The Trustees estimate the shortfall at 2.68 percent of taxable payroll, or half that percentage of GDP. This figure grows at roughly the same pace as GDP each year, which is about 3.5 percent in nominal terms. Assuming a 3.1 percent return (approximately the current yield on long-dated Treasury bonds), it would take roughly 100 percent of current GDP to cover the shortfall.

What that really means is that if our government is to fulfill its promises on Social Security, its debt isn't just $18.1 trillion, it's about $36 trillion—or twice our GDP. This means that, realistically, the current debt of the United States is greater than the debt of Greece relative to the size of our two economies—and Greece is currently flirting with bankruptcy! Some others have estimated the gap in our financing to be far larger.[7,8,9] For example, USDebtClock.org, a privately funded site that provides a continuously updated and detailed picture of America's finances, puts unfunded liabilities from entitlement programs at $123 trillion. The National Center for Policy Analysis, a nonprofit, nonpartisan center that advocates private sector alternatives to government intervention, estimates the figure to be $84 trillion, and Michael D. Tanner of the similarly pro–limited government Cato Institute places the amount at $90.6 trillion. Methodologies and assumptions can vary, but no matter how you estimate them, the numbers are staggering.

How the Ruling Class Got America into This Mess

To understand why we are in such terrible financial straits, recall the long-term Ruling Class strategy: expand the government and its reach and then limit the decision-making power of those elected by the people. A significant aid to the Ruling Class in this regard came in the form of the Congressional Budget and Impoundment Control Act of 1974. Passed and signed into law a month before Richard Nixon resigned, at a time when the president was vulnerable and unable to fight back due to the mounting crisis from the Watergate scandal that ultimately led to President Nixon's resignation, the Budget Act offered an opportunity for a Congress dominated by the progressive Ruling Class to push through far-reaching changes in the ways the government decides what it is going to spend.

At first, the Budget Act was known mainly for ending presidential impoundment of funds. Prior to 1974, the president, through executive authority, could simply refuse to spend money he thought imprudent.

This gave him important authority over the bureaucracy, as he could curb wasteful or inappropriate spending by refusing to authorize appropriations. Nixon used this authority in a wide-ranging way, and it made him lots of enemies. Congress banned his authority to impound funds largely out of frustration for how this impeded its plans. But in so doing, it made two significant changes: it removed one check on spending, and, perhaps more important, it shifted power away from someone who was elected (the president) and handed it to the Ruling Class in the bureaucracy. The bureaucracy, which supposedly works for the president, now got its money regardless of whether it followed his wishes or not. Woodrow Wilson's progressive goal of empowering the permanent unelected government at the expense of the voters had been advanced.

Although the Budget Act created the appearance of a process for budgeting, it actually made it easier for budgeting to proceed on autopilot, without congressional or presidential review. So-called mandatory or entitlement spending did not require an annual appropriation, or allocation of money by the Congress. Now any changes to these programs through a budget resolution would require sixty votes in the Senate instead of just a simple majority. Reining in this kind of spending, already politically difficult, became even more so.

But more important, if Congress did not act affirmatively to pass a new budget or a new appropriation bill, the previous budget resolution carried over. This made it much easier to simply put spending on a "continuing resolution" that allowed spending to continue at last year's level without the normal review by congressional committees as to its effectiveness.

Whatever the theoretical flaws, the proof is in the pudding—or more precisely, in our rising budget deficit. In the twenty-five years prior to the passage of the Budget Act, beginning in 1949, the federal deficit averaged just 0.6 percent of GDP.[10] This period included both the Korean and Vietnam Wars, which, like all wars, increased pressure to spend. But in the twenty-five years *after* the Budget Act's passage, up to the very end of the twentieth century, the deficit averaged 3 percent of GDP, or five times as much! And in the fifteen years after that, from 2000 up to the start of 2015, the deficit has averaged even more: 4 percent of GDP.

This key piece of legislation marks a breaking point in the control of the federal deficit. Before it, the deficit was a relatively minor share of GDP. Since then, it has become a large share and is growing. By any measure, the "reforms" of the 1974 Budget Act were a failure at limiting irresponsible budgeting and a boon to an ever more irresponsible federal fiscal program. The progressive goal of growing government and making it harder for the elected parts of government to control such expansion had been achieved.

Funny Numbers

The government's budget process has also created another dynamic that the Ruling Class have exploited to the fullest: what one could gently call "exaggeration" when it comes to projecting the economy. The reasoning is not hard to understand. The higher the assumption about the rate of economic growth, the higher the assumed amount of tax revenue that will be collected. The greater revenue that is assumed, the more expenditures can be built into the spending process. In effect, what the Ruling Class do is to assume that they are going to get a "raise" and spend as if they got that raise. And if the raise doesn't come in? They simply increase our country's debt.

Consider, for example, the assumptions of the Obama administration. When President Obama first came to office, he submitted a formal budget on May 11, 2009, for fiscal year 2010, which was due to begin on October 1, 2009. The budget was called "A New Era of Responsibility."[11] Over the first five calendar years covered by that budget, 2010 through 2014, he projected average real economic growth of 3.8 percent, with growth soaring to 4.6 percent in 2012 as his programs hit their stride. In fact, it averaged just 2 percent. One way of looking at this is that the incoming administration had predicted 9 percent more real growth over the next five years than was actually achieved.

Let's put that 9 percent extra real growth into perspective. In terms of GDP, it amounts to just over $1.6 trillion. When compared with a typical middle-class family earning $50,000, that 9 percent miss would have been an extra $4,500 to spend in 2014. Cumulatively, from 2010 through 2014, the miss to this family was worth $13,500 in total spending power. Given the way many run their finances, this probably meant that each family had $13,500 more in credit card debt than they would have had otherwise. So by no means should this be considered trivial.

The next year, the administration did the same in its 2011 budget, submitted on February 1, 2010.[12] Now, at that point, it sensed that growth from 2009 to 2010 was not going to come in quite as well as it had hoped, and so it cut the forecast for that period by a full half point. But that didn't stop the White House from predicting an even better 4 percent growth over the next five years, 2011 through 2015. The administration said that while the programs weren't working as planned, they just needed more time. Trouble is, growth over those five years also missed, averaging the same 2 percent. Again, the administration had predicted about twice the growth that actually occurred. It ended up missing growth over the next five years by a cumulative 10 percent, not just 9 percent.

By February 14, 2011, when the administration submitted its third budget, this time for fiscal 2012, it knew that it had been wrong twice.[13] The White House even admitted missing its first estimate for growth for 2010 and 2011 by a cumulative 1.8 percent. We know now that the combined miss was 3.2 percent, but, in fairness, the administration could not have known how big its miss was at the time—only that it had missed. Yet hope sprang eternal. The president's program is going to work, and we should budget for that success! The administration projected an average growth over the next five years, 2012 through 2016, of 3.9 percent. We don't know at this writing precisely how bad this miss is going to turn out to be, but we know it will be huge—roughly as big as the first two budgets.

To be fair, economic forecasting is imprecise—more so, even, than other fields where predictions are made. So forecasters are not technically being dishonest when they miss by big amounts, but they should be expected to learn from their mistakes. This administration did not. And the reason has everything to do with working for the Ruling Class. Again, the Ruling Class believe that they know best about everything, including budget forecasting. It follows that their programs have to work, if for no other reason than they are driven by superior insights. If the administration was to present a budget that forecast the kind of growth that actually occurred, that would present it in a negative light. In fact, during the eight years of George W. Bush, 2001 to 2009, growth averaged only 2.1 percent.[14] The Obama administration's eight years are going to come in about the same, maybe even a bit worse. Yet President Obama ran his campaigns and his policies as a change from Bush's failed policies. As his first budget declared, this was to be "a new era of responsibility," not a rerun of the previous eight years of failure.

In the end, the budget "reform" process passed in 1974 was a failure. As with so many Ruling Class initiatives, it was enacted under the pretense of creating a more careful and "scientific" way of getting things done. The end result was to make the budget process more political and less effective. It was not hard to predict that this would be the result. By relying more on "planning" rather than simply allocating what was available, the emphasis shifted from real-time choices regarding spending levels to ones based on fantasy. The key to planning is forecasting, so economic forecasting became even more politicized than it already was.

To make matters worse, this so-called planning process was easily manipulated by the Ruling Class. The gist of the budget rules is that a ten-year "baseline," or assumed budget path, exists that provides the holy grail of budget forecasting. It assumes that "current law" will exist for ten years and that what needs to be voted on is any change to that current law baseline over those ten years.

Consider how this affects the incentives for Congress to try to control long-term problems such as our entitlement explosion. No one thinks that current retirees and other beneficiaries should take an immediate big hit to their incomes. The right way to get control over our entitlement problem is gradually, over many years or many decades. As we have seen, the real budget calamity happens from 2025 to 2040. So changes need to be phased in. But that means that any Congress brave enough to take on this long-term challenge receives no political or budgetary credit for doing so because most of the effects of their reforms will happen outside the ten-year window.

On the other hand, those who wish to gradually turn America into a giant welfare state and have the patience to do so now have a tremendous budgetary tool at their disposal. Any expansion of welfare programs over the long term—that is, after ten years—are "free" from the point of view of budgetary accountability. The progressive Ruling Class therefore phase in programs over a long period, delaying their start for several years after they are proposed and therefore cutting down on costs in the ten-year budget window. For example, Obamacare was proposed in 2009, but subsidies didn't start until 2014. And the really expensive part of the program doesn't kick in until after the original ten-year window is past.

There is also an opportunity to game things in other ways. The tax code has a list of special interest provisions known as "extenders." These are tax programs that have been on the books for many years but have never been made permanent. Instead, they are extended year after year. Why? If they were made permanent, they would have affected the budget baseline for ten years, and the Congress that made them permanent would have to "pay for" or offset the cost of them for the whole ten years. But that Congress is going to be there for only two years, so it doesn't want to have to take the political hit of the offset. A simple one-year extension is much more affordable in terms of offsets. Besides, if you make something permanent—particularly something that has a fairly narrow special interest constituency, and most extenders do—you want to be able to turn to that special interest for campaign help every year. If something is permanent, there is no need to deliver the goods or to ask for help in order to deliver them.

If we are going to rein in this massive government debt, we must take away power from a system that puts most decisions on automatic pilot and hides them from regular review by elected officials. The fact that deficits are more than five times larger as a share of GDP since the Budget Act of 1974 was passed should be more than sufficient indication that Ruling Class budget "reform" has failed. What we have now isn't a real budget process at all but a charade that masks the budget challenge with a highly politicized and easily gamed set of rules—one that rewards those who increase our long-term fiscal obligations. Most of the Ruling Class think that ever bigger government is a good thing—it is certainly good for them! But once again, they have put their class ahead of the long-term interests of the people of the country.

CHAPTER 9

The Ruling Class Have Earned an F in Education

America's school system is failing our children. One in five students don't even graduate from high school, a figure that rises to roughly one in three among underprivileged groups such as African Americans.[1] International comparisons are dreadful. The United States spends more on primary and secondary education and gets a far lower return than our global competitors do. This harms our competitiveness in the world, reduces opportunity, and leads to increased inequality, as those who are behind fall even further behind as they progress through school.

Worse, the trends in student performance indicate that this failure is accelerating. The Organization for Economic Co-operation and Development (OECD) regularly analyzes the proficiency of fifteen-year-old students in math, science, and reading across its thirty-four member countries.[2] In 2009, America ranked twenty-fifth in math, seventeenth in science, and twelfth in reading, slipping to twenty-seventh in math, twentieth in science, and seventeenth in reading by 2012.

And these poor results are not from lack of money spent. In fact, the US government spends more on education than nearly every other country. A 2011 OECD report[3] on national education budgets found that, accounting for cost of living differences, the United States spent the fourth most of any country on its primary and secondary school students—32 percent more than average for primary school and 37 percent more than average for secondary school—less than only Luxembourg, Norway, and Switzerland. And for all that extra money, we came in at or near the bottom of the charts in terms of student performance.

Let's try to put that money into some perspective. Imagine a classroom of twenty third-graders—on average, there was $220,000 spent on that class. Where did the money go? The National Center for Education Statistics says that about 20 percent went to running the school, including capital cost, operation, and maintenance. That leaves $176,000 for salaries of all kinds. Of course, teachers don't earn anything like this. But in many cases, only around half of all school district employees actually enter a classroom. Education in America has become highly bureaucratized, where a variety of "services" are provided that don't have an impact on actual student performance.

A look at how American education developed throughout history provides a possible explanation for how our school system reached such a sorry state. From the earliest colonial times, literacy rates in America were among the highest in the world. Towns organized schools for their communities but in general stayed away from tax support, instead assessing the students a small fee to attend. By the time of the American Revolution, there was nearly universal schooling for boys under this model in New England. Even in quite conservative states such as South Carolina, "common schools" were established statewide within a couple of decades of the Constitution being adopted. But in all cases, these schools had to be responsive to the needs and wishes of the parents who were, after all, the school's customers.

In 1837, the secretary of education in Massachusetts, Horace Mann, introduced a series of reforms to "standardize" education in the state. Mann lived before the Ruling Class took hold in America, but his thought processes and approach were a precursor to today's progressive policies. On paper, his aims were noble: to provide a basic standard for teachers and curriculum. He set up a system of schools for teachers that became known as "normal schools." The argument was that it was necessary for teachers themselves to have a basic skill level in order to teach. Mann did not trust the parents to be able to judge the quality of their children's teachers and felt the state must take the lead.

Mann also expanded the notion of curriculum from the teaching of basic skills to include broader aims. One educational historian described these reforms as "social efficiency, civic virtue, and character, rather than mere learning."[4] These additional traits were, of course, well intentioned, but have provided the opportunity for Ruling Class exploitation. If "mere learning" becomes just one objective among many in the school curriculum, the emphasis on the acquisition of skills is diffused. Here is where the foundation for the problems we have today began. First, there is less instructional time. Second, it is the Ruling Class that would determine what "social efficiency and civic virtue" are. If one's ultimate goal is power, as it is with the Ruling Class, here is a chance to shape young minds. A lot of what is now taught in school has more to do with political correctness than with real information. Civic virtue has little to do with civics defined as "how government works," which the Ruling Class might not want to advertise. It has everything to do with how the citizen is supposed to behave. The more power they have and the more they emphasize what they consider to be "civic virtue," the more that test scores will drop in reading, math, and science.

As time passed, even Mann's better ideas on the professionalization of education have produced more of the problems we see in our schools today. For example, his original intention in creating normal schools was to ensure that in a variety of learning environments—different schools, different teachers—each student received a quality education. Today this ideal has led to a system where it is more important for teachers to have degrees in "teaching" than in the specific subjects they teach.

Examination of most state teaching requirements shows this to be the case. Nearly all states require the completion of teacher education programs and constant recertification through continuing education courses to keep one's teaching certification. Oftentimes, this overregulation hampers teaching quality. Consider, for example, the view of Ann Marie Corgill, 2015 National Teacher of the Year finalist and 2014–2015 Alabama Teacher of the Year.[5] Despite these accolades and National Board Certification that licenses her to teach children up to the age of twelve, Corgill was told she'd need additional state certification to teach fifth grade. Frustrated at what she termed a "wall of bureaucracy," Corgill wrote, "After 21 years of teaching in grades 1–6, I have no answers as to why this is a problem now, so instead of paying more fees, taking more tests, and proving once again that I am qualified to teach, I am resigning."

In addition, most states require teachers to be trained in child psychology, multiple styles of learning, and in the basic structure of education. By contrast, few, if any, have formal requirements that a math teacher must have majored in math, or a science teacher in science, and such qualifications are considered merely "helpful."

There is actually a standard joke about this: "Those who can, do; those who can't, teach; those who can't teach, teach teachers."[6] There is a complete lack of empirical evidence that teachers who attain advanced degrees in education produce better outcomes for their students (in other words, that their students actually learn more). Instead, the phenomenon of credentialism that was discussed in chapter 4 is now rampant throughout the teaching profession, leading to income that doesn't necessarily correlate with teaching quality. Teacher pay scales are driven by how many credit hours the teacher has spent in school, instead of by his or her merit in the classroom.

Critics of credentialism stress that its real purpose is to serve members of the profession and not the public—in this case, students and their families. Credentialism serves to falsely heighten the social status of an occupation by making it appear exclusive. The nineteenth-century German political scientist Max Weber called this "social closure," because it restricted access to the resources and opportunities in a field to a small number of people willing to jump through the necessary hoops. Conveniently for the Ruling Class, this means that those individuals most likely to disagree with their views have a difficult time entering the teaching profession. Attaining one's teaching certification today becomes a rite of passage that limits supply and allows current teachers to effectively maintain a monopoly. Similar practices date back to the guilds of the Middle Ages, and in both instances, the price of the service increases without necessarily improving its quality. None of this is the fault of individual teachers, most of whom are highly dedicated. It is the fault of a badly designed system founded on Ruling Class values and objectives.

Additionally, schools have further twisted Mann's theme of offering their students more than just the subject matter. A report by the National Education Commission on Time and Learning found that American students spent only about 41 percent of their school day on core academics, totaling 1,460 hours in a four-year high school career. Curriculums for same-aged students from Japan (3,170 hours), France (3,260 hours), and Germany (3,528 hours) more than doubled this time.[7] Part of this difference is accounted for by shorter US school schedules, but the main issue is that American schools allot less time for teaching these core topics. Further, a study commissioned by the US Department of Education indicated that disruptions for announcements, special events, and discipline problems in US classrooms produced significant reductions in the amount of classroom time actually spent on instructional activities.

Politics works to cement this unhappy state of affairs in place. The Ruling Class have become the beneficiaries of the political clout of the teachers unions.[8] Since 1989, the National Education Association was the fourth-largest political donor in the United States. In the 2002–2014 election cycles, the NEA gave more than $93 million. Moreover, the second-largest teachers union, the American Federation of Teachers

(AFT), gave an additional $70 million, making it the sixth-largest political donor in the country that year. To put these numbers into perspective, the infamous Koch Industries (owned by the Koch Brothers) gave a total of $28.6 million, making it the forty-eighth-largest donor. The Center for Responsive Politics finds that at least 94 percent of teacher union donations have gone to liberals and Democrats in every election cycle it has tracked.[9]

Bear in mind that all of this campaign money was collected forcibly from members' union dues. Most union members work in states with union shop laws that require joining the union as a condition of employment. The Ruling Class have every incentive to keep this situation in place. One of the biggest battlegrounds on this issue was Wisconsin, where public sector unions fought a battle to recall Governor Scott Walker, who tried to break the union monopoly. A 2011 law allowed teachers to keep their jobs without having to join the union, and from 2011 to 2015, membership in the state's largest teachers union, the Wisconsin Education Association Council, plummeted from roughly 98,000 to 40,000.[10] Union support extends beyond direct contributions to candidates that have to be reported as political spending and thus are not accessible publicly, including time spent on voter education and turnout drives. And buying access can take a variety of forms. In 2013, the AFT also gave $250,000 to the Clinton Foundation and $200,000 to the Clinton Global Initiative.[11] These foundations are charitable organizations in which Bill and Hillary Clinton are actively involved. Questions have been raised about some of the foundation donors and whether or not their donations were made in return for political favors. The link to direct educational interests is far from clear. A strong interest has developed for the Ruling Class to keep schools unionized, and union backing of political interests continues to play a significant role in policy decisions that affect education.

Take President Obama's repeated closure of the DC Opportunity Scholarship Program (OSP), for example. Signed into law by President Bush in 2004 as the District of Columbia School Choice Incentive Act of 2003, the OSP allowed students from low-income families who were currently attending failing DC public schools to switch to higher-quality private schools of their choice, allocating up to $7,500 a year per student. And for all intents and purposes, the program was a success. A congressionally mandated study of the OSP's effectiveness published in March 2009 by the Department of Education found that in its first three years, the OSP produced students with reading skills "equivalent to 3.1 months of additional learning," and that the OSP led to an increase in parents' satisfaction with their child's school and safety during the school day.[12] The previous school year, the OSP enabled 1,903 students in grades kindergarten through twelve from families with an average income just above the poverty level to attend fifty-four DC private schools.

Nonetheless, President Obama, under pressure from teachers unions, which felt the OSP was taking away from the public school system, cut all funding to the program in his 2009 budget proposal as one of his first acts as president. After Republicans retook the House of Representatives, the OSP was restored in 2011 under Speaker John Boehner's Scholarships for Opportunity and Results Act, with reauthorization for five years and increased appropriations to allow $8,000 per year for primary school students and $12,000 per year for high school students. Despite massive public outcry, President Obama again killed the program with his 2013 budget.

The Ruling Class attempt to justify limitations on parent/student school choice through their often-used rationalization that they know better. Consider the comments made by the school superintendent of Racine, Wisconsin, Dr. Ann Laing, who was speaking in opposition to an expansion of the Milwaukee Parental Choice Program, which is similar to the OSP. "The African American families are the ones who are most prone to enroll their kids in the fly-by-night schools that cropped up after vouchers existed," she claimed, going on to say that African American families "don't know how to make good choices for their children. They really don't. They didn't have parents who made good choices for them or helped them learn how to make good choices, so they don't know how to do that."[13] Admittedly, Dr. Laing's remarks represent the extreme end of the spectrum, but they are nonetheless emblematic of the Ruling Class's belief in their own superiority.

In addition to being explicitly racist, Dr. Laing's comments are completely false. A survey of parents whose children were part of the GOAL scholarship program, Georgia's equivalent of the DC OSP, revealed several reasons why so many families opt out of their local public school system when given the chance.[14] In naming what was the most important factor in selecting their choice school, 51 percent of parents responded "better student discipline," 51 percent selected "better school environment," 49 percent cited "smaller class sizes," 47 percent named "improved student safety," and 39 percent chose "more individualized attention for my child."

Contrary to Dr. Laing's views, parents understood *exactly* what was at stake. They were looking for an educational experience that would make the learning environment better for their sons and daughters. Also striking about the survey results is that the top responses were composed of intangible qualities not detectable by the standardized testing that the school systems of today prioritize so highly. (Only 10 percent of parents chose "standardized test scores" as their biggest reason for seeking an alternative to public education.) Intangible qualities regarding the actual learning environment were far more important.

These data offer insight into the hotly contested school testing debate. There has been a lot of talk about the need for a Common Core curriculum in order to facilitate decision making about which schools are succeeding and which schools are failing. Implicitly, this is buying into the notion that parents need more information about their schools and cannot judge based on what they see when they visit schools and hear from their sons and daughters. A school can be failing because students don't feel safe in the halls or the bathrooms, for example, and that has nothing to do with standardized test scores.

The GOAL survey results explain that the Ruling Class are failing to deliver more than just quality as measured academically. The parent responses indicate dissatisfaction in their children's state-run schools in nearly every area imaginable. One statistic that should horrify the unions: more than twice as many parents selected "more responsive teachers and administrators" as one of their top five reasons for switching schools than chose "standardized test scores." And these parents were by no means outliers. The survey respondents represented a cross section of Georgia's population: a quarter had incomes under $36,000, 27 percent were African American or Hispanic, and more than a quarter were single parents.

The notion that change is needed as conveyed by the GOAL survey is widespread. In 2012, the Friedman Foundation for Educational Choice, a nonprofit organization that promotes educational reform, commissioned a study that targeted the mothers of school-age children to gain insight into how well public schools are teaching American children from the people who'd know best. When asked if the federal government was doing a good or bad job with respect to public education, 79 out of 96 responded "bad job." So strong was this opinion that survey respondents drastically underestimated how much we spend each year on public school students. Only 11 percent guessed the correct national average of $8,000 to $12,000, while 35 percent estimated less than $4,000 a year. When asked to "grade" their local public schools, 54 percent gave them Cs, Ds, or Fs. The percentage dropped dramatically when parents were asked to rate their local charter schools* (16 percent, C, D, or F) and private schools (13 percent, C, D, or F). And 43 percent were in favor of the introduction of a voucher program (like those implemented in

---

*As defined by the Center for Public Education, charter schools are those that receive federal funding yet are free to operate as they see fit, with less government oversight. Because they are less regulated than public schools, charter schools are held to tighter academic standards, as detailed in the charter between the school and the state authorizing agency. Many feel that this system produces better results for students, because key decisions involving curriculum, staffing, and even how to spend appropriated funds are left up to those that know best: the school's officials. Because each school has its own charter, school administration can localize the rules governing the school to best fit its students, and aren't limited by the broad, one-size-fits-all considerations that must be made by public schools with governing bodies that regulate many different schools.

DC, Milwaukee, and Georgia), even without an extensive explanation of the program's details. When these were provided, support climbed to 66 percent. Clearly, our government is not delivering a value consistent with the high price tag of public education. People's natural instinct is to guess the cost of something is close to what they perceive as its value. The fact that the estimated spending per pupil was so far below the actual cost reinforces the low grades given by these parents.

One of the biggest problems with our public schools is that they lack competitive pressure. Any businessman will tell you that fear of competition is the biggest incentive to deliver a superior product. As summarized by Stanford's Dr. Caroline Hoxby, one of the leading researchers in the economics of education, school choice (even choice among public schools) benefits students and produces better outcomes because, ultimately, only those schools that are responsive to their customers' needs will survive. If there were exactly one car company instead of many, do you think the quality of its cars would be better or worse? Do you think the price would go up or down if there were no competition? Why would anyone expect it to be different with schools? In fact, we have laws on the books against monopolies in the private sector. Enforcement of monopoly laws does not even require 100 percent control of a market, just such extensive control that it gives the monopolist market power. The harm that monopolization causes is generally perceived as being so great that the sheer presence of market power is enough to initiate legal action. Monopolization is clear in public education. Given our legal and economic views of monopolies and the harm they cause, why do we encourage and protect monopolies in something as important as the education of our children?

And as we know from the private sector, monopolies tend to drive up the prices they charge relative to the cost of producing them. Consider again the details of the Washington, DC, OSP. At the program's inception, the vouchers were for $7,500, far less than the average cost of attending a public school in DC, which exceeds $17,000.[15] According to the program's website, more than 6,100 students have been awarded an

OSP scholarship since the program began during the 2004–05 school year. Taxpayers saved $9,500 on net for every student who signed up, making the total savings $60 million.

So, parents and their children clearly benefit, and taxpayers clearly benefit. The Ruling Class response, however, is that parents do not know what is best for their kids. This is the same as the Ruling Class's view about the rest of us: they know best. Their highly credentialed résumés combined with their supposedly higher intelligence mean that they should control the education of the nation's children—not parents. But their belief in their own superiority in making decisions hides the real reason for denying choice in education: power. The political coziness between the teachers unions—which are eager to drive up costs and protect incompetent teachers—and the Ruling Class is obvious. If there is any place where the grip of the Ruling Class needs to be broken, it is on their control of education.

CHAPTER 10

America's Infrastructure Is Crumbling Under the Ruling Class

Many of the Ruling Class's initiatives focus on America's infrastructure. President Obama came to office demanding investment in what he called "shovel-ready jobs" to repair our crumbling roads and bridges. Turns out, these projects weren't exactly shovel ready, and the phrase became a punch line for late-night comedians. In 2013, the president called for a new $300 billion program to fix our infrastructure,[1] saying that it shouldn't be partisan. And spending money on infrastructure is not—nearly everyone is for it. In December 2015, the House of Representatives passed a bill to spend $325 billion over six years on highways and mass transit by an overwhelming 363–64 vote.[2] But all of this neglects a simple question: Who exactly was in charge as our infrastructure deteriorated? Why did they get it wrong in the first place?

The go-to answer of "Spend more money!" needs some careful examination. The $261 billion authorized over six years by the highway bill is for the development of the 223,000 miles in the National Highway System: 47,000 miles of interstate and 176,000 miles of other roads. (The remaining $64 billion is to be spent on nonhighway infrastructure, such as mass transit systems.) That is $1,170,000 of federal money for every mile of road in the system. And this figure doesn't even include state spending. How does that cost compare with what any reasonable person would be willing to spend? Let's say that you were building and maintaining an asphalt driveway for your home. The driveway itself lasts about twenty years but has to be treated and repaired every six years. The total cost for this averages out to 37 cents per year or $2.22 per square foot every six years (the duration of the highway bill). A highway runs about 60 feet wide—the minimum is 12 feet per lane, and, of course, there are 5,280 feet in length per mile. If the cost of building, rebuilding, and maintaining were the same as for a driveway, we would be spending $703,000 per mile every six years.

A highway might be more complicated, but it should also be far cheaper per square foot, since trucking the men and materiel to your home is quite expensive. This phenomenon is known as economies of scale: it is cheaper to do something en masse than in small batches. But basically the federal government is building and maintaining the highway system at a price per mile that is two-thirds higher than what a homeowner would spend on his driveway! This hardly suggests we are skimping on our infrastructure spending.

International data reflect the same tendency toward higher costs. As with public education, we spend more on our infrastructure than other countries do on their national infrastructure. A 2015 report by the Organization for Economic Co-operation and Development (OECD) showed that the United States actually spends more than average, contributing 4.11 percent of our GDP, compared with 3.49 percent in the remaining OECD countries.[3] Moreover, nations with fabulous road and rail systems such as France, Japan, and Germany all spent a lower percentage of their national output on infrastructure than did the United States. So, once again, why are we spending more but getting less?

Research by the World Economic Forum, an international organization that aims to bolster economic development, might provide
the answer.[4] Surveying business leaders from around the world, the
study ranked the United States at just fourteenth globally in terms of
infrastructure—not great, but far from the biggest problem limiting our
country's growth. Instead, the survey respondents named inefficient
government bureaucracy as the greatest hindrance to economic development in the United States, followed by tax rates, tax regulations, insufficient access to financing, and restrictive labor regulations.

The real reason we're spending more and getting less is because of
the connection between the first problem on the list, bureaucracy, and
the fifth problem, restrictive labor regulations. Their combined effect
is to inflate the cost of infrastructure. Our cumbersome, overburdened
government and its overreaching labor regulations make for a horribly
inefficient use of our tax dollars. Our government continually spends
more to get less because of its now-bloated bureaucracy with too many
bottlenecks.

Consider the bureaucracy. When the federal Highway Trust Fund
was established in 1956, administration and research costs amounted
to 6.8 percent of total expenditures.[5] By 2002, these same outlays had
climbed to 17 percent of spending. But this measures only the direct
costs of these functions; there are a variety of indirect costs as well. Robert Farris, the former chief of the Federal Highway Administration, estimated that administrative restrictions increased the cost of road building
by 30 percent.

First among these are the contracting rules that limit who can be
hired—the kind of restrictive labor regulations outlined in the World
Economic Forum study. Chief among these is the 1931 Davis-Bacon
Act, which requires that all federal contractors pay the "prevailing wage"
to their workers. This, in effect, has become "the union wage," and is
unconnected to the actual cost of hiring road construction workers in
a given market. The law was passed in Depression-era America, when
many contractors competed for projects by hiring cheaper, out-of-region

labor. This undercut the local wage and thus deprived a congressman's constituents of the benefit of the pork projects he had brought home from Washington in the form of road spending. To stop this, Davis and Bacon required that all contractors pay the same—prevailing—wage. It has since become even more bureaucratic, breaking down work categories and adding more jobs for the bureaucrats who do the calculations. Individual job categories conform closely to union specifications. So ordinary laborers end up being paid the wages of much more skilled individuals in order to comply with the law. The net result is to raise the wages that must be paid an average 22 percent above the actual local average wage levels.[6]

Adding to the indirect costs is a 2009 executive order signed by President Obama that mandated the use of Project Labor Agreements that guarantee the hiring of unionized workers. A study by the National University System Institute for Policy Research found that this legislation raised the cost of school construction projects 13 percent to 15 percent.[7] In addition, another of the president's executive orders made it harder to use material or machinery manufactured outside the United States on any domestic construction projects, extending the regulation to go beyond roads and to cover all forms of construction. Projects *are* permitted to ignore this regulation if it's going to increase costs by more than 25 percent, but this figure alone should give a sense of how expensive the rule might be.

Local deals between labor unions and the politicians they back and elect also drive up the cost of the projects. Back in 2011, blogger Benjamin Kabak interviewed Michael Horodniceanu, president of New York Metropolitan Transportation Authority Capital Construction. When asked why things cost so much more in New York than anywhere else,[8] Horodniceanu cited work rules, noting that the MTA is required to overstaff projects so that the same tunnel-digging work, for instance, that can be done in Spain with nine workers must be done in NYC with twenty-five. As a result, everything costs far too much.

Other regulations affect costs. One of them is the extent of environmental review that must take place for any construction project to break ground. Representative John Duncan of Tennessee pointed out in hearings he held in 2011 that the approval of new projects often took two to three times longer in the United States than in other countries.[9] But the defense of the status quo in those hearings was even more interesting. Congressman Peter DeFazio argued with respect to one project in his home state of Oregon, "It wasn't a question of waiving environmental laws, but the bureaucracy was going to grind on for four or six weeks till this guy came back from vacation, went through his in-box, and then decided to check the box and send it back to Portland, and then it got to the top of the file there, and someone decided to check the box and send it on to the Department of Transportation. And by then, it might be too late." So maybe it isn't the rules themselves but the bureaucracy that administers the rules. This is yet another example of how the rules themselves are not an end, but a means to an end, and that end is power.

The National Environmental Policy Act (NEPA) requires that "environmental impact" statements be issued for most major projects, and since its passage in 1970, the act has been used to block or delay many construction projects. In 2011, it took more than eight years to clear the regulatory hurdles to build a project, four times as long as when the act passed. Two of those extra eight years were added just in the first three years that President Obama was in office. So the bureaucratic bottlenecks are getting longer at an accelerating pace. The issue is not so much the requirement that environmental impact be assessed, but *how* the Ruling Class carry out that mission. Since a bureaucrat's power is the power to say no and that bureaucrat can get in trouble only if he or she says yes, and the project goes forward, the process of approval has become needlessly complicated. In business, the incentive is to reach compromises to get the deal done. In a bureaucracy, power and justifying one's job involve extending the approval process as long as possible.

The NY-NJ-CT Regional Plan Association (which itself is not exactly independent of the Ruling Class) issued the following conclusions about why NEPA is failing in 2011. First: "lack of stakeholder consensus over fundamental aspects of a project forged during the planning phase, which are not efficiently resolved during the environmental review process."[10] This is its way of saying that the various parties disagree fundamentally about some aspect of the project and fail to work out their differences on these issues so that the environmental review can be effective. These side issues might involve the project's "purpose, design, location . . . cost, or some other consideration," as well as the environmental impact and mitigation procedures. In other words, NEPA provides a way of delaying projects through endless bureaucratic infighting that relate to nonenvironmental issues.

Second: "differing and conflicting interpretations of NEPA requirements, and inconsistent implementing policies and procedures among the multitude of government agencies," which cause delays. In translation, this means that various parts of the bureaucracy can't talk to one another because they use different languages. Or as the Regional Plan Association put it more delicately: "The various agencies, firms, and levels of government tend to interpret some aspects of the NEPA requirements, process, and vocabulary differently." This gets back to a fundamental failure of the Ruling Class: they are not driven organizationally to make things happen; their organizational focus is on acquiring power and control. There is no incentive to work together or even to agree to speak the same language, because that diminishes power and forces compromise.

Third, delays are caused by "administrative bottlenecks and outdated procedures within agencies that have insufficient staff capacity and training to efficiently complete environmental studies or reviews." Again, whose fault is that? In the private sector, the goal would be to remove the administrative bottlenecks and update the outdated procedures. Getting things done is the only way the business can survive. But in a bureaucracy, *not* getting things done is what justifies the institution's existence. The bigger the mountain of paperwork and the longer the backlog, the greater demand for more resources for the bureaucracy.

The Ruling Class have every incentive to run things the opposite of the way things are done in the business world. Their demand is always for even more resources to take care of the alleged problems of insufficient staff capacity and training. Of course, without updating and streamlining, that additional staff will be wasted.

Finally, the Regional Plan Association found that "misdirected response to the threat of environmental litigation, which leads to overly complex and technical environmental analysis and rigorous documentation efforts," delays the process further. Of course, the interagency process just described is only the *first* step in getting project approval. Disaffected parties who don't like the result can sue in court. The result is something that any lawyer would understand: increase billable hours by preparing for every possible contingency in case you have to go to court. This leads to higher bureaucratic costs because more work needs to be done "just in case," which obviously delays the process. The Ruling Class have not designed a system for project approval that reaches a final conclusion rapidly. That would actually be self-defeating. Instead, they have created an endless process that provides jobs, resources, and power to their component parts.

It is important to note that these are the conclusions from people who are generally *part of* the Ruling Class. They are, after all, planners. But even they are frustrated by just how bad the process has gotten and want it to work more efficiently—because, frankly, it has become an embarrassment. Indeed, even President Obama became frustrated with the process when his "shovel-ready jobs" didn't materialize and were becoming a political embarrassment. He issued Executive Order 13563[11] to try to speed things up. But as the Regional Plan Association noted in its report, "[I]n order for these agencies to fully reform their established procedures, they will need greater assurance and direction that the changes will not lead to an up-tick in lawsuits challenging the completeness and appropriateness of their environmental studies or reviews." Endless lawsuits to block needed infrastructure projects are part of the legal structure that has been built up over the years to empower the unelected. Advocacy groups and their allies in the bureaucracy are key components of the Ruling Class, and efforts to trim their power are not going to be enacted as long as the Ruling Class retain power.

The magnitude of the waste, fraud, abuse, and patronage involved in all of these projects is staggering. One of the most famous cases is the Central Artery/Tunnel Project, better known locally as the "Big Dig," which rebuilt the infrastructure in downtown Boston.[12] The chief congressional instigator of the project was Boston's own Tip O'Neill, who, as Speaker of the House, had the influence to make things happen. (One of the main parts of the Dig became the three-and-a-half-mile-long Thomas P. O'Neill Jr. Tunnel.) The project's planning phase was begun in 1982, when O'Neill was Speaker. Construction took place between 1991 and 2006 and was officially wrapped up at the end of 2007. It was originally supposed to be completed in 1998 and cost $2.8 billion dollars. In the end, the Big Dig cost over $14 billion (even after adjusting for inflation, it cost $8 billion), nearly three times the original estimate. The *Boston Globe*, however, estimates that the true cost will be more like $22 billion when interest is included.

The Big Dig points to the power of politics to drive up costs by allocating, or more accurately, misallocating money. An equally famous example, one that ultimately was not completed, was the so-called Bridge to Nowhere.[13] The bridge didn't quite go nowhere, but it extended from Ketchikan, Alaska, to Gravina Island, which had a grand total of 50 full-time residents. Ketchikan has about 9,000 residents. Gravina Island was home to Ketchikan International Airport, but a ferry has long connected the two. The ferry charges $6 per passenger and $7 per car and runs every thirty minutes year-round and every fifteen minutes during tourist season. A total of 350,000 people per year ride the ferry. Total toll collections amount to about $3 million. The bridge would cost $400 million. So if you did a simple cost-benefit analysis and considered the bridge as replacing the need for the ferry, the bridge would have yielded a return of 0.75 percent. Of course, since the bridge would also have to be maintained, the odds are that the real return on the investment would have been negative.

However, the local congressman, Don Young, chairman of the House Appropriations Committee, was joined by the equally powerful senator from Alaska, Ted Stevens, in pushing the bridge. Just like Speaker O'Neill, these men tended to get what they wanted. But media embarrassment and opposition from colleagues ended up dooming the project. Had it been built, it would have been an immense structure by any standard, let alone for its modest location. It would have been almost as long as San Francisco's Golden Gate Bridge and taller than the Brooklyn Bridge.

Our infrastructure problem is not so much a money problem as a problem of how the Ruling Class govern. They design projects based primarily on political need, not economic common sense. And in doing so, they encourage inefficiency. Next time you are in a traffic jam caused by some construction project, take a close look at how many people are actually working and how many are just standing around. And this pales in comparison with the costs imposed upon the planning and development process by delays caused by a bloated and growing bureaucracy. This process layers on cost drivers, ranging from labor rules to environmental restrictions that pump up costs higher and create endless delays in the construction process.

The final section of this book will consider how to streamline decision making to minimize these costs. They will never all disappear, because all public policy decisions involve trade-offs. But what we now have is a system that ignores that notion by creating a myriad of independent bureaucracies and judges, each of whom might possess an effective veto over a project. This is a generic problem with our current system of governance. It is the direct result of moving away from what the Constitution demanded: a system where Congress is the sole institution with legislative authority. The one thing we can know with reasonable certainty is that throwing more money into the current system will not solve our infrastructure problem. More money simply rewards the existing level of incompetence. Once this problem is fixed, we can actually determine whether additional resources are needed; but to do so, we must first fix the broken infrastructure approval system that the Ruling Class have put in place.

CHAPTER 11

The Threat of the Second Amendment to the Ruling Class

I f you listen carefully to speeches given by leaders of the Ruling Class, facts are remarkably scarce. Consider the press conference that President Obama held in Paris in November 2015 after a crazed gunman attacked an abortion clinic in Colorado. "Things like this don't happen in other countries," he said, to drive home his call for more gun control in America.[1] There was no sense of irony in his statement, and the Ruling Class media didn't object. But there in Paris, the president was standing within a few miles of where 130 people had been gunned down by a group of Muslim extremists associated with ISIS just a few days before.

Or consider his "commonsense" proposal to ban people on the no-fly list from being able to buy guns. There are a total of eight hundred Americans—either citizens or permanent residents—on that list. So stopping them from buying guns in a country where there are an estimated three hundred million firearms in circulation is not exactly going to make a dent. The no-fly list is composed of people who, according to the government (using a secret form of analysis), *might* commit an act of violence in the future, although not one has committed a murder by definition.[2] Nevertheless, this was put forward after the San Bernardino attack on December 2, 2015, where two shooters with ties to radical Islam opened fire on those attending a holiday party, as a straw man for a "commonsense" way of curbing gun violence through greater regulation. The Ruling Class's true goal, with comments like this, is nothing more than to weaken the impact of the Second Amendment, and they never miss an opportunity to try to take a swipe.

Their argument is not based on facts or analysis; it is entirely emotional. It is driven by the generic Ruling Class claim "Give us more money, give us more resources, and we will solve your problems." The trouble is, their "solutions" are ineffective at best; often the problem persists, and many times it gets worse. This book has shown that to be the case with their attempts to reduce inequality, manage America's finances, take over the public education system, and fix our deteriorating infrastructure. But once their failure is obvious, the Ruling Class argue that they just weren't given enough power or enough resources; that they need even more.

It's important to see through the falsehoods of the Ruling Class narrative and realize their true intentions when evaluating their proposals. Can their plan work as suggested, or will it fail like so many others and simply end up suppressing even more of our individual liberty? These are important questions to ask when it comes to gun control legislation. "Sounds good" isn't enough, or shouldn't be. "Will it actually make a difference?" is a much more powerful justification. That is why, with all of the calls for increased regulation of firearms, there's been precious little effort expended in researching actual gun crime statistics. If those in charge—the Ruling Class—were actually going to make a case based on facts, rather than emotion, one would think they would have used the resources at their disposal to marshal the facts. But they tend to use their marketing messages to further their goals, not objective facts. When they do reach for statistics, they tend to stretch them in ways that are objectively wrong, because the facts do not support their positions. Those facts that are available certainly do not make a strong case that further restrictions on guns will solve any problem.

This is mainly because existing gun laws are quite extensive. Yet despite this, there is still a significant amount of gun violence. It is now illegal for any individual who has committed a felony involving a sentence of more than a year to possess a firearm. It is also illegal for anyone convicted of domestic violence to own a gun. These seem like quite commonsense rules.

Trouble is, these laws aren't preventing criminals from getting guns and using them. They just don't care what any law says. A 1998 study of felony arrests in large urban areas found that 81 percent of homicide defendants had at least one prior arrest, 70 percent had one conviction,[3] and 60 percent had two or more arrests. A 1995 study by the Bureau of Justice Statistics noted that, by definition, stolen firearms are available for criminal use.[4] They cited the National Crime Victimization Survey estimates that there were 341,000 incidents of firearm theft from private citizens annually from 1987 to 1992. Moreover, they noted that the FBI's National Crime Information Center had files on more than 2 million stolen guns as of March 1995. If the theft rate of 300,000 per year was maintained, that number would be more than 8 million stolen weapons in circulation today. Stolen guns are unlikely to be surrendered under any "gun control" ordinance, and by definition, those in possession of these weapons are criminals.

Also indicative are the characteristics of murder victims. The Milwaukee Homicide Review Commission found that 77 percent of all murder victims had prior arrests, as did 90 percent of all suspects.[5] In New Orleans, the *Times-Picayune* reported that 69 percent of all victims had a prior criminal record.[6] *USA Today* reported that 91 percent of murder victims had criminal records.[7] In Philadelphia, the figure was 81 percent, and in Newark, New Jersey, it was 85 percent. Finally, the

New York Times reported that 70 percent of all murder victims had prior records in New York City.[8] The data on murder victims are more prevalent because the victim is, by definition, known, while the culprit is not. Still, it strains credulity that all of these criminals who are the victims of murders were killed by otherwise law-abiding citizens. If the victim had multiple prior arrests, the odds are that the perpetrator did as well, so it's highly likely that the person committing a gun-related murder was forbidden by existing law from having a gun! And thus continues the familiar Ruling Class story: "Current laws aren't working under our watch, so we need more laws."

Consider these statistics in terms of overall gun violence. Government data show that in 2013 there were 33,636 gun deaths in the United States.[9] Of these, 21,175 were suicides. While these suicides are all tragedies, they are not the target of proposals for more gun legislation. Another 505 deaths were deemed "accidents," a figure that has been dropping sharply over recent decades. Another 467 gun deaths were committed by police officers in the line of duty, and 286 were justifiable homicides committed by private citizens defending themselves against an armed attacker. That leaves 11,023 murders committed with guns.

So let's use data to try to estimate just how many murders could be prevented by tighter gun laws. As noted above, most of these murders were likely committed by someone for whom it was already illegal to own a gun. As the above data on urban violence make clear, roughly 80 percent of victims, and almost certainly a higher proportion of perpetrators had past criminal records and therefore had no legal right to own a gun. The US Bureau of Justice Statistics reports that between 2007 and 2011, only 9 percent of gun-related murders occurred between people who were or had been "intimate," and another 7 percent involved other family members.[10] Obviously some of those in-family murders were also done with guns that were illegal for the perpetrator to own because those convicted of domestic violence are also banned from gun ownership. So perhaps 2,000 murders were committed where the perpetrator probably could own a gun legally under current law. That number is the upper bound on the number of murders that might be potentially preventable by extending and successfully implementing additional gun laws.

Put that number into some perspective. There are an estimated 300 million guns in the United States. That means that there is roughly 1 potentially avoidable murder by further gun legislation for every 150,000 guns in the country! Every death is a tragedy, but from a purely statistical point of view, the amount of upside that can be obtained through further gun legislation—even assuming that it worked—is quite small by most metrics.

Another way of putting this into perspective is to consider that guns are also a way of preventing crime. Data on this vary widely. For example, the National Rifle Association (NRA) estimates that there are roughly 2.5 million instances per year in which a gun owner deters a crime due to the threat (implied or real) that it poses to the criminal.[11] The number is impossible to verify independently. In practice, most such instances are probably not even reported to the police because the crime technically did not occur. So let's place this on the "high end" of potential crime deterrence effect of gun possession. An intermediate estimate was done by Just the Facts, a statistical analysis outfit. It placed the annual number of defensive uses where "someone likely would have been killed" but for the threatened use of the firearm at 156,000, based on a 1993 survey. This is, of course, a much higher standard than the NRA uses, as there was the expectation of a death in the statistic.

There is also a "low-end" estimate provided by the pro–gun control group the Utah Gun Violence Prevention Center. Based on a "special run" of FBI statistics, they estimate that from 2007 to 2011, 235,000 violent crimes and 103,000 crimes against property were prevented by the threat or use of a firearm by the victim.[12] Because these statistics came from the FBI, these were cases of actual crimes that were reported by the victim and with sufficient evidence that the police included them in their official crime tabulations. But even if one takes this low-end statistic as the basis for comparison, that means that 47,000 violent crimes and 20,600 property crimes were prevented by the use or threatened use of a firearm. Combined, that is thirty-three times the maximum number of potentially preventable murders by the passage of and the completely successful enforcement of more gun laws.

This type of finding only makes sense. Compliance with any new gun legislation is only going to be made by those who comply with the law. As the trite but still accurate saying goes, "If guns are outlawed, only outlaws will have guns." The experience of other countries bears this out. India, for example, passed new gun legislation and found that 85 percent of its gun-related crimes were now committed with illegal weapons.[13] This is not unusual. In 2007, the Swiss-based International Small Arms Survey looked at seventy-two countries with various new gun control measures and found that after the laws were passed, there was an average of 2.6 illegal guns for every legal one.[14]

Further complicating the picture is that most Ruling Class proposals on gun control are very specific about the types of weapons they would ban. Most proposals have loaded words. For example, the word "assault weapons" sounds scary. But the definition included guns with pistol-type grips and adjustable stocks. There was no effect on the guns' ultimate lethality. The Bureau of Justice Statistics reports that 88 percent of all gun violence and 73 percent of all deaths involving guns were committed with handguns.[15] Ohio senator Howard Metzenbaum, a Democrat, opined tellingly at a 1989 hearing on gun control, "If you don't ban all of them, you might as well ban none of them."

Therein lies the real political rub. Gun rights advocates see gun control proposals as being driven toward their ultimate end of drastically limiting, or even ending, private gun ownership entirely. After the shooting of students at an Oregon college in 2015, Hillary Clinton spoke of what she called the Australian model of gun control. In practice, that model led to the confiscation of about a quarter of all the firearms in Australia. Though she did add, "I don't know enough detail to tell you how we would do it or how it would work."[16] She said she had no intention of confiscating guns. This points to two possible explanations of Ruling

Class politician commentary on gun control: either they really do intend to ultimately confiscate guns but they know they can't say that politically. Or they really don't know what the facts are. Let's consider both.

There is a good historical reason why the Founders put the Second Amendment into the Constitution: the right to bear arms was key to winning the War of Independence. Indeed, the "shot heard round the world" that started the war was at Lexington Green as the British made their way out of Boston to seize guns that the colonists had stockpiled in Concord. The Founders were also distrustful of federal power, noting that "a well-regulated militia [is] necessary for the defense of any free state."

President Obama, like Hillary Clinton, endorsed the Australian model in October 2015. Setting aside the Second Amendment, in America that would mean the confiscation of roughly seventy-five million guns. Presumably the government would have to compensate owners for taking their property. At an average cost of roughly $1,000 per gun, that would mean $75 billion for the program. (The Australian program cost more than $500 million to destroy just 650,000 guns.) By contrast, the entire budget for the US Department of Justice is just $27 billion. Setting aside simple dollar cost, consider the logistics involved in confiscating tens of millions of anything!

As the *National Review* pointed out, "The mandatory confiscation of the American citizenry's guns would involve tens of thousands of heavily armed federal agents going door-to-door to demand of millions of Americans that they surrender their guns."[17] Given that historically the Ruling Class were willing to arrest and fine a man for growing too much grain on his farm to feed his own horses (*Wickard v. Filburn*, discussed in chapter 6), one might suppose that carrying out a massive gun confiscation program is not beyond the realm of possibility.

But this is not the simplest explanation of the Ruling Class attitude toward guns. More true to form would be that their failure to provide an acceptable level of safety to the American people, those in charge need someone or something to blame. Since the Ruling Class can't accept blame themselves, blaming it all on guns serves that need. They try to convince us that people don't kill people, guns kill people. The most standard behavioral pattern we have discovered for the Ruling Class is to avoid blame for their failure to use the extensive powers they already have is to seek still more power.

As noted before, what is most startling is that given the power and resources at their disposal, those in charge have not provided the facts to back up their claim. There is no national evidence on the rate at which gun crimes are now being committed by those for whom existing law makes it illegal to own a gun. If there were, of course, and it showed that most gun crime is committed by people for whom existing law already bans gun ownership, then it would be hard to make the case for more bans on gun ownership. Maybe that's why the data aren't collected? A willingness to provide such data might provide good reason not to think the worst about Ruling Class motives; that it is not forthcoming is quite troubling.

So when one examines the evidence and does not rely on emotional rhetoric, two facts become obvious. First, that existing gun control legislation is ineffective. Second, that the incremental benefits from further tightening of rules would be ineffective, since there are far fewer potential gun murders caused by "legal" users.

So one does not have to believe that gun control is simply a power grab by the Ruling Class to explain their motive. They are in need of a defense for their failure to control crime. Their answer is, "It was the gun that did it."

CHAPTER 12

The Ruling Class and Your Property—Or Theirs?

Readers might recall from chapter 2 the story of John Hancock, president of the Continental Congress and wealthy New England merchant, whose ship *Liberty* was confiscated by the British and repurposed for use in their navy. In addition to radicalizing Hancock, the seizure helped shape the Founders' vision of what America should *not* be, inspiring part of the Fifth Amendment: "No person shall . . . be deprived of life, liberty, or property, without due process of law; nor shall property be taken for public use, without just compensation."

Hancock received neither due process nor just compensation. His case never went to trial and the smuggling charges against him were eventually dropped. Nonetheless, the *Liberty* was never returned. This represents one of many outrageous abuses of power perpetrated by Britain and is illustrative of the type of governmental abuse that the Founders fought so hard to escape. Despite their explicit intention to create a country where cases like Hancock's would never happen again, we live in an America today where innocent citizens' possessions and property are no more protected from the government than was Hancock's *Liberty.* Through both direct action and indirect support of increasingly ambiguous legislation that favors their interests instead of those of the people, the Ruling Class have warped our country into a nation where laws and law enforcement are used against the public instead of for them.

Consider the actions of Loretta Lynch, US attorney general. Just before her nomination, Lynch's office announced, with some pride, that between 2011 and 2013 alone, it had confiscated over $113 million in assets through civil asset forfeiture proceedings[1]—seizures in which there was only a belief of criminal activity, not any formal charge or conviction. Intended originally to hinder organized crime through confiscation of different pieces of its enterprise, civil asset forfeiture has since become a means for the federal government and local law enforcement to capture the private resources of Americans, unimpeded by the original protections of the Constitution. Directly contrary to our Founders' intentions, citizens in these cases are robbed of due process, and instead are forced to fight costly and time-consuming legal battles where they are seen as guilty until they can prove their innocence. Worst of all, in nearly all states in our country, the police departments are allowed to keep the funds and property they seize, an approach that has been dubbed "policing for profit."

One prime example reveals a lot about Lynch's attitudes toward personal liberty. In 2012, federal agents seized the bank account of a small business owned by brothers Jeffrey, Mitchell, and Richard Hirsch, amounting to roughly $447,000.[2] Their business distributed small items such as cigarettes and candy to stores throughout Long Island, New York. Most of their income was cash, which they deposited regularly in increments of $500 to $9,000—as they had for nearly twenty-seven years. Despite this consistency and the clear justification for such deposits, the Hirsches were accused of "structuring": deliberately depositing in such a fashion in order to avoid IRS reporting requirements for transactions over $10,000. No charges were ever filed, yet their business was effectively shut down in the case handled by Lynch, then US attorney for the Eastern District of New York.

Only because of intense political pressure did the Hirsches' case have a happy ending. Partly because of her history of overaggressive confiscation, Lynch's seizure of their account attracted considerable attention from several US senators who were highly critical of Lynch's approach. The Hirsches ultimately got their money back, but only after a two-year court battle. As Jeff Hirsch commented rightly, "Nobody in America should have to live through the nightmare we've experienced."

There is even circumstantial evidence that Lynch's office knew it didn't have a case: the US Attorney's Office offered to return a portion of the Hirsches' business capital if they agreed to cease their efforts to get the rest of it back. Lynch and her associates were willing to settle in order to prevent the Hirsches' case from reaching the objective scrutiny of a court of law. What does that say about their integrity or their view of proper judicial process?

Instances like the Hirsches' are by no means unique. Take the case of Russ Caswell, the seventy-year-old owner of Motel Caswell in Tewksbury, Massachusetts.[3] Based on a few drug-related arrests at the motel, a local fixture since 1955, the US Drug Enforcement Administration (DEA) and the local police department seized Caswell's motel, though these crimes occurred behind locked doors by people with no connection to Caswell except that they stayed in his motel. Similar to the Hirsches' case, no charges were filed against Caswell, and he provided a likely explanation for the government's true interest in his business worth an estimated $2 million: "This had nothing to do with drugs. It was just an excuse to steal property from us."[4] Ultimately Caswell prevailed in court, as the judge ruled that the authorities had engaged in "gross exaggeration" in presenting evidence.

Then there is the case of Straughn Gorman, who was traveling across Nevada in his motor home to visit his girlfriend.[5] He was pulled over for driving too slowly in the passing lane and refused the officer's request to search his vehicle. After allowing Gorman to continue on his way, this officer radioed ahead to another trooper, who stopped Gorman again, this time with a drug-sniffing dog. During a search spurned by the dog's alleged detection of drugs in Gorman's vehicle, the deputies found $167,000 in cash. Though no drugs were ever found, they seized this money, along with Gorman's computer, cell phone, and the vehicle itself. While Gorman eventually reclaimed his property, it took over two years of expensive court battles. In delivering his decision on the case, US District Court Judge Larry Hicks admonished the Nevada US Attorney's Office in Reno for withholding critical case information, arguing, "[T]he government has a duty of candor and fair disclosure in the court." Further, Hicks assessed, "No matter how this can be viewed, the two stops were for minor violations, and they both were extended beyond the legitimate purposes for such traffic stops." As in Caswell's case, the government stretched the law to line its pockets, hoping that Gorman would forgo the difficult battle necessary to win back his property.

The alarming trend that is emerging in our country is that if police can seize your property, they will. And they (rightly) assume that in most cases, people won't expend the resources or time necessary to reclaim their possessions. Take, for example, the Philadelphia Police Department's seizure of Christos and Markella Sourovelis's home. The police claimed their property, leaving the Sourovelises homeless, because their son had sold $40 of heroin to an undercover officer from the property.[6] Similar to Caswell's case, the Sourovelises had no knowledge of their twenty-two-year-old son's drug activity. Of course, selling heroin is a serious crime, but does this response seem appropriate? Philadelphia officials have seized more than 1,000 houses, 3,300 vehicles, and $44 million in cash in the last ten years in cases that often bear an uncomfortable resemblance to those discussed here.

Or consider Tan Nguyen's experience in Humboldt County, Nevada.[7] Mr. Nguyen was stopped for driving three miles an hour over the speed limit and declined the deputy's request to search his vehicle. The officer searched Nguyen's car anyway and confiscated $50,000 in cash and cashier's checks from a closed briefcase, which Nguyen claimed were casino winnings. The deputy didn't charge Nguyen with any crime, nor did he write him a traffic ticket. In a lawsuit filed against the Humboldt County Sheriff's Department, Nguyen alleged that the officer violated his civil rights through "unconstitutional search and seizure." According to the legal complaint filed by his attorney, the officer threatened to seize and tow his vehicle unless he "got in his car and drove off and forgot this ever happened." Unsurprisingly, the Sheriff's Department settled, returning all of Nguyen's cash plus $10,000 to cover his attorney fees.

Further increasing the perverse incentives driving law enforcement agencies in these cases, cops are given a wide berth in deciding how to use confiscated funds. For example, the *Milwaukee Journal Sentinel* reported that the Milwaukee County Sheriff's Department used $25,000 of seized funds to send fifty officers to the Walt Disney World Resort for customer service training via Disney's "Approach to Business Excellence" program.[8] Texas district attorney Ron Sutton flew his entire office and their spouses and a local judge to Hawaii for a six-day "law conference" using $27,000 of confiscated funds. In Georgia, the Camden County Sheriff's Department bought a $90,000 Dodge Viper with seized assets, a purchase it justified by using the car for antidrug outreach programs.[9] Sheriff Bill Smith of the same department was investigated by a federal grand jury for several instances of spending confiscated assets questionably, including a $250,000 donation to his alma mater.[10] Texas district attorney Michael McDougal purchased alcohol and even a margarita machine for a community cookout with seized funds.[11] Though civil asset forfeiture doesn't usually fund such extravagant purchases, the underlying principle is the same: law enforcement in today's America is driven by motives completely contradictory to protecting its people, and *that* is a real problem.

Even in the few states that protect their citizens from such egregious abuses, a process known as equitable sharing provides a loophole for local authorities. Through equitable sharing, police restricted by more rigorous state seizure legislation can confiscate property in accordance with federal law, keeping as much as 80 percent of the proceeds. Americans are truly out of luck in terms of finding a branch of law enforcement that isn't incentivized to work against them.

In fact, the rigging of the system is so complete that the official advice is to surrender your rights as a citizen and cut a deal. Consider the case of Lyndon McLellan, a convenience store owner in Fairmont, North Carolina.[12] Mr. McLellan had his life savings of $107,000 all invested in the working capital of his business. The IRS seized the funds in December 2014, alleging deposit-structuring violations like those in the Hirsches' case. The Department of Justice joined in the suit. However, as in so many other related cases, McLellan was never formally charged. It's important to note that this seizure occurred after supposed reforms were implemented in the scandal-plagued IRS to prevent such practices.

McLellan did what every American has a right to do: he complained to his congressman. In February 2015, Representative George Holding, a member of the House Ways and Means Oversight Subcommittee, had IRS commissioner John Koskinen before him. Without naming the case, he outlined the facts, and Commissioner Koskinen agreed that the IRS had violated its own guidelines in going after McLellan.

This was too much for the authorities. The assistant US attorney in charge of the case notified McLellan's lawyer and accountant that he was "concerned" that the case had been brought to the attention of Congress. "Whoever made [the document] public may serve their own interest but will not help this particular case," he wrote. "Your client needs to resolve this or litigate it. But publicity about it doesn't help. It just ratchets up feelings in the agency. My offer is to return 50% of the money. The offer is good until March 30th COB." The American people are being shaken down by their government, and the attitude that "We can take your money; what are you going to do about it?" pervades our justice system.

When the US attorney's "final offer" was made public, McLellan received a more generous counteroffer, but not one that would cover all he had lost since the start of the case. While the US Attorney's Office agreed to return the money it had seized, it refused to pay McLellan's legal fees, which at this point amounted to $22,000, or to pay for the interest that would have accrued if McLellan's capital had remained unperturbed. This is how the Ruling Class operate in the "Land of the Free." It seems that your money is theirs for the taking even if you are innocent. And all this from a case about which even the IRS commissioner agreed the IRS was in the wrong.

The practice of seizing money for rather ambiguously defined cash deposit and withdrawal patterns has exploded in recent years. In its 2015 report *Seize First, Question Later*,[13] the Institute for Justice describes this alarming trend. Between 2005 and 2012, IRS seizures have increased by more than 450 percent, netting $242 million in seized funds during this period. Moreover, this rise in seizures has led to a 166 percent increase in revenue obtained through forfeiture. Of these structuring confiscations, 80 percent were labeled civil, and not criminal, meaning that seizures could occur more easily and the citizens affected had less protection under the law. Worst of all, perhaps, there's a large difference between what's initially seized and what's actually forfeited: of the $242 million seized by the IRS, $116 million, nearly half, was returned.

Most of the increase in IRS structuring seizures occurred during President Obama's first term—as did most of the evidence of overreach. In Obama's first year as president, seizures for structuring violations totaled $16.4 million, with $12.4 million forfeited. By 2012, the amount seized had nearly tripled to $48.6 million, while the amount permanently forfeited increased to only $22 million. Further, the instances of forfeiture have not kept pace with the increases in seizures. In 2009, the ratio of cases where assets were forfeited to those where they were seized (which can be thought of as an approximate "guilty rate"—how frequently the IRS was actually keeping the funds to which it laid claim) was 83 percent. In 2012, this statistic plummeted to 57 percent. It seems the IRS is expanding its definition of what qualifies as a structuring violation, so much so that its asset seizures are incapable of withstanding the court's judgment.

This is alarming behavior by the government because it illustrates the attitude of the Ruling Class pattern of failure linked to demands for more power. Back in 1994, the Clinton administration argued unsuccessfully before the Supreme Court in *Ratzlaf v. US* that "structuring is not the kind of activity that an ordinary person would engage in innocently." Therefore it was "reasonable to hold a structurer responsible for evading the reporting requirements without the need to prove specific knowledge that such evasion is unlawful."[14] The administration found the Supreme Court rejection of this argument so restrictive that in 2000 it persuaded Congress to remove the need to prove that there was a "willful" attempt to evade the law. Most shamefully, authorities justify structuring seizures under the auspices of being more vigilant regarding terrorist money laundering activities post 9/11. Do the aforementioned stories sound like activities perpetrated by those involved with terrorism?

In arguing for more power in 2000, the point was made that proving "willful behavior" would needlessly hamper prosecution of drug dealers and money launderers. But, of course, money laundering and drug dealing are now more rampant than ever, and the Ruling Class have instead used the additional power they were given to go after ordinary citizens.

The power seizure is made worse by the fact that it creates a profit incentive for law enforcement. The combined resources in the US government's main forfeiture accounts—the DoJ's Assets Forfeiture Fund and the Treasury Forfeiture Fund—rose from $763 million to $3.2 billion between 2001 and 2012.[15] This is money these agencies can use as they please without federal oversight.

This raises an important issue about how the Ruling Class view the role of the police and the courts. In our civics books, the police protect the public from "the bad guys." But, of course, this presumes that they know who "the bad guys" are. If the police start punishing the innocent in the name of punishing the guilty, then the distinction disappears. And policies that are geared toward securing maximum numbers of arrests—regardless of who is arrested—blur the distinction. In the extreme case, the public might come to have reason to fear the police, something called "the police state." There can be no clearer example of a "police state" attitude than the case of Lyndon McLellan, who was threatened by a federal prosecutor for the temerity of reporting the abuses of the police to his local congressman.

Contrast this with the attitude of the Department of Justice and the Internal Revenue Service toward the behavior of their own officials. Lois Lerner, the presidentially appointed IRS official in charge of approving the application of nonprofit organizations, came under fire for delaying the approval of groups with whom she and the administration disagreed.[16] Her emails were destroyed. Copies of her emails were apparently retained by the IRS and destroyed after the date at which they had been requested by the Congress. The emails of friends in political organizations were destroyed around the same time. Ms. Lerner herself took the Fifth Amendment when she was asked questions about what happened.

Moreover, the Department of Justice found "substantial evidence of mismanagement, poor judgment, and institutional inertia leading to the belief by many tax-exempt applicants that the IRS targeted them based on their political viewpoints."[17] But despite this pattern of misbehavior, the Department of Justice, under Attorney General Loretta Lynch, found that "[P]oor management is not a crime," and so no charges were filed.

What does this say about the difference between the Ruling Class's attitude toward ordinary citizens and the standards to which they hold themselves accountable? Members of the Ruling Class might engage in widespread mismanagement and poor judgment that leads people to believe they are acting for political motives. They might also destroy evidence and refuse to testify on their behavior, and they are held harmless. But if an ordinary citizen happens to make cash deposits or withdrawals of his or her own legally obtained funds, those funds are confiscated, and the victim of the seizure must use his or her own money to fight the government to get the money back.

This is the state to which Americans have now been reduced by the Ruling Class's progressive seizure of power. This section has shown that despite their massive grab of power and resources, the Ruling Class have not delivered on their promises to make the lives of "ordinary" Americans any better. Inequality has increased. The debt load has skyrocketed. Schools are high cost and low quality, abysmally so. Infrastructure creation is overpriced and hindered by special interests that are political supporters of the Ruling Class. Demands are made that gun ownership be restricted even though past Ruling Class efforts to limit guns have failed, and crime has risen under their watch. Finally, the Ruling Class feel free to seize lawfully earned money without any need to build a burden of proof. They use police-state tactics to go after the few who fight these injustices, while at the same time protecting their own from the consequences of their actions.

This is what the Founding Fathers called "a long train of abuses and usurpations." Fortunately, we Americans still have recourse. But we must act to prevent further depredations of our liberty. The final section of this book describes what must be done.

PART 3

Securing Our Liberty Once Again

CHAPTER 13

The Pro-Liberty Majority

Part 1 of this book explored how the Ruling Class are fundamentally different from the rest of us. Deep down, they believe in their own natural superiority, so much so that they feel infinitely more qualified to run our lives than we are. To reach this end, they have steadily increased their clout as rulers, greatly expanded the scope of the federal government's authority, and shifted power away from the elected branches of government toward nonelected power centers in the judiciary and the bureaucracy. These power centers are the natural positions from which they rule.

Part 2 considered what they've done with all of this assumed power. Despite access to virtually unlimited resources and far more authority than our Founding Fathers ever intended in the Constitution, the answer is: not much. Inequality has increased, and economic performance has decreased as the Ruling Class have steadily amassed more power.

Government services are overpriced and underperforming. Yet Ruling Class politicians still attempt to solve these problems by giving themselves ever more power and more resources.

Most Americans are fed up with these trends, and if you've read this far, chances are that you agree that the Ruling Class need to be stopped and that power should be returned to the people, to whom our Founders gave it originally. This section explains how we, united, can bring about such a change.

There are three steps in this process. The first is political. Although powerful, the Ruling Class still require the consent of the governed, and We the People need to say "No more!" This chapter outlines how believers in liberty can build an unassailable majority at the ballot box to reverse these trends. The second step is institutional. A lot of the Ruling Class's power grab is reversible. It will require getting that unassailable majority in favor of liberty to do so, but once we have it, we can make changes that will break the Ruling Class's current grip on the levers of power. The final step is to remind ourselves and our countrymen just how great a force for good an America based on liberty has been. Just as most political discourse today is geared toward Ruling Class thinking, we need to reestablish a belief in our country. We need to reestablish that our Founding Fathers really had the right idea—that liberty is the natural order of things and a way of thinking that we cannot give up.

Winning Elections

Elections are all about numbers. For example, why did the Ruling Class get as many votes as they did, and how can we get those votes? Polling data and actual election returns provide the basis for answering those questions. As with most such questions, the answer is multitiered; solving it is like peeling back the layers of an onion. The first and most obvious question is: How do the Ruling Class ever win an election given their poor performance in office? If it were stated honestly, the platform would be, "Give us more money and power so we can continue to do a mediocre job of running the country." Not a very attractive offer, is it?

In fact, polling data suggest that the overwhelming majority of voters think the Ruling Class have failed. A common polling question meant to gauge Americans' opinion of how the country is doing is known as "Right Direction or Wrong Track." According to a Rasmussen Reports survey of likely US voters from December 2015, 68 percent believe that we are on the wrong track,[1] compared with only 25 percent who agree with the country's current direction. Moreover, the feeling that we are headed in the wrong direction is overwhelming across nearly every subset of the electorate: Men voted "wrong track" 66 percent to 28 percent. Women agreed, 69 percent to 21 percent, as did white voters, 73 percent to 21 percent. Although black voters' pessimism is less strong, they too responded "wrong track," 50 percent to 32 percent, as did Hispanics and other ethnic and racial groups, 57 percent to 36 percent. Unsurprisingly, Republicans strongly responded "wrong track," 83 percent to 14 percent, as did Independents, 73 percent to 19 percent. Even Democrats weighed toward "wrong track," 49 percent to 40 percent. Voters over forty said "wrong track," 71 percent to 24 percent, while those under forty responded "wrong track," 61 percent to 30 percent. Of course, those who voted for whoever is in office tend to be more optimistic about America's future, so there are small differences among these groups. Taken as a whole, however, these data represent a resounding and widespread rejection of the direction in which the Ruling Class are taking the country.

Then there is the central part of the Ruling Class agenda: that they, the people in charge, should have more power and resources than they do already. There are a lot of ways to ask this. The simplest is, "Would you like more control over your own life, or would you like to give the government more control?" Obviously, more control for the individual would win hands down. But it is not a real choice. Life is about trade-offs. A more realistic question is, "Would you like more control of your life on the condition that you accepted responsibility for the consequences of your decisions?" Pollsters can't ask questions like that, as voters might find them offensive. So most polls get at the "trade-off" idea with a set of less personal questions, and ones more geared to real policy choices.

Let's start with basic questions about the size and roll of government. A March 2015 Rasmussen poll asked, "Generally speaking, do increases in government spending help the economy, hurt the economy, or have no impact on the economy?" The one thousand likely voters surveyed responded 52 percent to 28 percent that increased government spending hurts the economy.[2] From the same survey, in fact, the public feels that actually cutting government spending would be beneficial economically by a margin of 44 percent to 30 percent. And by a split of 52 percent to 23 percent, voters think that cutting taxes would help the economy. More taxes and more spending are both considered bad ideas—not a good sign for the Ruling Class. But there is an even more sophisticated version of this question that gets to the heart of the "trade-off" issue.

In December 2012, just after President Obama was reelected, Rasmussen asked voters whether they would prefer "a more active government with more services and higher taxes or a smaller government with fewer services and lower taxes." The response was 56 percent to 34 percent in favor of fewer services and lower taxes.[3] This question not only got the public policy trade-off correct but also went to the core of the different views that political parties tend to have on this issue. Republicans were for fewer services by 88 percent to 8 percent, and Independents agreed, 56 percent to 31 percent. Democrats, on the other hand, favored more services and higher taxes by a margin of 59 percent to 31 percent.

Voters were also asked a question about government "power": "If the government got more involved in regulating the economy, would society become more fair, less fair, or remain about the same?" The results, when this question was asked in April 2012, echoed the public's views about taxes and spending and also reflected the same partisan differences. Overall, 50 percent of voters said that more regulation would produce a less fair society; 22 percent believed that it would make society fairer;[4] and 21 percent said it would make no difference. So the idea is fairly widespread that the Ruling Class regulate society in their interests and not in a way that increases societal fairness. The partisan differences were telling. Republicans said "less fair" by a margin of 74 percent to 13 percent, while Democrats said "more fair" by a margin of 40 percent to 17 percent. Independents tended to side with the Republicans, saying "less fair" by a margin of 56 percent to 14 percent.

These data show clearly that there is a strong majority in the country for liberty, and strong opposition to giving more power and resources to the Ruling Class. They also show that the voters for each of the two parties had decidedly different ideas on this issue; in fact, it was the biggest divide of any issue. Republicans wanted lower taxes, less government spending, and less regulation by overwhelming margins. Democrats wanted the reverse. So in the minds of the voters who voted for each party, the distinctions couldn't have been clearer.

Now comes the first puzzle. Overall, voters wanted less government and fewer taxes by a 22-point margin and thought that government regulation made society less fair by a 28-point margin. People who identified as Republicans were overwhelmingly on the winning side of both issues; Democrats were on the losing side of both. The polls were taken in 2012, yet the Democrats won the presidential election by 4 points that year.

There can be only one conclusion. The 2012 election was not fought on the issue of more government versus less government. It was not fought as a Ruling Class versus liberty election. If it had been, the party that favored more government would not have won. It is therefore worth looking at the results to see why the election turned out the way it did. This requires further digging into the numbers, because, ultimately, that's what elections are all about. This is why we have to take the next step in peeling back the onion.

Why People Vote

There are two keys to winning elections: (1) turnout—how many come out to vote; and (2) persuasion—convincing people to vote for your party rather than for the other one. While it might seem on the surface that campaigns are all about persuasion, and it would be comforting to think so, the data show that turnout is key. All that negative advertising is designed to make voters angry at "the other guy," and, unfortunately, that anger is one of the most powerful motivators there can be. In addition, both parties go to some length to identify their voters and make sure those voters are registered and actually turn out. It is not that persuasion is not important, but most "swing" voters, who may switch from year to year, are persuaded already by events. They have a strong view about whether things are going reasonably well or not, and vote either to give the incumbents four more years or to "throw the bums out."

When viewed in this light, we can begin to understand the puzzle of 2012. In surveys, voters did not think things were going well, that less government and less regulation were the way to go, and so normally would have been inclined against four more years. But turnout was key. The incumbent party turned out its voters, the challengers did not.

To see this statistically, it is necessary to separate "turnout" factors from "persuasion" factors. Social scientists (including economists and political scientists) do this by creating a "control" or "counterfactual" of what would have happened if one key variable were kept unchanged. In this case, the key is to keep "turnout" unchanged and see what happens. So we have created a "control" model to project this and compare it with actual voter turnout. The table below presents data from the 2004, 2008, and 2012 elections to see how this works.

The party identification of voters is listed on the left: Republican, Democrat, and Independent. Each row shows how many members of each party voted for the various candidates in 2004, 2008, and 2012. The votes are calculated from exit polls on how each group voted.

Table 2. Turnout Matters: Votes Cast in Millions by Party Identification

	2004		2008		2012	
	Bush (R)	Kerry (D)	McCain (R)	Obama (D)	Romney (R)	Obama (D)
Republican	40.7	4.4	37.8	4.2	37.2	4.1
			(42.7)	(4.6)	(44.7)	(4.8)
Democrat	4.4	40.6	5.1	46.1	4.9	44.1
			(4.6)	(42.6)	(4.8)	(44.6)
Independent	16.9	14.0	17.0	19.2	18.8	17.7
			(15.3)	(17.2)	(17.6)	(16.5)
Total	62.0	59.0	59.9	69.5	60.9	65.9
			(62.6)	(64.4)	(67.1)	(65.9)

Source: *National Election Pool*, surveys conducted by Edison Research; Dave Leip's Atlas of U.S. Presidential Elections; and author's calculations.

Our projected numbers are in parentheses below the actual vote totals, and our extrapolation begins from the 2004 turnout by party. These projections show what the number of votes cast would have been if we simply extrapolated turnout from 2004 to later years based on the normal growth of the electorate. Over the last ten cycles, the number of voters has increased by an average of 5.3 percent per cycle,[5] or around 6 million more voters each election. Of those 6 million additional voters, roughly 2.2 million are Republicans, 2.2 million are Democrats, and 1.6 million are Independents. So to build our projections, we added these numbers to each category and put them in parentheses below the actual result. Historically, around 90 percent of voters who identify with a party vote for that party's candidate, and so we apportioned them accordingly. For example, in our projections, the extra 2.2 million Republicans and Democrats were assigned to their parties, with 2 million going for the candidate of each party, and 200,000 going for the other party. (So in 2008, Republican voters voting for the Republican candidate, John McCain, rose from the 40.7 million who voted for Bush in 2004 to 42.7 million.) Independents swing back and forth, so we apportioned those according to how Independents actually voted in that year's election. For example, in 2008, Independents split for Obama by a margin of 53 percent to 47 percent, so we assigned the "new" Independent voters the same way.[*]

The 2004 election is a good place to start our analysis because it represented a shift toward both parties emphasizing turnout after the closeness of the 2000 election. The results on election night 2004 were startling. Both the media and the Kerry campaign thought that Kerry would win because of Democrats' much improved turnout operation. To their surprise, the Bush campaign had actually improved the Republican turnout operation even more. Typically, the additional 6 million voters gained in an election year would split about evenly for the two candidates—say, 3 million for each. In a marked increase from this trend, 11.5 million more people voted for Bush in 2004 than in 2000, and 8 million more people voted for Kerry in 2004 than voted for Gore in 2000.

Remember our projections represents a hypothetical trend: how each party's voters could have been expected to vote had they simply shown up to the ballot box and voted according to the pattern that had been observed in previous exit polls. When the facts deviate from the trend, we need to look for an explanation. Start with the 2008 election. Democrats were excited, and Republicans were demoralized. This a natural phenomenon after eight years, as the incumbent party tends to be tired, and the opposition is hungry to come back into office. In addition, that year there was a desire for change, concern about the deteriorating economy and housing situation, and fatigue with the wars in Iraq and Afghanistan. One can see this in all categories. Republican turnout was about 5 million votes below trend; Democratic turnout was about 4 million votes above trend. In addition, there was a lot of "persuading" going on. In 2004, 55 percent of the Independent vote went to the Republican candidate. In 2008, this share fell to 47 percent. That was a dramatic

---

[*] Of the total 32.5 million new Independent voters in 2008 (2004's 30.9 + 1.6), 53 percent voted for Obama, so our projections became 17.2 million Independent votes for Obama (53 percent of 32.5).

swing among Independents, but even so, it accounted for only half of the increase in the Democratic vote. The other half came from increased turnout.

This shows how important turnout actually is. Of Obama's 9.6-million vote margin over McCain, 7.4 million came from a margin among partisans—fewer Republicans and more Democrats—while only 2.2 million came from Independents. And this was driven by the fact that 4 million more Democrats and 5.3 million fewer Republicans turned out than our projections indicate.

Now consider what happened in 2012. There was a lot of persuading of Independents. They swung back to giving 52 percent of their vote to the Republican candidate, Mitt Romney. And Independents were still excited about voting; their total vote was well above trend. The problem for the Republicans came in getting their own people to turn out. While Democrats turned out in numbers almost exactly on trend, the total Republican vote fell more than 8 million below trend. Had Republican turnout not dropped, Mitt Romney would have won the election.

This raises yet another puzzle and requires peeling back yet another layer of the onion. There is no doubt that Republicans did not like Obama very much. The problem seems to be that they did not find Romney to be the right kind of alternative. He could not persuade voters who believed in liberty that he was actually going to deliver what they wanted. Let's take a close look at more data, this time from the 2012 exit polls, to see why voters for liberty might have been let down.

Picking the Right Candidate

Consider the qualities that voters seek in choosing a leader. They tend to break down into two sets: qualities that will make a good president for the country, and qualities that will make a president look out for their own personal interests. Both are quite natural things to be concerned about. Four values are cited most often in exit polls: strength, vision, values, and "cares about people like me." These also tend to represent a sliding scale from what the country needs compared with self-interest, with "strength" being most country oriented, and, obviously, "caring about people like me" being most self-oriented.

Let's look at how those broke down. Strength is all about the fact that the president is the country's projection on the world stage. For the 18 percent of voters who thought having a strong leader was the most important trait, Romney beat Obama 61 percent to 38 percent. Foreign policy was a relatively minor issue in 2012; hence presidential strength was a primary concern for less than a fifth of the voters.

The second trait is vision, and here the most important point is that people can have different views about what kind of future they want, but a vision is a fairly general thing that applies to more than oneself. Among the 29 percent of voters who thought vision for the future was the most important trait, Romney beat Obama, 54 percent to 45 percent.

Values differ among individuals, of course. In seeking a candidate that shares one's values, a voter is looking for a hybrid of the personal and the general. Values define how a president is likely to respond to a national issue, and voters are looking for someone who will approach the issue with the same predispositions as they would. Among the 27 percent of voters whose most important candidate criterion was that they shared the voter's values, Romney beat Obama 55 percent to 42 percent. So to sum up, in terms of the leadership qualities—strength, vision, values— Romney clearly beat Obama hands down.

The final candidate quality in the poll was "cares about people like me." This is the most personal one can get. The pollsters are very careful about the phrasing. They understand that a president can't know a specific person, and they don't want it to sound too selfish, so "people like me" is substituted for "me." But since goodies, or government favors, are dispensed to groups of people, caring about "people like me" means a very personal benefit to the individual voter. It is not about something broad such as values, vision, or strength, it is about having a president who understands their needs on an individual level, including one they feel can help them when they need it. Among the 21 percent of voters who stressed this trait, Obama beat Romney 81 percent to 18 percent. That and that alone was what gave Obama the win.

This suggests that Romney might have had the right message and image in terms of what the country might have needed, but that he was just not the kind of person voters thought cared about them. He might have been from central casting on leadership issues, but Romney did not exactly resonate as having an understanding of the common man. In a period where the "rich" were demonized as having caused the financial crisis, a man who was a centimillionaire investment banker was not exactly the kind of fellow that people thought would identify with their problems. Voters wanted liberty, but it was hard to see Romney as significantly different from the Ruling Class. He looked like one of them, his record did not suggest he was significantly different from them, and his résumé was filled with Ruling Class accomplishments. Liberty-oriented voters were not going to vote for Obama, but they were not about to turn out for Romney, either.

The same type of story came through when one looks at the issues people considered most important, not just candidate qualities. Three issues scored in double digits as the "most important": the economy, the deficit, and health care. The most important was the economy, with 59 percent identifying it as the most important issue. But there was no consensus on how to deal with the economy. Voters identifying the economy as most important preferred Romney over Obama, 51 percent to 47 percent. Of the 15 percent of voters who identified the deficit as the most important issue, 66 percent voted for Romney, and 32 percent for Obama.[6]

The story was different for health care. Of the 19 percent of voters who thought this was the most important issue, Obama won, 75 percent to 24 percent. At first this might sound odd. Obamacare was not a popular bill overall. In most surveys, it was unpopular by margins of between 10 and 20 points.[7] In the exit poll, in which voters tend to be more likely to link issues with the candidate they voted for, it was still underwater by 5 points in terms of popularity. But people who thought it was the most important issue favored Obama by a three-to-one margin. Romney appeared to fudge on this issue. As governor of Massachusetts from 2003 to 2007, he had brought in something like Obamacare on the state level, but then was critical of the national program. The result was confusion and a distrust of Romney on this issue.

Here is the classic issue of Ruling Class advantage: they offer a tangible benefit to those who support them with their vote. Those who were losers under Obamacare (and that was the majority of the population) vote on other grounds: a deteriorating economy or fiscal situation or poor leadership. When it comes to attracting voters on something that they feel the government has given them, it is very hard to beat something tangible with "Let's repeal."

But that does not mean that the right answer is to get into a bidding war with the Ruling Class. They will always win. The key is that voters must feel that the candidate who is for liberty is for it because he cares about voters like them. Voters don't have to be bribed with goodies. However, they do have to believe that the president is looking out for them. Voters who feel that they are being abused by an overly powerful bureaucracy can feel the same about a president who shrinks government and reins in the bureaucracy.

The good news is that there is a clear pro-liberty majority in the country. The key is to get that majority to turn out for a pro-liberty candidate. A candidate who can frame the election as a choice between liberty and the Ruling Class will win. But the candidate must be believed. The lesson from recent elections is that a candidate must appear to voters to be a genuine champion of liberty and someone who truly understands that less government control is something that people value. Candidates who simply propose alternative schemes that are more efficient and better run are not going to be credible. They are going to simply look like a slightly different version of the Ruling Class.

The 2016 presidential selection process has seen voters take that to heart. Candidates who are viewed as having close ties to the Ruling Class are not faring well. Prior government service is a definite drawback in the Republican primary. Jeb Bush, the former governor of Florida, has been hurt in particular. At this writing, the primary process is likely to be based on who is viewed as the most genuine candidate to carry the banner of liberty in the 2016 election. It is very much a personality-driven choice, since candidate qualities are key. But issues will also be important. The next chapter turns to how a pro-liberty candidate might frame key issues in order to hold the already existing pro-liberty majority together and get its members to turn out in the November election.

CHAPTER 14

Policy: Philosophically Populist, Operationally Libertarian

As the previous chapter noted, while there is a clear majority in favor of increasing liberty in America, the problem is that the 2012 election was not fought on that basis. This was true even though one party's supporters (the Republicans) identified strongly with smaller government, while the other party's supporters favored bigger government. Despite this, millions of supporters of increased liberty stayed home on Election Day. The reason appeared to be that the Republican candidate did not seem like he understood or cared about the needs of the ordinary voter. If the Republican Party (or any other party based on the principle of liberty) is going to win, it must convince voters that its programs will give them more control over their lives and not leave them at the mercy of Washington. It is not enough to say that they will still be at Washington's mercy but with a different group of people in charge.

In short, a winning party must ask itself constantly, "How can we make sure voters know that their lives will be improved by what we are proposing?" The philosophy of a winning campaign is focused on improving people's lives. The way that will be achieved is by giving them more independence and control. These can be thought of as the difference between an end and the means to that end. The end must be to improve people's lives; the means to do so is by increasing their liberty. Historical experience going back to the Declaration of Independence and Adam Smith's *Wealth of Nations* shows that increasing liberty will improve the economy, as people will be more motivated to improve their lives, so we can be sure from historical experience that we are on the right track.

Liberty will deliver the results that the progressive Ruling Class have not. Their end is to increase the power of government, and in doing so, they increase their own power as well. Their means are to promise people that their lives will improve through the Ruling Class's "giving" them something. Historically, this has failed time and again because it cannot be sustained. But it still makes for a great short-term marketing message for a campaign. We must take on that campaign directly. Below we present a set of issues on which the progressives have failed and how liberty can succeed.

Inequality and Taxes

We showed in chapter 7 that inequality has increased continuously, but it increased faster under Clinton than it did under Reagan, and it increased faster under Obama than it did under Bush. This was despite the fact that Clinton and Obama raised taxes on the rich and promised to spend lavishly on programs to help the poor. Voters know instinctively that the progressives' plans don't work. From the March 2015 survey discussed last chapter, voters thought that tax increases hurt the economy rather than help it by a margin of 50 percent to 23 percent, and that tax cuts help the economy rather than hurt it by a similar margin. The same survey found that voters felt that increased government spending hurt the economy rather than help it by a margin of 52 percent to 28 percent. Not only do tax-and-spend policies not work, voters know they don't work.

Why is it painfully obvious to the electorate, but not to the Ruling Class, that tax-and-spend policies fail? Taxes hurt not just because they take money out of people's pockets but also because they discourage people from doing things that stimulate the economy, such as working, investing, and starting new businesses. To make matters worse, the government tries to use the tax code to manipulate people into doing what it wants, thus accomplishing the social engineering that the Ruling Class covet. That is the reason for all the tax deductions, exemptions, and loopholes. But by steering people into things the government wants and not necessarily into what is best for economic growth, the Ruling Class tend to make the economy grow more slowly—all while adding enormous complexity to the tax code.

Complexity has its costs. The Tax Foundation, a nonpartisan Washington think tank that compiles statistics on taxation, estimated that in 2011 it cost taxpayers $392 billion to comply with the income taxes in the tax code.[1] That's 21 cents of every dollar collected. That doesn't include the economic distortions caused by the income taxes, just the cost of complying. Stated plainly, the cost to the taxpayer of sending $1 to Uncle Sam was not just that dollar, but $1.21. To put that $392 billion in compliance costs into perspective, Americans spent $337 billion on new homes that year. We spent $328 billion on new cars and replacement parts for old ones. We spent $375 billion on new computers, peripherals, and software. Imagine: the cost of just complying with income tax regulations was more than what we spent on new homes, on new cars, and on new computers!

Progressives have learned to talk the language of tax cuts, but listen carefully to their plans. They will give you a tax cut, but only if you jump through a bunch of hoops that they design. You must spend your money in a particular way—the way they say—to be able to keep more of what you earn. This fits precisely within their agenda of power: controlling our lives is necessary for them to engineer society into their vision of the future. But doing so makes the tax code more burdensome on the economy and raises compliance costs. People hear the plan and think "Oh! That sounds like a nice idea," and that is the point. Only later is the extra burden on the taxpayer realized.

To be philosophically populist and operationally libertarian, we need to propose tax code simplification as the core of the tax change, not propose new loopholes, gimmicks, or rules. The idea of a flat tax gets to the heart of this. But care must be taken in designing the flat tax to be not just simple but also fair in terms of the share of taxes paid by different groups. It must also raise sufficient revenue to fund the government. There are a variety of proposals around: the FairTax, the Hall-Rabushka plan, and a plan I call the KISS tax[2]: Keep It Simple Stupid. The latter plan would involve really radical simplification: abolishing the current personal income tax, corporate income tax, and payroll tax, and replacing them with a single two-tier tax paid only by businesses. Under the KISS tax, April 15 would become just another day for American households. Some candidates have their own versions of these ideas, and some are more sweeping than others. Whichever plan is chosen, the simpler the tax, the more it fits with this electoral model.

One of the key points to make about tax simplification is that it is philosophically populist by definition. Who is the beneficiary of complexity? It isn't the ordinary taxpayer. It is the taxpayer who can afford the lawyers and accountants to figure out how to exploit the complexity — and, of course, the lawyers and accountants who run up billable hours figuring it all out. These are not ordinary voters; they are part of the elite. And by empowering them and moving resources in their direction, the progressive idea of tax complexity is helping to make society more unequal. It is not just income inequality but also a more fundamental form of inequality that our Founding Fathers would have recognized and understood. If society is governed by complex laws and regulations, we might have formal equality before the law, but in practice, the rich, the powerful, and those who can afford lawyers, accountants, and lobbyists are the big winners. Equality and simplicity therefore go hand in hand as a populist idea.

Simplicity is operationally libertarian because it leaves decision making in the hands of individuals, without government pressing on the scales. There aren't differential tax treatments such as deductions and credits that lead taxpayers to decisions they would not make in the absence of these hidden subsidies. Common sense—exercised with a sharp pencil—would decide where an investment should be made or whether buying a house and how much to spend would actually make sense. Simplicity is operationally libertarian for another reason that has everything to do with math. The broader the base of a tax, the lower the rates have to be to collect revenue. And the lower the rate, the less the tax has an influence on the decision making of the taxpayer, be it a business or a family.

Taking Care of Obamacare

A second issue that a winning campaign must talk about is health care and how we can give people more control over their lives in that sphere. Obamacare has been a disaster. It was designed as a political document and not to be an operational success. It increases demand for health care services by subsidizing them for those who do not currently have access. It decreases the supply of these services by driving doctors and other professionals from the business. And it was supposed to cut costs, but they are going up, not down. That is what one would expect from any program that cut supply and increased demand. Despite its programmatic failure, a frontal assault by simply repealing the law is not a political winner. Here is where being philosophically populist is key. Many voters see repeal as taking away something that they find valuable. So instead of taking something away, the right strategy is to give people something else: increased liberty.

As noted in the last chapter, voters who identified health care as their main issue voted overwhelmingly for Obama despite the overall un-popularity of Obamacare. The reason was personal. Of those who cared about it the most, a large majority thought they benefited from it. In fact, in terms of nationalized health care, most Obama voters wanted even more. For example, the 26 percent of voters who thought Obamacare should be expanded supported Obama 92 percent to 5 percent.[3] Stated differently, roughly half of all the people in the country who voted for Obama's reelection wanted Obamacare expanded. They wanted more government, not less. They believed Obama when he said he wanted to help them. Or perhaps more precisely, voters preferred the candidate that gave them something over the candidate who wanted to take away something. Phrased that way, it goes back to the old political nostrum that "You can't beat something with nothing"—and you certainly can't beat something with the threat of taking something else away.

This, however, does not mean we should play the Ruling Class's game. They will always be able to offer more, and, indeed, because it will give them more control, they will always be happy to offer more. It enhances their power and their grip on the electorate. Instead, the issue must become what giving the Ruling Class more power means for *your* health care. The alternative offer to Obamacare must be freedom to choose. The Ruling Class offer a warm, cuddly blanket that in reality smothers those who take it; it is one-size-fits-all because that is how government and the Ruling Class work. Increasing personal liberty instead offers variety and choice. Voters can understand this if it is presented as a positive offer, not phrased negatively as "Abolish Obamacare!"

There are three parts of Obamacare that are a direct assault on personal liberty. Repealing these three specific provisions would "solve" the Obamacare problem without directly threatening anyone who currently receives benefits from the program. This is where the emphasis should be.

First, repeal the individual mandate. This requires people to buy coverage or face a fine, or what the Supreme Court managed to call a tax. The individual mandate is a direct assault on liberty because it requires individuals to buy something that is solely for their own benefit. It is not like a state mandate to buy liability insurance, since the beneficiary of the insurance isn't the individual but the owner of the car the driver may hit. The only beneficiary of the payments from an Obamacare plan is the specific individual who is insured.

Second, repeal the employer mandate. This part is so unworkable that even President Obama has extended its effective date twice. Why should a worker be forced to take his or her compensation in terms of health insurance (which might not be needed if the worker is covered by another family member) instead of salary? Workers and their employers should be free to decide the terms of their contracts.

Third, end federal mandates and restrictions on what policies must cover and who may offer coverage. One of the reasons that premiums, deductibles, and copayments are so high in Obamacare plans is that they mandate that the policies carry a variety of provisions that the great majority of the individuals covered neither want nor need. These range from expensive policies with mental health and drug addiction coverage, to policies that cover the cost of contraception. It makes little sense to force expensive coverage on small employers, when the extra thousand dollars or so per employee for a specific provision might mean the difference between operating and hiring workers and shuttering their doors. Contraception was added as a talking point. In fact, the purpose of insurance is to cover high-cost, surprise, and uncontrollable events. You do not pay an auto-insurance company to cover the cost of putting gas in your car or to change your oil. It is inefficient and a waste of bureaucratic overhead. The same is true of medical coverage. The rationale had nothing to do with "insurance" or "health." In fact, most common forms of contraception were not even covered. It exists as a political talking point. More fundamentally, shouldn't the person buying the insurance decide what he wants and needs, and what he does not want?

Not only is this approach philosophically populist (meaning that people will like it) and operationally libertarian (meaning that it will eliminate wasteful regulations), but also it happens to be what the voters want. And this is a chapter on making sure that there is a pro-liberty majority at the ballot box. A December 2015 Rasmussen survey asked voters whether they wanted to keep the law, repeal it in its entirety, or work on its provisions on a piecemeal basis. Only 11 percent wanted to keep the law, while 37 percent wanted full repeal. But 49 percent wanted to go through the law piece by piece and improve it.[4]

Allowing people more choice is both good politics and good government. President Obama knows this as well. So early on in the fight, he argued that his plan would not affect individual choice. For example, in his weekly radio address in June 2009, the president said, "If you like the plan you have, you can keep it. If you like the doctor you have, you can keep your doctor too. The only change you'll see are falling costs as our reforms take hold." Later that year at a town hall meeting in Wisconsin, he said, "No matter how we reform health care, I intend to keep this promise: If you like your doctor, you'll be able to keep your doctor; if you like your health care plan, you'll be able to keep your health care plan." And four days later, on June 15, the president told the American Medical Association, "I know that there are millions of Americans who are content with their health care coverage—they like their plan and, most importantly, they value their relationship with their doctor. They trust you. And that means that no matter how we reform health care, we will keep this promise to the American people: if you like your doctor, you will be able to keep your doctor, period. If you like your health care plan, you'll be able to keep your health care plan, period. No one will take it away, no matter what."[5]

Now, none of this is true, and the president almost certainly knew it at the time. Limiting choice was the only way to make his plan work. But for the Ruling Class, the ends justify the means. In 2013, as it became obvious that the president had not been truthful, the spin changed. He told his campaign organization, Organizing for Action, "Now, if you have or had one of these plans before the Affordable Care Act came into law, and you really liked that plan, what we said was you can keep it if it hasn't changed since the law passed."[6] There are a couple of problems with this. First, that isn't what he said. Like in Orwell's *Nineteen Eighty-Four*, the goal was to make what he had actually said to get the law through disappear down the memory hole. But, again, to the Ruling Class, the ends justify the means. Second, the Obamacare regulations forced changes in health care policies. The only way you could "keep your health care plan" was if the provider made absolutely no changes to it. But minor changes are a natural part of the insurance process, so the president was being dishonest in that he knew that all policies change. And new rules being imposed by his own administration virtually guaranteed that would happen. So to say that you can keep your policy if it doesn't change at all and then force changes on the system meant that he intentionally knew that people would not be able to keep their plans.

The sensitivity over this issue of being able to keep what you have in terms of health care shows the vulnerability of the Ruling Class when they provide something. Defenders of liberty need to stress what it is going to cost people on an individual basis—what it means to them personally, as well as what it will mean for the country. There is an old saying that has been attributed wrongly to Thomas Jefferson (although he certainly would have agreed with it!): "A government big enough to give you everything you want is a government big enough to take away everything that you have." * The lesson is that if the election is going to be fought on the basis of increasing liberty, we must remind people that the Ruling Class can take what they have in the process of supposedly giving people what they want.

---

*Gerald Ford used this saying during his inaugural address to Congress on August 12, 1974, though it was informally ascribed to him as early as 1954. Reference: Bernard L. Brock, "President Gerald R. Ford's Inaugural Address, 1974," chapter 19 in Halford R. Ryan, ed., *The Inaugural Addresses of Twentieth-Century Presidents* (Westport, CT: Praeger, 1993), 241. See also: Gerhard Peters and John T. Woolley, The American Presidency Project, http://www.presidency.ucsb.edu/ws/?pid=4694.

Don't Take Away Anyone's Liberty

The 2012 exit polls discussed last chapter showed that there is a clear pro-liberty majority in the country. Being perceived as standing for increased liberty is a valuable political asset that should not be discarded lightly. This is particularly true for the party that makes increasing personal liberty its unifying feature. However, the Ruling Class try to manipulate the electorate by moving the focus of the election away from a choice between liberty and big government. They confuse and obfuscate by using a common ruse: attack their opponents with criticisms that are really a reflection of their own guilt. They claim it is they that are for increased happiness and "leveling the playing field for everyone," though they fail to state that their means of accomplishing this is by expanding the government. The only way the Ruling Class can win an election is to persuade the voters that liberty is not the question before them. That case becomes a strong one when those supporting liberty use phrases that imply they are taking liberty away.

The most glaring issue on which the Ruling Class have handled this most successfully is abortion. The formulation of their position is very well thought out and focus-group tested. They say abortion should be safe, legal, and rare. Obviously, no one is against abortion being "safe" when it does occur, so this is a clear winning lead. The implication is that the other side is for "unsafe" abortions that occur in back alleys by shady operators. Again, that is untrue, but it works. The real emphasis of their platform is on the word *legal*: they are against restrictions on access to abortions. *Rare* is thrown in as a nonthreatening afterthought: "Sure, they should be rare, why not?" However, there has been nothing "rare" about the policy result, unless one considers 1.1 million abortions a year a "rarity." There are roughly 3.9 million live births, so roughly 22 percent of pregnancies are aborted.

Those are the facts. What are the politics? In the 2012 exit polls, 29 percent of voters said that abortion should *always* be legal. They voted for Obama 76 percent to 22 percent. Another 30 percent said that abortion should be legal in most circumstances. They voted for Obama 58 percent to 40 percent. And 23 percent of voters said abortion should be illegal in most circumstances; they voted for Romney 76 percent to 22 percent. Just 13 percent of voters said abortion should *always* be illegal, and they voted for Romney 79 percent to 13 percent.

As is usually the case, the majority of voters are somewhere in the middle. It would be impossible to win an election with a platform that said that abortion should "always be legal" or "never be legal." Voters think abortion should be legal but regulated—there should be limits on the practice. In other words, the key word really is *rare*. The winning political position is one that says abortion should be safe, legal—but not all the time—and rarer than it is.

It is easy to understand the views of those who think it should never be legal. They believe that life begins at conception, that abortion takes a human life, and that should never occur. Does that mean that they would oppose making abortion rarer? Some might, on the grounds that abortions would still be occurring, and that must never happen. The problem for people with that view is that it is not a winning position; it scores just 13 percent. So the real choice is whether to have the current law, with 1.1 million abortions, or a different law that would garner a political majority and would result in fewer abortions.

One such idea would limit abortions to the first half of a pregnancy (20 weeks) and allow it thereafter only in a medical emergency. When voters are asked what kind of restrictions should be put on abortions, the answer almost always involves later-term abortions. They are grizzly events. There is also the sense that the unborn child is more of a "person" later in life, deserving of the protections accorded such persons.

The abortion issue is a good one for the Ruling Class because it involves competing rights, or alternatively, competing liberties. There are the rights of the unborn and the rights of the mother. The extreme pro-abortion position gives the unborn no rights. The extreme antiabortion position gives the mother no rights. The challenge is to find a position that recognizes the rights of both. People who believe in liberty certainly also believe that taking the life of someone who might be born soon and who could survive on his or her own is not a pro-liberty position. But liberty is also not consistent with a government so big that it can regulate the most intimate details of a fertility cycle. Communist China tried that to enforce its one-child policy. Having the state know the moment a woman becomes pregnant and set mandates on her pregnancy is simply not a view consistent with the notion of liberty.

But liberty is also consistent with the notion of traditional values. Indeed, freedom of conscience was the basis of the notion of liberty in the English-speaking world. There is an established way of doing things consistent with both religious and secular traditional values that is not necessarily consistent with the current teachings of the state. Indeed, without an individual's established values, there would be no basis for ever doing something other than what the government of the moment and its Ruling Class demanded.

That is the reason why supporters of traditional values have tended to join forces with defenders of liberty at the ballot box. As the Ruling Class become increasingly antagonistic toward traditional values, this political alliance should intensify. In such an alliance, a common political plat-form on a variety of issues such as abortion would have to be forged. The key in all political alliances is to find common ground that is acceptable to all sides even if it is far from ideal to any particular side. Making abor-tion rare is a good thing: it is good governance and supportive of the rights our Founders established, and it is also popular. Banning abortion outright would be unpopular, involve an enormous government, and probably could not be achieved anyway. Similarly, defending those insti-tutions that object on moral or religious grounds to supporting abortion is both a popular and pro-liberty choice. In the current environment, that is where our emphasis should be.

Populism and Liberty Can Be Tied to All Issues

In addition to these three issues—taxes, Obamacare, and abortion—all of which are difficult to address politically, the goal of being philosophically populist and operationally libertarian can work for virtually all issues. After all, if we can find a majority position on the tough issues, the rest will be easy. And it is not just a campaign slogan but also a governing philosophy.

How do we build infrastructure? It is certainly not by making the government contracting process more complicated. Nor should it be to give more regulatory commissions and bureaus veto power over every detail of the construction. It is philosophically populist to speed up the construction process, to open the bidding to more small business contractors, and to reduce the congestion on our highways. It is operationally libertarian to do so as well. Additionally, it is the essence of good government.

Or when it comes to public education, should we give parents more control or less? And by more control, we do not mean sending more homework home so that more learning must take place outside of the school environment, since it cannot occur in school. Shouldn't parents be treated like customers when it comes to making decisions regarding their children's education? Certainly more choice, however that is accomplished, is both philosophically populist—as it gives more power to people—and operationally libertarian, in that it cuts down the power of public school monopolies and the role of government in schools.

Should government be allowed to confiscate the bank accounts of individuals who have committed no crime other than not filling out some paperwork? Should people have to sue to get back what has been confiscated, even though no charges have been filed? Again, it is certainly populist to protect people from this type of civil asset forfeiture and seizure of assets. It is operationally libertarian to stop such extortionate exercise of government police powers. It is also good government to respect the use of money that is, after all, issued by the government.

And when it comes to respecting the Second Amendment right to bear arms, it is both populist and libertarian to guarantee these rights. Beyond that, respecting the Constitution of the United States is an exercise in good government.

In sum, a candidate promising increased liberty and building his or her campaign around the subject can win an election. As our Founders knew, desiring liberty for oneself also means respecting the liberty of others. It cannot mean taking away something from others, and instead means providing opportunity for all. Coupled with a candidate who projects a genuine belief in liberty and an understanding of why liberty is important to ordinary voters, it is a campaign that can set us on the path to breaking the grip of the Ruling Class forever.

CHAPTER 15

Cementing the Restoration of Liberty and Democracy

Securing a political majority for a return to liberty is our first step. But we need to remember that the Ruling Class have systematically changed our system of government in order to increase their power and limit our ability to challenge them through the ballot box. Restoring liberty will also mean restoring at least some of the constitutional practices that our Founders drafted to protect us. Many of those will require changing the attitude of the courts or possibly passing constitutional amendments to reestablish liberties taken away through judicial fiat. These are very long-term battles. But there are three very practical reforms that can be accomplished right away that will do much to cement our freedoms back as they were intended.

This chapter considers those first important steps that must be taken once a political majority for liberty has been reestablished in Congress. It proposes three specific changes.

First, Congress needs to reassert control over rule making, a function that the Constitution gave the Congress, but which it has since relinquished to unelected officials in the executive branch.

Second, we need to limit the terms of the right people—specifically, people who have no accountability at all to the elected. We need to focus on term limits for the many permanent unelected officials who have amassed enormous power without accountability to the people before limiting the time in office of elected officials who can be voted out anyway.

Third, we need to reform our budgeting process to include real discipline so that we can steer clear of the fiscal cliff over which our country is headed.

Reasserting Congressional Control over Rule Making

Earlier in the book, we showed how legislative power has moved to an unelected bureaucracy that writes rules that have the force of law. This is done in the name of supposed "delegation" of rule-making authority to commissions or agencies that have "expertise" in these matters. There is nothing wrong with expertise. But expertise and ultimate decision-making power are different things. For example, we go to doctors when we are ill or for routine checkups because they know more about the science of how our bodies work than we do. Sometimes they might prescribe medicine or even recommend surgery, and when they do, they tell us the benefits and risks of what they recommend. Then the decision is ours. Usually we take their advice, sometimes we seek a second opinion, and sometimes we may decide that the "cure" they recommend is worse than the disease. Regardless, the decision is ours, not the doctor's.

The same relationship between expertise and decision making should apply in government as well. Indeed, that is how the Constitution was set up, and it is the best model of how things are supposed to work in political science—at least in democratic societies. Our government has what should be three equal but separate branches: legislative, executive, and judicial. Legislative power means rule making. The Constitution says, "All legislative Powers herein granted shall be vested in a Congress of the United States." This couldn't be simpler. Neither the executive nor the judicial branches should create legislation.

The role of the executive branch is to enforce laws, and in that capacity to recommend new laws. The Constitution grants executive power to the president and says that "He shall from time to time give to the Congress Information of the State of the Union, and recommend to their Consideration such Measures as he shall judge necessary and expedient." So in addition to enforcing laws, the president and the rest of the executive branch may play the role of expert on what the country needs. But, the key words are "recommend to their Consideration"; it is Congress that ultimately makes the decision.

Third is our judicial branch, which ensures that the laws the Congress passes and the president enforces are in accordance with the rule of law. The Constitution sets up a court system to do this. The courts are not supposed to "make law," nor are they there to "enforce laws," only to adjudicate their enforcement. Seems pretty straightforward. But that is not how things are working now, and, consequently, things are not working well. Courts are making decisions that legislatures and the Congress should be making. Many legislators don't seem to mind this because it saves them from making tough decisions and then taking the blame. This creates increased political friction in the public, because voters end up not having any say in important matters. Limiting federal judges' terms would have the effect of increasing voters' say, if only indirectly, by shortening the tenure of these unelected policy makers.

Power is attractive, and there is a natural tendency for the Ruling Class and their institutions to try to take more of it. "Expertise" is most often the excuse they use: "We know better than Congress." For example, the US Environmental Protection Agency (EPA) was granted regulatory control of "navigable waters" under the 1972 Clean Water Act. Control of other bodies of water was left to the states. Now, most of us might think that the word "navigable" means a body of water in which one could go boating. Not so. In 2014, the EPA proposed that "navigable" meant any body of standing water. And the water didn't have to "stand" on a permanent basis; it could be there for just a few days. That means the agency could regulate a puddle in your backyard or a drainage ditch alongside your street.[1]

This is not the Ruling Class's first attempt to expand its power in this way. For example, in 2001, the courts rejected an attempt by the US Army Corps of Engineers to regulate isolated bodies of water simply because migratory birds landed there and then might move on to navigable waterways.[2] In 2006, the courts rejected an EPA claim that its jurisdiction extends to all water with a "hydrological connection" to a navigable waterway. This latter claim would have included all water, since ultimately it all runs into some other body of water that ultimately ends up in a navigable waterway.

Having failed to control everything, the EPA and the Army Corps are proposing a rule to effectively accomplish the same thing with a much more vague set of rules that they hope no one will understand. They have come up with a 370-page rule on which bodies of water they regulate and which ones they don't. A farmer wishing to spray fertilizer will have to consult this massive rule first to see if the drainage ditches on his land that sometimes fill up with water after a heavy rain make those ditches "navigable." If they do, then he will have to apply to the EPA before he can add fertilizer to his crops. If he fails to "comply," he is subject to a fine of $37,500 per day. The same would apply to a state or locality trying to repair a road. Most roads have drainage ditches alongside them, and under the proposed rule, the EPA and the Army Corps would have to sign off before the road repair was approved.

This is, of course, the type of ultimate power grab that the Ruling Class covet. They create broad but very vague rules and then decide for themselves whether or not an individual is in compliance. They can then descend on whomever they choose and hit them with crippling fines for having been "out of compliance." And, of course, to be "in compliance," you have to first apply to the agency and pay a permitting fee that can run between $15,000 and $30,000, with the money going to support their bureaucracy. Then you have to wait for the agency to get around to approving your application. Under this rule, the EPA and the Army Corps take all the powers of government into their own hands. They become the legislature, deciding what the law is; the executive, deciding when and how to enforce the law; *and* the judiciary, deciding who is guilty. Not much room left for liberty—or for democracy.

But there are more practical issues than just the loss of freedom and democracy. These rules all assume that the "expert" is the one who should make all decisions, and not the person who is affected. This goes hand in hand with the Ruling Class notion that they are inherently smarter—so smart, in fact, that they know how to run other people's lives better than the people do.

But experts are never expert in all things. In fact, that goes with the definition of expertise. An expert's talents might be deep, but they are rarely wide. Almost by definition, "experts" are specialists. That may make them very knowledgeable about a specific issue, but it means that they are not very good about making trade-offs. And trade-offs and com-promise are what public policy is all about. When one asks only experts to do something, the result will be something that does a wonderful job in their area of expertise but might not do such a good job in other as-pects of the project.

For example, say we want a bridge built across a river, and we want to have only the best experts design it. Go to an expert civil engineer who specializes in making sure that everything he builds lasts a long time and ask him to build a bridge that won't fall down. He will design a bridge that won't fall down. It will survive almost every imaginable event: all earthquakes up to the strongest one ever recorded, or a massive tidal wave hundreds of feet high. It might even survive a terrorist attack if it's made difficult enough to blow up, and, of course, it will survive the usual problems of rust and corrosion. Naturally such a bridge would be truly massive, take up enormous amounts of extra land, be unsightly, and cost tens of billions of dollars.

Now go to an accountant and ask her to build a bridge, but tell her that it can't cost more than $300 million. She will come in under budget. The bridge probably won't survive an earthquake—not even a small one, or even a small wave, let alone an act of terrorism. It won't look very nice. But it will come in under budget.

Similar incongruities will occur if you go to any kind of expert. A regional planner will design a bridge with maximum interconnections with the regional road network as well as room for transportation needs that might arise generations from now. An environmentalist will emphasize other things, and might even conclude the bridge is not eco-friendly. The problem becomes obvious: experts not only tend to know a lot about their chosen profession, but also tend to believe that what they studied is the most important aspect of the world, so they will emphasize it to the exclusion of other things.

One way to handle this is to involve multiple panels of experts and give each one control over his or her area of expertise. So the civil engineers would have to say that the bridge won't fall down, and the accountants that it won't go over budget, and the regional planners that it will meet the transportation needs for the next hundred years, and the environmental experts that it'll be eco-friendly. If you were to give each a veto power on the project over his or her field of expertise, one could hope for a strong, environmentally sound bridge that met the area's needs for a hundred years, *and* came in under budget.

However, more likely than not, you would end up never building the bridge. And that is what has been happening in our country's infrastructure projects, as chapter 10 showed. Stronger bridges cost more and might well be less eco-friendly. Eco-friendly bridges might not be designed to meet future needs, as they emphasize preserving the current environment. Bridges built for future needs are necessarily bigger and more costly than what is needed at present.

By definition, one cannot leave compromising to the experts. It is not what they do—or like to do. They like to study and obsess about their field of expertise. By contrast, the one thing that the political process is good at is achieving compromise. Trading this for that is what politicians do and what they love to do. It is also what we elect them to do. And if we don't like the trade-offs they make, we elect new ones. We never get to "elect" new experts.

So the first reform that will not only restore liberty and democracy but also produce a better result is to move decision making away from panels of "experts" and put it back in the hands of Congress. That means restoring rule-writing authority to Congress and leaving individual agencies as the executors of the law, not its writers.

Consider the case above regarding the jurisdiction of the EPA and the Army Corps over waterways. If Congress thinks that more waterways should be covered, and not just navigable ones, then it should legislate the change. If nitrous oxide emissions should be cut further, let Congress pass a law to do so. If securities laws need a different emphasis or a different burden of proof, then let Congress enact it.

Or consider the recent regulation of the internet by the Federal Communications Commission. Congress had no say in giving the FCC regulatory control over the internet; the FCC gave it to itself by a vote of 3-to-2, with no input by our elected representatives.[3] It might have been a good decision or a bad one; it doesn't really matter from the viewpoint of good government, liberty, and democracy. However, does anyone seriously think that having a group of five people decide whether or not it should have more power is the way things should be done in a democratic society? Will it enhance or detract from liberty in a society to have panels of experts decide whether or not they should become the legal legislators, executors, and judges in a certain area? If an expansion of regulatory power is a "good" idea, then is it too much to ask that someone other than the regulators make that determination?

One can easily imagine the Ruling Class objections, and there will be many. The most obvious is that asking Congress to decide on new

regulations will give "special interests" the power to block them. However, isn't a regulatory agency that gives itself more power acting in its
own special interest? What the Ruling Class really object to is having
competing interests involved in the process. By including these, "control" is more diffuse, and the Ruling Class would have to relinquish their
monopoly on control and power over the process. Groups other than the
regulators should have a chance to persuade Congress that the idea is a
bad one—for example, that it will cost too much, weaken the economy,
and eliminate jobs. The regulators need not be silent in this process.
They have the power through their congressional testimony and through
their use of the press to persuade Congress that the regulation is worth-
while.

Then there is this old Ruling Class standby: "Congress is not composed of experts, how can it possibly know what the right regulation is?"
But, of course, congressional expertise is not in any particular field but
in making trade-offs among particular areas—something in which the
regulator is *not* an expert. When deciding whether or not to expand a
regulation, the regulators can give their expert testimony, and other "experts" in the field of that regulation can also be called. People from other
areas of expertise are also allowed to comment on those aspects of the
regulation. Congress must then use its judgment about which experts it
trusts most.

There is also the possibility that regulations and regulatory emphasis might change over time. The Ruling Class will project this as a bad
thing and use a phrase such as "regulatory instability," as opposed to the
"predictability" supposedly offered by the current system. But the only
real predictability in the current system is that regulators will, over time,
grant themselves more power. Actually, regulation will likely increase
over time under a congressionally driven scheme as well, especially if
Congress were only to approve new rules. Existing rules would stay in
place, so regulation would not "weaken" but could only strengthen.
Some members of Congress might want to revisit existing rules, and
could, but there is a lot of inertia in the political process, and proponents

of regulatory relaxation would have the same challenge of persuading Congress as those who favor increased regulation.

One other possible development is that the congressional taste for more or less regulation might change with economic conditions. When an economic recession occurs, Congress might be less willing to pass new regulations that impose economic costs. Our legislators' sense of what the "trade-offs" are might change. Alternatively, when the economy is booming, Congress might decide that the country can afford more emphasis on the goals of regulation, as job creation and real wages might be far from its members' minds.

Ultimately We the People are the ones who should decide what makes sense, and our members of Congress, unlike the regulators themselves, are ultimately subject to our votes. We are the final arbiters of trade-offs. We breathe the air and drink the water, so we are the beneficiaries of controls on air and water pollution. We also want to be able to support our families and enjoy the occasional luxury. So ultimately we are the ones who should make the trade-offs because we are the ones who will have to live with them. That does not make us experts, but it does make us the ones who should weigh the options. This is what a republic—a representative government—should be doing. This function is lost when the executive branch violates the Constitution and assumes legislative powers from Congress.

One other thing might happen if Congress actually had to approve new regulations: we might elect better (or at least different) congressional representatives and senators. It is, after all, past Congresses themselves that created the regulatory bodies we are talking about. They created these bodies for political reasons and authorized them to make the decisions without having to involve Congress, even though Congress does not have the congressional authority to give up this power. What does that say about the congressmen and congresswomen who shirked their responsibilities to make decisions? Did any of them really campaign saying, "I'm not able to make this decision, so I want someone else to do it?" Our representatives are generally not self-deprecating people. They think quite highly of themselves. Few of them actually thought themselves incapable of making judgments.

No, congressmen who gave up their decision-making power didn't do so because they thought someone else was smarter. They did it because that way they didn't have to answer for the results and be accountable to the people. They did it out of cowardice. If a regulation didn't work out as well as intended (and most do not), the congressman doesn't have to admit, "I made a mistake." Depending on which way the wind is blowing, he might give some great speeches attacking the regulatory agency that made the decision. Or she might say, "Even more regulation is needed." But under the current arrangement, members of Congress never actually need to come clean that they did anything wrong. Perhaps if they had to be accountable for their responsibilities, the voters would be in a better position to make decisions in the voting booth.

Term Limit the Right Offices

One of the most popular reforms of our government among the public is to impose term limits on members of Congress. It is easy to understand why: Congress is one of the most unpopular institutions in our country. Many of its members spend a good portion of their lives there, and in the process, they might forget what "real life" is like.

However, there is an incentive for states and congressional districts to return the same senator or congressman that has little to do with their attitude toward policy. Congress works on a seniority system. In general, the congressman or senator who has been there the longest or who has served on a congressional committee the longest tends to become the chair of the committee. That means power. And a powerful member is naturally in a position to trade favors on issues that he or she controls for favors that help the state or district that he or she represents. So in that sense, the process is somewhat stacked for incumbents and against challengers. In addition, states tend to draw their congressional district lines to protect incumbents regardless of party, as many legislatures designate

advantages to the state in having a long-serving congressional delegation. On top of that, being in office a long time and becoming a powerful member makes it easier to attract contributions to mount successful
campaigns.

This is particularly true when one party controls one or both houses
of Congress for an extended period. One such period was from 1954
to 1994, when the Democrats controlled the US House for forty years.
In that case, there was never an alternation of chairmen or a sharing of
power. Over a long period of time, it could become harder and harder
for the minority to recruit candidates or get contributions, making one-
party control almost self-perpetuating.

So it is easy to understand the case for term limits. One of the most
popular proposals, pushed by a citizen-based lobbying group known as
US Term Limits, would limit members of the House of Representatives
to three terms, or a total of six years, and members of the Senate to two
terms, or twelve years in office. After serving, the member would have to
live as an ordinary citizen under the laws that he or she passed. The idea
is that Congress would become an institution of citizen legislators, as our
Founders intended.

While the idea is intriguing, the real power of the Ruling Class is in
institutions that are never subject to election and have no limitations on
the period of time over which people can serve. When you don't even
have to face the voters and never face the possibility of being fired unless
you commit a serious crime, you really can come to view your job as a
sinecure to which you are entitled. And if you have the Ruling Class
mentality of believing that you know better how to run the lives of the
country's citizens than they do, being in a position for a very long time
can only reinforce your sense of self-importance and superiority.

The composition of Congress—and particularly the control of
Congress—has rotated quite a bit in the last twenty-five years or so.
For example, at the start of the 114th Congress, the one in office when
this book was written, only 54 of the 435 members of the House of
Representatives—17 Republicans and 37 Democrats—had served more

than twenty years. An additional 91 members, 47 Republicans and 44 Democrats, had served between ten and twenty years. That means that two-thirds of the House—290 members—had served fewer than ten years. Sixty-two were in their first term (47 Republicans and 15 Democrats), and an additional 71 (33 Republicans and 38 Democrats) were in their second term. Basically, a third of the House has been there ten or more years, and an almost equal number are either in their first or second terms. That is hardly a lot of longevity.

The same is true of the Senate, perhaps more so. Just 7 Republicans and 5 Democrats have served more than twenty years, and an additional 18 have served more than ten years. That's less than a third of the Senate. By contrast, almost half the Senate (32 Republicans and 16 Democrats) are serving in their first term.[4]

What has caused that to happen has been a series of large partisan swings in the control of both the House and the Senate.[5,6] Ronald Reagan came to office in 1981 with 192 members of his party in the House and left in 1989 with just 173. The number of Republicans in the Senate dropped from 54 to 43 while Reagan was in office. Bill Clinton came to office in 1993 with 258 members of the House from his party and left eight years later with a minority of 213 (and having dropped to as low as 199 at one point). Clinton also saw the number of Democrats in the Senate drop from 57 when he came in to office to a low of 45 before recovering to 50 when he left. George Bush came to office in 2001 with 220 Republicans in the House and 50 in the Senate; and left in 2009 with 178 in the House and 45 in the Senate. And Barack Obama came to office with 257 House Democrats; in his final term, this had dropped to 188. His party's showing in the Senate dropped from 60 when he took office to just 46 currently.

So even if individual senators and representatives have an advantage in their reelection, all other things being equal, the swinging pendulum of American public opinion has had the effect of limiting the terms of members through the electoral process. Perhaps if the control of the House and Senate were more stable, then the advantages of incumbency would add to the advantages of being a member of the party in control and greatly lengthen terms. But that is not the case today.

The biggest problem with limiting the terms of Congress members is that they confront a permanent bureaucracy and a permanent judiciary that never face election. Congress is by and large the only tribune available for increasing liberty, and to merely limit terms in Congress might place the Ruling Class at a distinct advantage. The statistics tell a daunting story.

The US Government Accountability Office (GAO),[7] an internal government organization that audits various parts of the government and reports to Congress, found that in 2013, just 3,500 of the roughly 2.5 million government employees were terminated. That is roughly 1 in 300. In the overall economy, employers terminate approximately 1 worker in 80 each and every month. That is around 1 in 7 over the course of the year. Granted, many of these individuals in the private sector were let go because their jobs disappeared, something that almost never happens in the federal government. But the rate of termination in government is so low primarily because it is almost impossible to fire someone.

Getting rid of someone takes six months to a year. First, the person's supervisor must notify him of his substandard performance. Then he is put on a performance improvement plan. Only if that fails does the firing process actually begin. The employee is granted numerous rights of appeal and is generally placed on paid administrative leave in the interim. In the highly publicized scandal at the Veterans Administration, there has been only one person fired so far—*ever*—and that was after months of being on paid administrative leave while the appeals process dragged on and on.

Of course, this is all wasteful and contributes to the overall poor performance of government. But it also creates a problem for trying to change bureaucratic behavior. It might take years of constant oversight and public hearings to expose the incompetence and arrogant behavior of portions of the bureaucracy. In the meantime, malfeasant bureaucrats can just wait it out. The name in Washington for those who are elected is "short-termers." Bureaucrats can simply wait until the congressman who is exposing their actions moves on. The departure of congressmen trying to effect positive change could be accelerated greatly by term limits.

Most government workers are dedicated people who do their jobs. But these are the workers who are affected most adversely by the system. It is difficult to retain a strong work ethic and avoid cynicism about one's job if a fellow employee is obviously not doing his. This creates a corrosive work environment that is bad for morale and innovation. It is also a bad environment for whistle blowing. If a good employee reports bad behavior, he or she will become a pariah in the office and will have to confront the bad employees who resent the reporting of their inappropriate behavior.

The process also has an ideological component. Political appointees who are dedicated to the Ruling Class mission of their agency often do something called "burrowing" late in an administration's second term. This means converting from a political employee who must depart at the end of the administration into a career civil servant who can carry on the ideological agenda well into the next administration. Given their former position and connections, these burrowers can lead rear-guard actions that make life difficult for the incoming team, while also making reform and policy changes almost impossible. Typically they do this by providing ammunition to the press against their new bosses to embarrass them and make it increasingly difficult for them to do their jobs.

The other long-serving and unelected part of our government—and a bastion of the Ruling Class—are our courts. Five of the nine justices on the Supreme Court have served more than twenty years each—longer than only about a sixth of the members of Congress. On average, they are appointed around the age of fifty. Today one justice is already over eighty, two more will turn eighty in 2016, another is seventy-eight, and the other five are in their sixties.[8]

The Constitution is silent on term limits for the court. It says merely that they shall "hold their Offices during good Behaviour" and that their "[compensation] shall not be diminished during their Continuance in

Office." This is subject to many interpretations. It is clear that Congress can't punish the court's members by cutting their salaries. But what about "good Behaviour?" Some allege that this means they can serve for life unless they are impeached. But this might be a stretch. On a plain reading of Article 3, Congress can set up the court system pretty much as it wishes. So limiting judges to a fixed term would certainly be in its purview, although a change to a term of office might have to be prospective. That is, if a term were imposed, time already served would not count toward the term.

The case for giving judges life terms is to insulate them from politics. Of course, as we learned, the courts have not exactly been models for resisting political pressure, particularly when it comes to progressive politicians pressuring Ruling Class judges. They have rewritten the Constitution on numerous occasions in ways that defy its plain reading. They have expanded both the role of the federal government in our lives and their own power in decision making far beyond what was intended. And they have turned a blind eye when it comes to taking away fundamental liberties from the people. It is therefore hard to justify lifetime appointment in the name of political independence, when the people being granted those terms act like typical politicians.

A reasonable compromise can be found in the way the Federal Reserve is constituted. Members of the Board of Governors are definitely involved in the process of setting policy. They set overnight interest rates and also have extensive regulatory decision-making power. The institution is supposed to be independent of the politics of the day—one would not want interest rates set to meet the political agenda of the current president, for example. They are given fourteen-year terms, and the chair and vice chair are given four-year terms for those special offices. Since there are seven members of the Board of Governors, technically a new governor is appointed every two years. At that pace, a sitting president would not fill a majority of the board until his last year in office. That certainly creates a significant amount of political independence.

A parallel structure for the Supreme Court would involve eighteen-year terms, with one member being appointed every two years. Assuming there are no resignations, an incoming president would never be able to fill the entire Supreme Court during his or her two terms in office. That is probably enough political independence for the court. Moreover, it eliminates the randomness that now occurs, where some presidents get to appoint a lot of justices and some appoint few. Justices themselves often "game" their retirements to avoid the possibility of giving a president with whom they disagree ideologically the chance to replace them.

Eighteen-year terms would also make sense for lower federal court judges. Although the need for a new appointment every two years to spread them out at an even pace does not apply to appeals courts or circuit courts with varying numbers of members, it is certainly a long enough tenure to avoid the threat of political pressure. If a justice were appointed at age fifty or so, he or she would serve for the rest of his or her normal working life. Justices would therefore be independent for the term of their careers. That certainly should be enough. One technical issue to be decided would be how to count the years of service of judges appointed to fill the unexpired terms of other judges who have retired or died. Congress could either decide to limit judges to eighteen years or one full term. In the latter case, a judge could serve for far more than eighteen years if he or she took office to fill the unexpired term of another judge.

This would not necessarily make the courts more pro-liberty or more pro–Ruling Class. But it would send an unmistakable signal to unelected officials that the public is tired of having policy set by people with no accountability to the electorate. More than any other single group in our society, they have handed power to the Ruling Class (and themselves), and that was never intended by the Founding Fathers when they wrote the Constitution. Judges, like everyone else, need to spend time outside of the institutions of power.

Budget Reform

Earlier, in chapter 8, we saw how the Ruling Class have made a hash of our nation's finances. Sound budgeting is the heart of good governance, and right now America is on the path to fiscal ruin. To make matters worse, it seems that each year the country teeters on the brink of fiscal meltdown, as Congress and the president are unable to put together a plan—any plan—to keep the country running. The 1974 Budget Act supposedly laid out some rules for budgeting on a timely basis, but that law has utterly failed. Once the defenders of liberty break the grip of the Ruling Class, they will need to put the government back on a sound footing and show that our system can work.

The first step is to take the budget off autopilot and subject all government spending to the appropriations process. Right now Congress does control the actual level of spending on about 30 percent of the budget. It can say, for example, that the Department of Defense is allowed to spend only $600 billion, and that's the law—the Pentagon can't spend a penny more. But on the wide swath of programs known as entitlements, Congress never passes an actual limit on how much is spent. Instead, bills are passed with "estimates" of entitlement program costs, but if those estimates turn out to be wrong, it doesn't matter; Congress never revisits the issue.

A recent example of this came with the passage of Obamacare. To get the bill through the House in early 2010, Speaker Nancy Pelosi insisted that the ten-year "cost" of the program come in under $1 trillion. Magically, when the bill hit the floor, the cost was just $944 billion. When the Congressional Budget Office (CBO) released its 2011 estimate, the price tag was now $1.442 trillion, more than 50 percent larger. (What a surprise.)[9] There was no need to go back and make changes to bring the bill down to its original cost estimate. No, the policy is "let it ride." The cost overrun is built into the system automatically. It is, of course, impossible to prove that any one particular person lied, but the entire system produces dishonest numbers, and no one is ever held accountable. Even if one thinks that an "honest mistake" was made, shouldn't Congress have to go back and address and rectify the mistake?

The errors become really large over time. Former Kansas senator Sam Brownback made this point at a Joint Economic Committee hearing in July 2009, when Obamacare was being considered. He noted that when Medicare was enacted in 1965, the projected cost of the program in 1990 was set at $9 billion. But when 1990 finally rolled around, the actual cost was $67 billion.[10] The "estimate" on which the program was passed was off by more than 700 percent. That is one heck of a large "honest mistake."

Entitlement spending, unlike other forms of spending, depends on factors such as program participation and how much costs rise. These might not be entirely predictable, but that doesn't mean they should be ignored. Consider what happens when a major weapons system experiences a "cost overrun." Spending is not automatically increased. Not a dime above that which was authorized and appropriated ever leaves the Treasury. Instead, Congress must make a change in its appropriation in the next fiscal year to make up for the overrun. And that change is subject to budget rules, which require that such a change be offset against other spending and revenues.

In the case of an entitlement, the money might have to go out the door in the year of the error. One would not want to deny a beneficiary his or her Social Security check or Medicaid reimbursement. But if there were an error in one year, Congress should be obliged to cover that error in the next fiscal year, and the "make-up" money should be subject to the same rules as other spending with regard to finding offsets. The budget law should also require that if the target were missed two years in a row, automatic across-the-board spending cuts in the program subject to repeated budget breaches would have to be made in the third year to make up for the overruns. So, for example, if Medicare had two consistent years of 2 percent cost overruns, then reimbursement in the third year would have to be cut by 4 percent to make up for it.

Would this be painful politically? Most certainly. But one suspects that the Congress would make extra efforts to get it right if confronted with such political pain. The days of "letting it ride" and just passing on the cost overruns to our children and grandchildren in the form of mounting public debt would be over.

The second piece of entitlement reform would be to force a Congress and a president enacting either a new entitlement or changing an existing entitlement to confront the full long-term cost of what they are doing. Unlike a new weapons system or a new road in which the costs disappear after the project is completed, entitlement programs last forever. Long-term estimates of the cost of the program are made but are not incorporated in the legislation. For example, the trustees of the Social Security and Medicare trust funds submit annual estimates of the cost of these programs over the next seventy-five years, so that the mission can be accomplished.

When a change is made in a program, the present value of the change over the next seventy-five years should be incorporated into the program's cost, and the Congress enacting the change should have to take those costs into account. Otherwise we set up a system where one Congress enacts very generous programs, claims credit, and then leaves future Congresses and presidents to clean up the mess.

Currently Congress and the president game the rules. Typically cost estimates are made for just ten years of a new program. So legislative changes are often tucked into the ninth and tenth year of the program, leading to explosive costs. But those costs are not counted in the ten-year estimate because they occur outside the so-called budget window.

One important point to note about this reform is that it would also reward good behavior. Nearly everyone agrees in theory that we need to reform our entitlement process. Moreover, it should be gradual. Changes to programs such as Social Security and Medicare should not force rapid adjustments by people who have become dependent on those programs and who are at a stage of their lives where adjustment is difficult. Instead, changes should take place over many years and allow people to prepare.

An example of this is the 1983 Social Security Reform Act passed by President Reagan and Congress based on the recommendations of the National Commission on Social Security Reform (also known as the Greenspan Commission, as it was chaired by Alan Greenspan).[11] One of the big changes was an increase in the retirement age at which full benefits could be received, from sixty-five to sixty-seven. However, this did not begin until 2000, seventeen years after the bill was passed, and then it was phased in over twenty-seven years—a full forty-four years after the bill was passed. At this point, most changes in the system will have to take less than four decades, because we are running out of time. Consequently, it will be a brave Congress and president who enact these changes.

So the politicians who make the changes should get the credit for their political courage. The Social Security Trustees estimate that the present value of the shortfall in that fund and the Medicare fund amounts to $37 trillion.[12] So a Congress that even makes a start should be able to claim credit for "taking $10 trillion off the debt" if it makes the change. Its members might even give themselves a little reward and spend a small fraction of that savings on programs that win them votes. That might not make them an exemplary profile in courage, but at least the men and women who take these steps would be moving the country in the right direction.

Third, liberals and conservative alike need to bear in mind that long-term budget scoring in present value terms should apply to both taxes and spending. Those who favor expanding the size of government have tended to resist a more honest approach to scoring the costs of program expansion because they think it biases the system against them. But taxes should be scored the same way. If there were a tax cut, the long-run budget implications need to be taken into account. Otherwise the system will be "gamed" on the tax side just as it has been on the spending side.

One great example of this was the one-year "repeal" of the inheritance tax, or "death tax," in the 2001 tax cut. Congressmen had campaigned on the platform of repealing the death tax. The bill, which was scored only over ten years, did enact a repeal, but only in 2010, the tenth year of the bill. This sharply cut the estimated budget cost of the bill. The hope was, just as it is for spenders, that in year ten, the politics would make it difficult to bring back a tax that had disappeared. Whatever the policy merits of the concept, it is not a good way to run the government or its finances. It creates needless uncertainty and therefore undermines sound tax policy.

The right goal of defenders of liberty should be good government and not just smaller government. We cannot engage in the same dishonesty as the Ruling Class, or we will take the country on a path to ruin just as surely as they have—more slowly perhaps, but with the same end result.

Fourth, so-called PAYGO rules need to be changed in accordance with long-term honest budget principles and not left in their current state. PAYGO is a rule that supposedly requires that any increase in spending or cut in taxes is offset by other changes. But, as George Mason University scholar James Capretta described it, "The real aim of PAYGO, however, is to stop tax cuts. PAYGO does not place any constraint on the 'natural' (and inexorable) growth of entitlement spending that occurs under current law. . . . PAYGO is the embodiment of the view that fiscal responsibility entails 'paying for' newly enacted spending commitments. That's very different from the view that sound fiscal policy is focused on spending control to allow private actors to keep and use as much of their own money as possible."

One other aspect of PAYGO is its fundamental dishonesty in how it treats tax changes, which are scored as ten-year changes unless they say otherwise, and discretionary spending increases, which are scored as one-year increases unless specified otherwise. Consider the preposterous idea that Congress starts a new spending program and expects it to lapse after just one year. But that is what PAYGO does. Of course, Congress is going to renew the program year after year. But by doing it this way, Congress is allowed to get the proverbial camel's nose under the tent and only score it for PAYGO reasons at a fraction of what it will ultimately cost. Now, the tax cutters caught on to this trick and began enacting provisions known as "extenders." These are supposed one-year tax cuts that have been extended year after year for twenty or more years. The reason for this is to game the PAYGO rules.

When one has a set of rules that are open to gaming by both tax cutters and spending increasers, it is time to admit that the rules are broken. Either we must get rid of the rules or decide that if a change is made that does not have an intrinsic sunset quality to it, or is a true one-off expense, that it must be scored as a ten-year program on both the tax side and the spending side. Suppose there is a bill to permanently acquire new land for a national park. That land, once it is acquired, does not have to be reacquired every year. The spending naturally sunsets and is not likely to be recurring. The same can be said of a specific weapons program, or of the construction of a particular road or school. But if a new bureaucracy is being created or a new set of program beneficiaries is being established, then the odds are that a permanent set of spending increases is occurring. PAYGO makes no recognition of that difference currently.

Fifth, we need a mechanism to avoid government shutdowns. The power of the purse is a very valuable tool for keeping a government from overstepping its bounds. But history has shown that the Ruling Class exploit shutdowns by closing only those parts of the government that have a big visible impact while keeping most of the government functioning. This has meant that they deliberately stall the process of negotiating a compromise, knowing that in the end they will win the public relations war by painting those who want to slow down government as causing a "shutdown." In fact, it was their refusal to compromise that led to the shutdown.

So rather than let the Ruling Class game the system, we need a systematic method of dealing with any political impasse that is caused by a refusal of the various parts of government to reach a compromise. The easiest method is an across-the-board rule. Whenever any appropriations bill is not passed by the start of the fiscal year, a system should be in place that spreads an across-the-board reduction in spending to the agency where there is no compromise. For example, for the first month of the fiscal year, the agency may continue all operations (including salaries) at the same rate as in the previous fiscal year. After one month, spending can continue at a pace of 99 percent of the previous fiscal year. After two months that figure drops to 98 percent. So over time, the power of the purse begins to bite, but never in a Draconian way. Faced with this and the political pain within the government that even modest cuts cause, a path to compromise will be forthcoming soon.

Sixth, and most important, we need a way to enforce all of this. And so, dear reader, let me let you in on a little secret that congressional leaders learned long ago. It involves the most important lobbying group that ever existed. No, it is not a big money group. Not business, not labor, not a special interest group at all. It is the lobby of family members. Leadership uses this lobby shamelessly as congressional sessions come to an end. For example, they threaten to keep members in town and Congress operating through Christmas if need be. All of a sudden compromises that could never be reached are reached, deals brokered, and those airplane reservations home do not have to be canceled.

What we need to do is to take advantage of this by making Congress work full-time until it gets its work done. Then, and only then, can its members go back to their districts and their families. Right now Congress operates under what is, in effect, a three-day workweek. Members are due in town Monday night so that work can begin Tuesday morning. Often there is a "bed-check vote" late on Monday night just to create an incentive to be there. Then members are out of town by Friday, typically taking the last plane out on Thursday night.

So a reform that might meet all needs is to have a five-day workweek in Washington, three weeks at a time, and then one week at home for "district work." To incentivize a productive use of the time, this three-on, one-off system would stay in place only until all of the next year's appropriations bills were enacted. Then members could spend all of the remaining time back home if they wanted.

In conclusion, we can get the budget under control, but we must insist that the people we send to Washington do so. And as with all of us, rules must be designed and incentives created to follow those rules, to make us do the right thing. Defenders of liberty have a stake in making this happen. The Ruling Class would just as soon see the system continue on as it is.

CHAPTER 16

Reforming the Fed:
The Right Way to Take Back
Control of Our Money

This book was inspired by the fact that the public is angry. The people have seen the Ruling Class take more power and more resources and deliver declining services and less liberty in return. Calls for change are everywhere, and the need for change is real. In this third and final section of this book, we are considering the changes that will take back the power that the Ruling Class have seized, the reforms that will return our government to a footing that restores our constitutionally granted liberty, and the choices we need to make to place our country back on the path to prosperity—what Jefferson called "a wise and frugal government."

One of the areas of greatest public distrust of our institutions involves the institution that is responsible for our money: the Federal Reserve. A November 2013 Rasmussen survey showed that only 34 percent of those polled had a favorable view of the Fed, while 50 percent held an unfavorable view. When asked whether there should be an "audit" of the Federal Reserve, the public was for the idea by a margin of 74 percent to 10 percent.[1] There are even widespread calls to "end the Fed" driven by suspicion that the Fed is a secretive institution that manipulates the economy in favor of the Ruling Class and their well-to-do friends on Wall Street. The fact that the economy has seen three bubbles form in the space of a quarter century (two of which ended painfully, and if history is any guide, the one that we're in now will too) lends credence to this suspicion.

Yet there is a widespread misunderstanding of the Federal Reserve, and so it is important that any changes made are based on the reality of the situation, not assumption and suspicion. Start with the fact that the Fed is already audited, both internally and externally. Its entire balance sheet is made public down to the specific identifying number—the CUSIP—of each bond it holds. In terms of the transparency of its operations, it is at least as open to public scrutiny as any other governmental institution. That doesn't mean reform isn't necessary, just that we need a better understanding of what calls for change. The place to begin is with a brief history of what our money actually is, how it affects the economy, and the Fed's role in regulating this system.

Money and the Federal Reserve

Money is probably the least understood yet most talked about invention of mankind. Of all of our creations, it is arguably the ripest for abuse, and always has been. The often-quoted phrase "The love of money is the root of all evil" couldn't be more true. But it's important to realize that despite its potential to corrupt, money itself is a necessary tool for a functioning and cohesive society. Only when people pursue something for its own sake—money or power—do things turn ugly; and when people who have control of money and the instruments of power abuse them, then we all get into trouble.

The Constitution granted two very important enumerated powers over money to Congress: "[t]o borrow Money on the credit of the United States" and "[t]o coin Money, regulate the Value thereof, and of foreign Coin, and fix the Standard of Weights and Measures." What has the Ruling Class done with these powers? Chapter 8 provided the gory details on what they have done with the power to borrow on credit. Clearly, the Ruling Class have stretched beyond what is allowed by the Constitution, and that's a big part of the reason our country's in so much trouble financially. We mentioned that there is now $56,000 of total debt for every man, woman, and child in America, and that for all practical purposes, there was no way to pay that back—and that in reality, the government never intends to pay that back. Even worse, the government has an "implied debt" many times that size in terms of promised payments to individuals in the future that far exceeds the practical taxing authority of the government.

But what about the government's authority to coin money? What stands behind the money the government (actually the Federal Reserve) prints? Unfortunately, our currency is backed by nothing more than US government bonds—yes, the same ones that are never really going to ever be paid back because new ones will be issued as soon as the old ones expire. Go ahead and pull out one of those pieces of paper in your wallet. On the top of the front side are the words "Federal Reserve Note." These are actually debt notes of the Federal Reserve—an IOU, in effect. Our money is the liability of the Federal Reserve, and, like any bank, the Fed has an asset standing behind those liabilities: one dollar in assets for every dollar in money the Fed creates. Those assets are the "safest" in the world. When the Fed issues money, it gives that money to the government to spend in return for the bond the government issues. (Note: the transaction is not direct; both sides make the exchange through the market, but the effect is the same. The Fed gets US government debt, and the government gets Federal Reserve debt—known as money.)

So our money is the debt of one government institution that in turn is backed by the debt of the government. And what stands behind the debt of the government? The credit of the United States. If this all sounds a little circular, that's because it is. In the end, what stands behind our government's credit? The same thing that stands behind the credit of any individual or any company: the ability to pay it back. And that is based on the ability to generate income to pay it back, or to borrow from someone else. Of course, the government ultimately has only one source of income: its taxing authority, or, more precisely, its ability to tax more than it spends. Therefore, what stands behind both our money and the debt of the government is the same thing: the government's ability to borrow—and tax—to pay all of this back. We have already gone through the math of how this is never going to happen in practice, in chapter 8. This brings us to the term "full faith and credit" of the United States. The key word is "faith." What stands behind the government's debt and the money in your wallet is faith. It's the faith that this money will always be accepted, that "dollars" will always buy you something, and that the government will never get so over its head in debt that no one will lend to it anymore.

It turns out, thankfully, there's a lot of faith going around. At present, the Federal Reserve has roughly $4.5 trillion of bonds on its balance sheet, comprised of US Treasury debt and debt issued by agencies guaranteed by the US government. Those are bonds that the Federal Reserve bought with money that it printed. That works out to nearly $14,000 for every person in America, so much money that it would never fit in our collective wallets. Only about a quarter of it is in cash ($3,500 per person); the rest sits at banks in electronic form in something called "reserves." But consider that amount: When was the last time you had $3,500 in your wallet as spending money? The Fed has put far more money in circulation than could ever conceivably be needed. Money is no longer being supplied merely to carry on its normal functions and is instead being created for entirely different reasons. Starting in 2009, the Federal Reserve printed money and bought government bonds and other bonds guaranteed by the government for the express purpose of driving up prices of things such as stocks traded on the stock exchange, as well as residential and commercial real estate. The jury is still out on whether this will turn out to have been a good idea. But it is unusual, or in Fedspeak, "extraordinary." How we got to this point is a long story.

Remember that in reality all that stands behind money is faith — particularly faith that you can exchange money for something you want to buy. Of course, the key to this is that someone else is willing to take your money and give you the good or service that you want, and that also requires faith on his or her part, which, of course, depends on being able to pass on that money to someone else.

This faith should be well founded no matter what kind of money you're using. It is true for gold coins as well: you have to have faith that someone will take your gold coins in return for what you want to buy just as much as you have to have faith that the other person will take paper money. Neither paper money nor gold has any "intrinsic" value; both are mediums of exchange, the value of which depends on someone else's willingness to accept them.

The difference between paper money and gold is that human beings — the Ruling Class, to be precise — can make paper money; they can't make gold. So you have to have a little bit more faith to go for paper; faith that those who are printing it won't print so much that the paper money they create becomes worthless. History is full of cases where this has happened. In fact, it is fair to say that all currencies eventually end badly, either when the government prints too much or when the government itself fails. When that happens, gold and other mediums of exchange are the only items of value.

Even in our 240-year history, since the Declaration of Independence was signed, our faith in paper money has risen and fallen dramatically. Prior to forming the United States under our Constitution, each state printed its own version of paper money. They printed too much, though, so eventually the money became worth less than its face value. Then, when the Constitution was signed in 1787, the federal government redeemed that paper money and started minting coins made out of gold and silver. This lasted until the Civil War, when both the Union and the Confederacy ran out of gold and silver and resorted to printing paper money. The Confederate money became worthless, and the Union's money went up and down during the war, depending on the fortunes on the battlefield, but ultimately became stable, though this printing caused some inflation. After the Civil War, we went back to predominantly using gold and toyed with the idea of using silver as well. Then in 1913 we created the Fed and began an experiment with paper that was partially backed by gold. That ended in 1933 with the Depression, when, under the Roosevelt administration, the government confiscated all gold held by individuals and corporations, paying $20.67 per ounce, only to raise its "price" to $35 an ounce when it held nearly all of the country's gold. Since then, the constraints on printing money have been eroded, so now we are back to a pure paper standard.

That is the short story. It goes paper, to gold, to paper, to gold, to paper. Now, at some point, dear reader, you probably took a test where you were given a series and asked what came next in the sequence. So in the historic series of paper-gold-paper-gold-paper, what comes next? There's no date on when the next step will be made, but history is fairly convincing.

Trouble is, the logical answer is not the best one. Both gold (and other forms of specie, or coined money) and paper have advantages. The right public policy is to find a way of creating a system that maximizes the *faith* in the currency so that the advantages that money offers society can be utilized fully. What follows is a brief history of how America has tried to make this happen. Studying history is the best way to avoid repeating its mistakes, and some of the historical details will help you to understand why the modern Federal Reserve is the way it is.

Our conclusion and suggested reform stem directly from this history. This erratic switching of currency regimes does no one any good. Each regime is carried to the point of excess, and only when trouble emerges are changes made. What we need instead is a dynamic balance between paper money and gold. The right people to ensure this balance aren't an unelected group or some unchanging law or rule, but the people themselves. We need to restore on a constitutional basis something that we lost in 1933: the right to settle contracts in terms other than US dollars. The history provided below shows why this is our best solution.

How We Got Here

It seems a bit strange that in the Constitution, the power to print money and regulate its value is lumped in with establishing a system of weights and measures, but that is how the Founding Fathers thought about currency. Money has value only when compared with something else. The word "dollar" is just as meaningless as the word "ounce" when taken out of context. Different states had issued their own "dollars," gold and silver coins were circulating, and some basic standard was needed.

But there was also the problem of debt. The various states, through their own banks and congresses, had issued debt and paper currency during the revolution. Already that debt was viewed as unserviceable and too large to be paid back. These debt notes were often trading at 20 percent to 50 percent of their face value, routinely yielding much less than promised originally when traded for gold.

Alexander Hamilton, the first secretary of the Treasury, came up with a solution to both problems: that the states were in debt and that the nation lacked a common currency. First, he had the new federal government assume all state debts and those that Congress had issued during the war and during the time of confederation. Everyone got paid back at par—that is, the full amount that was lent. Hamilton's reasoning was that these debts had been incurred to win independence, so they were the new government's natural responsibility. Now, with a clean slate for the finances of the states, Hamilton went about establishing a credit system on the national level, starting a sinking fund for the repayment of all the new debt issued by the federal government; it was not to be perpetual but paid back at 5 percent a year and retired for good after twenty years. The money to pay for this retirement of debt would be collected from taxes on imports and whiskey. Hamilton's plan worked. For all intents and purposes, the United States's debt was cleared. Both the states and the federal government were essentially debt free.

Hamilton chose to issue money in the form of gold and silver coins, instead of paper, for the express purpose of facilitating business. Most of the previous American coinage was actually Spanish and had been divided into "eighths," which made transactions cumbersome. Hamilton replaced this system with one not unlike the basis of modern American currency: there was a $10 gold coin that weighed about as much as the Spanish coins; silver-based dollars; and smaller copper coins ranging from a half cent to ten cents. Hamilton reasoned that these smaller coins would be of particular benefit to the poor and would also help people become comfortable with using money.

Hamilton also created the first Bank of the United States. It was owned 20 percent by the government and 80 percent by private investors. The purpose was to facilitate the borrowing and lending of money, although the bank was forbidden from buying US government bonds, which Hamilton viewed as a potential conflict of interest. The bank could lend money to other banks and businesses, and did so primarily to finance internal improvements for the country: what today we would call infrastructure. It also acted as a fiscal agent for the Treasury, a place to collect and store tax revenue, and as a means of covering short-term funding gaps, should they arise. This bank lasted twenty years. Five years later, the second Bank of the United States was constructed along similar lines. Although it possessed only limited ability to create money, Andrew Jackson, the seventh president of the United States, opposed the extension of the bank on the grounds that it violated the concept of "sound money," and led to its closure twenty years after its inception, in 1836. This left young America without a central lending source for another seventy-seven years.

During the Civil War, the national government faced a severe cash crunch. Tax collections were not enough to pay for the war effort. President Lincoln tried to borrow from New York banks, but they demanded interest rates of 24 percent or more. Instead, the government began printing money—at first with caution, but then more brazenly. Richard Taylor, a colonel in the Union army and an Illinois businessman, reportedly told Lincoln, "Just get Congress to pass a bill authorizing the printing of full legal tender treasury notes . . . and pay your soldiers with them and go ahead and win your war with them also. If you make them full legal tender . . . they will have the full sanction of the government and be just as good as any money, as Congress is given the express right by the Constitution."[2] The key was making the notes legal tender, which meant that under the force of law, they had to be accepted for all debts, both public and private. Earlier forms of money had been usable only for taxes and other debts to the government. Congress authorized the printing of $150 million worth of these notes.

However, because they were legal tender only if the Union won the war, their value as measured in gold coins fluctuated with the North's progress. At one point, it took $258 of these so-called greenbacks (because they were printed in green on their reverse side) to buy $100 of gold coins. Yes, it was the law that you had to take them, but that did not mean people wanted to, and there was passive resistance to their acceptance. Fortunately, the Union won the war, and the greenbacks were ultimately retired.

But the story of legal tender in the Civil War is an interesting one and involves one man: Salmon P. Chase, who was secretary of treasury when the greenbacks were issued. Later he was named chief justice of the Supreme Court. In 1870, as chief justice in *Hepburn v. Griswold*, he reversed his actions as treasury secretary, declaring that making the greenbacks legal tender for past debts was unconstitutional. The idea was that if you made a contract saying that you were going to be paid $100 in gold coins and were paid back in greenbacks, which were worth only a fraction of that in terms of gold, then you'd basically had some of your property stolen. This is known as a "taking" in the Constitution. Shortly thereafter, President Ulysses S. Grant appointed two new justices to the Supreme Court, and they reversed this precedent in January 1872. This case is important because it made clear the problems that come about when the government says that its money must be taken "for all debts public and private," even when some of those debts might have been incurred in something other than the government's legal tender.

But we also discovered in the late nineteenth century that there is a problem with using just gold and silver as the basis for money: there's only so much of these precious metals available. So when economic booms take place, particularly those that involve big investment projects, reserves are easily spent. The nineteenth century saw many of these rapid expansions: America's great railroad network was established, and telegraph lines crossed the country. Building of the infrastructure required to bring electricity throughout the United States began. Financing these projects used up much of the money that was in circulation. So, late in these boom periods, the price of borrowing money—the interest rate— rose sharply. All of a sudden projects that were under way could no longer be financed affordably, and work stopped. The country went from boom to bust very quickly, and then recovered again. The fixed supply of money acted as a rationing device for economic activity in a way that led to a very volatile business cycle.

Additionally, there was the issue of long-term supply. In general, our country's economy was growing faster than the rate at which silver and gold could be mined. There is a tendency for a certain amount of economic activity—the volume of transactions in the economy—to require a proportionate amount of funding. For example, if the economy doubles in size, it needs roughly twice as much money to maintain its former level of growth. So if economic production is high, the only way to keep the volume of transactions in line is for the price of each good or service to drop.

When money ran out, it led to panic, as people scrambled to find new sources of funding. They sold what they could—frequently assets such as stocks—and prices plummeted. Of course, when stock prices went down, people whose wealth was grounded heavily in the market panicked, as their shares became worth less and less. In 1907, during a particularly bad scare, the famous banker J. P. Morgan provided enough funding to alleviate the public's anxiety, likely saving the country from a deep recession or large depression. Morgan summoned the country's leading bankers and financial experts to his home in Manhattan. They effectively set up shop in his library, making deals and moving money to back up weak institutions to prevent them from failing. He had done the same a dozen years earlier during the second Grover Cleveland administration when the government was running low on cash. Morgan led a consortium of bankers to sell government notes in order to buy gold for the US Treasury.[3]

But Morgan wasn't happy being the guy America turned to whenever it grew desperate. After all, at times he was taking real risks with his bank's money, and even his own fortune. If his intervention didn't work, prices would keep dropping, and he and his bank could be wiped out. And for taking this risk, he really wasn't appreciated and (except in emergencies) was often criticized for having too much power. Morgan thought that the country needed a central bank to step in as "lender of last resort" when things got tough, to bail out the economy's finances. So he assembled a small cadre of the Ruling Class of the day at a duck-hunting club he belonged to on Jekyll Island, off the coast of Georgia. At this secret location, they drew up the plans for what would become the Federal Reserve.[4] The original plan was amended slightly and passed into law as Congress was headed for its Christmas recess on December 23, 1913. This circumstance of this beginning and the players involved provide the basis for the belief today that the Fed is a secretive institution.

The key provision of the Federal Reserve Act allowed the Fed to print Federal Reserve notes that were legal tender throughout the United States. This was a return to paper money creation similar to what happened during the Civil War. But rather than have the paper be legal tender with no gold backing, the Fed was empowered to print money as long as it had 40 cents of gold for every dollar of paper money it created. The other 60 cents could be government bonds. So, technically the Fed could issue $2.50 in paper money for every dollar of gold on its books. America now had an "elastic" currency that could be created when needed to "stretch" its potential money supply. But it could be stretched only so far. Alongside these notes, gold and silver coins were still in circulation, with set prices for each. Therefore, if the Fed printed too much money, and people feared inflation, they could go down to the bank and convert their paper money into gold. The designers of the Fed thought that this would be a good check on any excesses on America's money printing. If too much paper money was created, people could simply dump their Federal Reserve notes and go back to gold and silver. But if there was too little gold and silver around, then money could be printed to meet the growing demand. This would be a particularly valuable tool in the case of a panic, and so it was hoped that panics could be minimized.

This arrangement came to an end when President Franklin Roosevelt issued an executive order on April 5, 1933, outlawing the possession of gold, silver, or any foreign currency.[5] All gold was to be surrendered to the government at $20.67 per ounce, its pegged price, under punishment of confiscation, severe fines, and up to ten years' imprisonment. Once the government had seized all of the privately owned gold, it promptly raised the price to $35 an ounce, effectively expanding the amount of money that the Fed could print by 70 percent.

The plan greatly expanded the net worth of the government and the money-creating power of the Federal Reserve. Now 70 percent more dollars could be issued on the same amount of gold. Similarly, because some of each dollar was backed by government bonds, it also expanded the amount of government debt the Fed could buy. And needless to say, the wealth of the government expanded tremendously. It shelled out $20.67 for every ounce of gold in the country and forced people to sell at that price. Then, after it had the gold, it declared each ounce worth $35, thus making a profit of $14.33 on each ounce it had acquired through a forced sale.

But the real long-term impact was on removing a check on how far the Fed could actually stretch its gold holdings in terms of dollars. Remember, if Americans thought the Fed was printing too much paper money, they could always take flight into gold. In fact, some Americans acquired gold as the Depression set in precisely because they thought that gold would have to be revalued. They were right; it's just that the government wanted all the profits from revaluation for itself.

There was one more check on the government printing more money in relation to its gold reserves: foreign governments could still convert their dollar holdings into gold at the official price. The law limited only Americans from doing this. The Fed continuously expanded the money supply, and over time, much of this ended up overseas in the hands of foreign governments. By the early 1970s, foreign central banks owned $14 billion in US currency, but only $3.5 billion of this debt was backed by Treasury gold. So, on August 15, 1971, President Richard Nixon ended the convertibility of dollars into gold entirely. Then he followed Roosevelt's lead by revaluing the gold to $42 an ounce and finally letting it trade freely.[6] And in 1974, with all gold constraints on printing money removed, Nixon's successor, Gerald Ford, made it legal once again for Americans to own gold.[7]

Gold is now trading around $1,100 per ounce. So when the government sells one of those ounces of gold that Roosevelt forced people to sell for $20.67, it is making a profit of 5,500 percent! But from a policy perspective, once the Fed became unconstrained by gold, its ability to print money also became unconstrained. Gold used to put a check on excess money creation, as people could switch into the precious metal if they felt that too much money was being printed. Now they no longer had this option. And with its greatly expanded ability to print money, the Fed could buy government debt. There are few more important decisions in terms of shifting wealth, power, and borrowing power to the Ruling Class than FDR's forced gold sale. It opened the floodgates on money creation and, with that, expanded the ability of the Fed to finance government spending by printing money to buy government bonds.

The Effect of This on Prices of Goods and Assets

Following the Fed's creation, the money supply began expanding, initiating the gradual decline of the US dollar's purchasing power. When FDR ordered the confiscation of gold, what could be bought for $100 in 1913 now cost $131. Between the time of Roosevelt's action in 1933 and Nixon's in 1971, inflation rose further. Goods purchased for $100 in 1933 now cost $311 in 1971. But in just the first ten years after Nixon's move, the cost of living more than doubled. What cost $100 in 1971 was now priced at $224 in 1981. Altogether, over those eighty-two years, what used to cost $100 now cost $913.

Who wins and who loses? When prices rise, all other things being equal, someone who borrowed wins, and the person who lent loses. That is because the debt is repaid in dollars that buy less than they did when the debt was made. Now, here's the best part: Who is the biggest debtor in the country, or for that matter, in the world? Uncle Sam and the Ruling Class were winning, and they were winning at a pace that began threatening the "faith" part of the "full faith and credit of the United States." Long-term interest rates on US government debt skyrocketed as savers began to demand that they be paid for the risk they took in being paid back in dollars that didn't buy as much. The yield on the ten-year bond soared from 6.5 percent in 1976 to 16 percent just before Reagan took office in 1981. Something had to give.

The Federal Reserve began to raise rates sharply and began to focus on the supply of money in the economy. The rhetoric from the government and from the Federal Reserve was decidedly anti-inflationary. And the rate of inflation began to drop quickly. In early 1980, prices rose 2 percent in a single month—or more than 24 percent a year. But by the mid-1980s, the rate of price inflation had dropped to just 4 percent per year.

When we look back at this period, something strange happened, or didn't happen: price inflation dropped rapidly, but the Federal Reserve continued to expand its balance sheet (in other words, build up its bond holdings and issue money in return) at the same pace as it had been doing. Financial assets on the Fed's balance sheet roughly doubled from $94.6 billion in 1971 to $181.9 billion in 1981. They nearly doubled again in the next ten years, to $364.6 billion. The process of rapid monetary expansion continued unabated until 1999, when the Fed balance sheet listed $696.9 billion in assets. Even though there was no slowdown in the money machine, inflation began to relax. The 124 percent rise in prices in the decade after Nixon took us off the gold standard dropped to just 50 percent in the 1980s and 30 percent in 1990s. It turns out that when the price of goods doesn't go up as fast as money is being created, it doesn't mean that there isn't inflation; it just occurs in different sectors of the economy.

Where did all the money creation go? Even though the inflation rate for goods and services dropped sharply, assets such as houses and particularly stocks rose extremely rapidly. Between 1981 and 1991, stock prices (as measured by the Standard & Poor's 500) climbed 190 percent even though corporate profits over that same period increased only 105 percent. Between 1991 and 2001, stock prices soared an additional 217 percent, with corporate profits lagging behind at 67 percent. In fact, from 1997 up to their peak in early 2000, stocks surged more than 60 percent even while corporate profits were falling!

The evidence shows that the money being generated by the Federal Reserve went toward accelerating asset prices but not those of consumer-purchased goods. Why? At this point, it should be admitted that as smart as the Ruling Class and the economics profession might be, they really don't have an answer, although there are reasons to guess. Most important, the supply side of the economy expanded very rapidly in the twenty years after 1981. Deregulation of American enterprise was a cornerstone of President Reagan and continued right through President Clinton. Tax rates had come down sharply. At least as important was the very rapid expansion of the global workforce after the American victory in the Cold War. Workers from Russia, Eastern Europe, and particularly China were incorporated into the global trading system. World trade blossomed, competition rose, and the result was a restraint on the ability to pass through price increases on goods. New technologies arose in this environment, which brought us goods and services never before dreamed of—particularly in electronics and information technology—and the technological improvements brought us a rapid drop in the prices of services. When you increase the supply of goods and services, their price drops, other things being equal. So all of the extra money the Fed was creating could not push up prices of goods and services if their supplies were growing rapidly. Instead, the increase went into things not affected by supply—the price of assets.

In fact, this mismatch among consumer price inflation, money creation, and asset prices has gotten worse in the last few years. Between 2007 and 2014, the Federal Reserve has increased the amount of financial assets it holds by 379 percent, from just under $1 trillion to more than $4.5 trillion.[8] In the same time, the stock market has risen 42 percent, while consumer prices have increased just 14 percent. In fact, the Fed has stated its policy was to expand its balance sheet in order to drive up asset prices such as stocks, with the goal of increasing economic growth and encouraging inflation. The balance sheet rose by a huge amount, and stock prices did climb, but economic growth has failed to accelerate, and the rate of inflation has declined.

What developed was a series of asset price bubbles shown in figure 3. It shows the ratio of household wealth to income. This is usually a stable relationship, but it began to swing wildly in the last twenty-five years.

Figure 3. A Third Asset Price Bubble

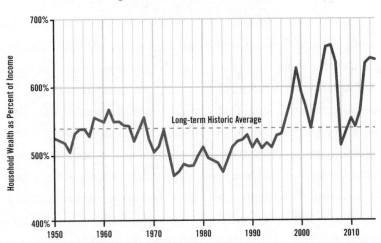

Source: Federal Reserve Flow of Funds, line 51 of Table B-101.

Each time asset prices rose too high, the bubble burst. Then at the bottom, as asset prices were crashing (as they did in stocks in 2000 and houses in 2008), the Fed rushed in to the rescue, cutting interest rates and trying to push more money into the economy. In the current bubble, it announced a policy known as quantitative easing, which the Fed said was deliberately geared toward increasing asset prices again. And the purpose of pushing up asset prices was to stimulate the economy and try to get inflation to start rising! In the process of doing this, the Federal Reserve has taken the size of its balance sheet from roughly $900 billion to more than $4.5 trillion—or $14,000 per person! This means that there is so much money sloshing around that it can't readily be used in the real economy, but instead pushes up the price of financial assets. People might choose to hold these assets, because if the money were ever to enter the real economy, inflation would likely result, and it would be better to hold inflation hedges that might include assets such as stocks and real estate. In truth, we have no idea how this will end—we are in uncharted territory. And many people are concerned that an unelected group of individuals have embarked on a bold and unprecedented experiment without knowing for sure how it will work out.

Lessons from This History

A strong case can be made that some reform is needed, but what kind? First, neither we nor the Fed are sure what happens when money is created; history shows that the effects varied over time. From 1933 to 1981, the answer seemed clear: prices of goods and services soared. Then a shift in focus occurred during the 1980s. And from 1991 to the present, inflation in goods and services has continuously come down. Instead, prices of assets such as stocks and housing have risen rapidly, and then collapsed, and then begun to rise again. When these prices rise, they do not count in our usual "inflation" measures. And what is particularly strange, the lowest inflation in a half century occurred in just the last few years, just when the Fed balance sheet rose fivefold! At a minimum, this suggests that we need to be quite modest about what we know and how to fix it.

Criticisms That Aren't Solutions

This modesty should apply to both current policy makers and those pushing reform. For example, some people have suggested that we need to reform the Fed by forcing it to obey a "rule" when it comes to monetary policy. Some have suggested a price rule or an inflation rule. Some have suggested a formula that balances inflation and unemployment. But what good is a rule—particularly one based on prices and inflation—if history offers no guide to the relationship between Fed policy in the short term and its effect on inflation? A rule that might work at one point in time might prove disastrously inaccurate and inappropriate at another.

Another popular idea is to "audit" the Fed. It is not clear what this means. Every expense of the Fed is already audited extensively by both internal auditors and external auditors. The composition of the Fed balance sheet is disclosed fully and is audited. Most of the proposals for auditing the Fed involve having the Government Accountability Office audit the reasons why Federal Reserve governors and other decision makers made the decisions they did and how effective those decisions were. This is also known as "second guessing." The question is, "If you knew then what you know now, would you have made the same decision?" Of course not. Policy making always involves uncertainty. Little would be gained and time would be lost. And the most predictable effect would be to shift decision makers toward a cover-their-you-know-what mind-set in which they never wanted to take bold action for fear they would be second-guessed later.

Bubbles are politically very popular—until they burst. When things are going up, people like to brag about how much a stock they bought has risen, or about how the price of their home has increased. Of course, no one talks about how this was caused by the Fed printing money. No, it is always because the person talking had a particularly great insight into stock selection or home price appreciation. The Federal Open Market Committee (FOMC)* knew that it was causing a bubble as early as 1996.[9] It did nothing, but Chairman Alan Greenspan gave a speech in which he talked about "irrational exuberance." With money exploding, the stock market laughed and danced to ever-higher highs. The political establishment certainly didn't want this to end. President Clinton was faced with impeachment; his popularity depended on a booming stock market and the spending power it produced. It was no different in the housing bubble. Home appreciation is great when two-thirds of all families and roughly 80 percent of all voters own their own homes. The word went out from Washington policy makers and Wall Street houses alike: "Home prices can only go up!" The Ruling Class have a similar interest in the current bubble as well. The Fed is financing government spending and pushing asset prices ever higher. Imagine how popular incumbents would be if we didn't have quantitative easing to deliberately push household wealth up to new records!

The "End the Fed!" cry is the most curious. What would you replace it with? Should Congress decide on interest rates and money supply targets? What about Bitcoin? Do you really trust this computer algorithm and the people who design it but keep it secret? Didn't we want to get away from secretive institutions? The only real substitute if we end the Fed is to go back to an inelastic currency, with the risks of sudden crashes like we had at the end of the nineteenth century and in the early twentieth century.

A Modest, but Radical, Proposal

The Fed is a useful creation, but it is far from omniscient. It is better to have an elastic currency than not. It is better to have a lender of last

---

*The FOMC is the main policy making body of the Federal Reserve. It meets eight times a year to set interest rates and make other policy decisions that affect the money supply and economic conditions in America.

resort than not. But the Fed cannot be expected to do things that are not within its ken. And frankly, it doesn't really know much for certain about the intermediate-term relationship between money creation and prices or economic performance. Its forecasting record in the last few years has been dismal, continually overestimating the positive effects of its actions on growth and continuously underestimating the pace at which the labor market would tighten. If there is any lesson for the Ruling Class in how they have run monetary policy, it is that modesty is the best approach.

The most effective change we could make would be to recognize these limitations. Continue to appoint smart people to the board to figure out what the economy might need, but don't put all the pressure on them to get it right, because they won't. Instead, limit their ability to get it really wrong by giving the American people a choice. There is nothing like competition (or the potential for competition) to focus the mind of the businessman and to improve the quality of the marketplace. We need to enshrine the concept of competition in the provision of money into the system. Specifically, we need to pass a constitutional amendment that protects people's right to use something other than Federal Reserve notes (Fed-printed dollars) both as a store of wealth and as a medium of exchange:

"Congress shall pass no law nor shall any branch of government issue any regulation restricting the right to hold any tangible asset or any currency issued by any country with which the United States is not at war or engaged in a similar congressionally authorized state of conflict; nor shall there be any restriction on the ability to make contracts or settle debts in the same; nor any restriction on the courts from enforcing such contracts."

In plain English, if you want to hold or write a contract in gold, or Bitcoin, or yen, you may do so. Of course, we can do so now, but the government can change that at a moment's notice, as Roosevelt did in 1933 by executive decree. And we didn't have that right for the next forty-one years. All this amendment would do is to prevent that from happening again.

This stops the government—and the Federal Reserve—from getting us too far in over our heads. If too much debt is issued or if too much money is created, we simply stop using it and start paying for things and making contracts in terms of something in which we have faith. Remember, all of the debt and all of the money are based solely on the full faith and credit of the United States. If that faith is lost, it is all worthless. This amendment might not prevent that from happening, but it might prevent the government from taking the people down with it.

More to the point, it would concentrate the minds of the Federal Reserve and political decision makers on the need to behave responsibly. They cannot simply use money creation to solve their problems and compel us to put up with it. In my experience, decision makers then take that into account in their earlier decisions. The seemingly endless resorting to quantitative easing—printing more money—would be far less attractive if there were an obvious alternative to holding the freshly printed (if potentially worthless) paper.

What would the Ruling Class say to such an amendment? First, they would say it is unnecessary, as we Americans can do that now. When pressed, they might have to add that *of course* they would never take away that right, as Roosevelt did. But if you believe them when they say that, then heaven help you. Second, they would say, "Gold is a barbarous relic." This is a quote of the twentieth-century British economist John Maynard Keynes that has been recited by many Ruling Class economists ever since. Of course, they are right, from their perspective. Gold and similar assets are barbarous because they limit the freedom of action by the Ruling Class. If people can hold and transact business using any medium they want, then the rulers' ability to force us to take the paper they have made worthless is gone.

But if they object too loudly, then one might ask them why they object to giving people the constitutional right to do what they can do now. And then we will know what their plan really is. I cannot imagine any chair of the Fed objecting to this amendment, especially given the alternatives now being considered.

The amendment is an alternative to proposals now out there. But it is one that is philosophically populist and operationally libertarian. It is populist because it puts a potential limit on an elite institution that is viewed with suspicion by a majority of the population. But it does not change their day-to-day operational efficiency, so we are not simply adding to ever-increasing complexity in government, playing one part of the Ruling Class against another. It is libertarian because it guarantees a constitutional power to the people. One suspects that at the writing of the Constitution, this right was assumed, since all manner of coins were in circulation, and people got to negotiate their value. But times have changed, and now this right needs to be enshrined. And it restores something that is now sadly lacking but vitally important: *faith* in liberty and our system of government.

CHAPTER 17

America Is a Cause, Not Just a Country

In a few years, Americans will celebrate the 250th anniversary of the Declaration of Independence. We will still be an independent country, but where will the ideals of liberty that accompanied the Declaration stand in 2026? America was founded on a principle that was quite different from those of other countries: that government was created to serve the people by protecting their rights. By contrast, most countries are founded on the principle of geography, and their people are merely incidental to the territory the ruler has acquired. That is what makes America a *cause* as well as a *country*. It represents a unique principle in how humans govern themselves.

Listen carefully to members of the progressive Ruling Class. They rarely speak admiringly of the cause of liberty, but say instead that America should emulate the forms of government that are common in Europe. They admire the power of European governments and the cradle-to-grave care those governments provide their people, along with the higher taxes that pay for that care. To them, America should be more like Denmark or Sweden, where the relationship between government and the governed is quite different.

In the 1830s, a Frenchman named Alexis de Tocqueville was sent by his government to tour America and identify how Americans were different. He reported back, "There are some nations in Europe whose inhabitants think of themselves in a sense as colonists, indifferent to the fate of the place they live in. The greatest changes occur in their country without their cooperation. . . . They think that such things have nothing to do with them, that they belong to a powerful stranger called 'the government'. . . . They are so divorced from their own interests that even when their own security and that of their children is finally compromised, they do not seek to avert the danger themselves but cross their arms and wait for the nation as a whole to come to their aid."[1]

That was not the case in America, where people took initiative and did not wait for government and certainly did not expect its permission before helping themselves.

De Tocqueville also predicted that, over time, America risked the same fate, not brought about by the emergence of a tyrant but through the tyranny of government complexity and the resulting tyranny of a bureaucracy. "Society will develop a new kind of servitude which covers the surface of society with a network of complicated rules, through which the most original minds and the most energetic characters cannot penetrate. It does not tyrannise but it compresses, enervates, extinguishes, and stupefies a people, till each nation is reduced to nothing better than a flock of timid and industrious animals, of which the government is the shepherd."

That is the fate that awaits us if we continue much longer on our current path. For the past century, the constitutional protections of our liberty have been eroded by a Ruling Class that have amassed power for themselves. They did so by claiming that our new "complex" society could not be run under the rules on which the country was founded.

The representative institutions of a democratic society simply did not have the necessary knowledge or judgment. Instead, committees of "experts" were needed. Government itself was not to be limited in its scope, but unlimited. The logic was that something an individual might do entirely privately might somehow have an effect on the nation as a whole and therefore had to be regulated. Finally, the rule of law no longer required the vote of the Congress, which was vested with all legislative powers, but instead could be pilfered as time passed by executive decree.

So as de Tocqueville said, we are gradually being reduced to "a flock of timid and industrious animals of which the government is the shepherd." Timid animals do not produce a vibrant society or economy. It shows. We have just had the slowest economic recovery following any recession in our history. This is despite the fact that usually steep contractions are followed by rapid recoveries. Real living standards are declining. Even the willingness to participate in the economy is diminishing. Labor force participation rates are down to levels not seen since the 1970s, before the Reagan Revolution increased incentives to work, save, invest, and start new businesses.

We are a less united society than ever before. The Ruling Class hold onto the reins of power by intentionally dividing us. They constantly emphasize differences based on race, or gender, or sexual orientation, or religion, or national origin. These are superficial differences that camouflage the fact that we are all in this together. America is still the greatest land of opportunity the world has ever known, where someone from any background can get ahead. But those opportunities are being eroded, since the goal of the "shepherd" is to reduce us to the status of docile beasts. Government is actively compressing, enervating, extinguishing, and stupefying us with complex rules, taxes, and obligations.

The failure of this vision is also shown by our standing in the world. In 2008, we were not popular. We were playing the role of global policeman and were resented for it. So we gave up that role. But today there is not a single country on the planet in which America is more respected or admired than we were in 2008. Instead, we are taken as patsies, pushed into a full-fledged retreat. And as we have retreated, we seem to feel the need to apologize for our existence. We are even warned against speaking the truth about what is happening lest we "offend" others. For example, we are told not to name the Islamic extremists for what they are out of fear of being seen to criticize Islam. Speaking the truth by calling these people what they are is not an attack on Islam but on the extremists who are corrupting that faith.

Similarly, our current government shrinks in other areas of foreign policy. It fails to criticize Russian president Vladimir Putin for the thug he is, instead insisting that it is putting Putin in a corner; that its strategy is prevailing. Again, the facts don't seem to matter. First it was Crimea, which our government claimed at the time "would not stand." It has. Then it was western Ukraine. Then Syria. The language of our government is designed not to speak the truth but to hide its failings in order to protect itself from domestic political criticism.

The truth is that the progressive Ruling Class do not view America as a cause, only a country. Therefore, they feel little compulsion to protect the cause of liberty that America stands for. Do not expect a robust defense of American interests from them unless they themselves are threatened. Their purpose is not to protect our liberty or the cause of liberty around the world, but to ensure their own positions of power.

That power is increasingly well entrenched. As we saw in chapter 5, they themselves acknowledge their control of the news media, of the entertainment industry, and of academia. These are the commanding heights of "thought leadership" from which they define the terms of debate and censor the information we receive so that we get only the news that fits their tint. They believe that they are naturally entitled to these positions because of their supposedly superior intelligence.

This all seems to paint a bleak picture.

But the public is now on to their game. In a May 2015 survey, voters said they do not trust the political coverage provided by the news media by a margin of 61 percent to 21 percent. Needless to say, people who said they were strong supporters of Obama "trusted" the coverage three times as much as those who were not strong supporters, and self-identified liberals and Democrats were also the most trusting. But even among those groups, there is widespread suspicion of the coverage. And while voters think overwhelmingly that wealthy people have too much influence on politics, when asked whether campaign cash or media bias was the bigger problem, they chose media bias 48 percent to 44 percent.[2]

The final section of this book began with the view that there is a clear majority for liberty in the country. It then suggested ways that majority could be turned into a movement that could defeat the Ruling Class at the ballot box. But there is another, much longer-term battle than the contest between the rulers and liberty in any particular election. It is reclaiming the narrative on the value of increasing liberty over the long term. The Ruling Class will always find an excuse for reducing our liberties. All of their promises will sound well intentioned, but their proposals all have one thing in common: more power for the government and themselves; less freedom for the people they govern. Our narrative must focus on the unique values that increasing liberty offers everyone.

The Beacon of Liberty

The best protection against oppression is to constantly stress the value of increasing our liberty. We in America have a unique obligation to liberty because of how and why we were founded as a country. People all over the world admire us for that. When asked what country people would most like to move to, America tops the list. A 2012 Gallup survey[3] from around the world determined that 640 million people would like to leave the country in which they live now. Of these, 150 million wanted to move to America, more than three times as many as the United Kingdom and Canada (second and third on the list, respectively), more than five times as many as Germany, and twenty-five times as many as Sweden. Denmark failed to make the fifteen-country list.

Sweden and Germany provide greater material help to people

emigrating there than does America, so the motivation to move is not based simply on the generosity of the welcome. It is based on what follows that initial welcome. Immigrants, by definition, do not want to sit back and take what life—and government—gives them. It takes a lot of motivation to want to move to a different country. People want to come to America for the opportunity it offers: the chance to make one's own way in life. This is quite different from starting one's journey in a new land in as high a position as possible. Liberty therefore has a global appeal, one that trumps mere material well-being, and one that America stands for. We therefore need to take advantage of this in order to change the narrative on immigration to one that links immigration and what the Founding Fathers called "the blessings of Liberty."

The Ruling Class claim that only they support immigration. In fact, what they want is unlimited immigration; more people dependent on the government, more of what de Tocqueville called "docile beasts" that they can shepherd and will ultimately turn into voters. As a country, we don't benefit from people that want to be shepherded; we benefit from people who want to pursue the blessings of liberty. They possess the energy and determination to drive our country forward; they are the people who will be pulling the cart, not riding in the back. So part of the narrative of liberty should include the fact that a country where people want to go for freedom has a real advantage—and can, if it wants, pick and choose who it admits (since it can't admit everyone), with a focus on those who will help build our economy and our society. America is a beacon of liberty, so we should put those who are attracted to that beacon at the front of the line.

The Crucible of Prosperity

America holds just 5 percent of the world's people. It produces 22 percent of the world's output. Its citizens have about one-third of all the wealth on the planet—$85 trillion out of a total of $250 trillion. We are also the most charitable, according to the World Giving Index.[4]

Those supposed model countries that progressives cite—Denmark and Sweden—are ranked between eighteenth and fortieth, depending on the year. Access to key signs of consumer well-being are also high in the United States. Ownership of major household appliances is almost universal. Even automobile ownership is widespread. More than 85 percent of US households have a car, and 63 percent own a home.[5] We achieved world-class leadership in the basic indicators of prosperity decades ago. For example, there were 430 and 500 cars per 1,000 people in Denmark and Sweden, respectively, in 2010. America hit those levels in the 1960s.[6]

None of this is the result of the fact that we call ourselves "Americans." It is because of what the Founding Fathers called the blessings of liberty. When individuals are allowed to pursue their own dreams, they can accomplish amazing things. So our success is not due to America the *country* but to America the *cause*. We need to stress this and to remind ourselves and our countrymen that our prosperity cannot be taken for granted. It was earned through the hard work, creativity, and entrepreneurial spirit that liberty encourages.

Many in the Ruling Class say that we need to imitate others to get our country going again—though the countries they point to are hardly models of success at the moment. But the simple truth is that America is not going to succeed by acting more German than the Germans, more French than the French, or more Chinese than the Chinese. We are going to succeed by making the most of what makes us American. And that is our liberty.

A Force for Peace

Americans have never been eager to get involved in foreign entanglements. And when we have, we have not done so to pursue imperial status. After World War II, for example, we set the countries that we had defeated back on the path to freedom and prosperity. Though it is fashionable among progressives to assault America's role in the world, one cannot find in the history of the world defeated countries that have been treated more generously than Germany and Japan were by America. In fact, although some claimed that the Iraq War was just "for oil," the fact is that we did not claim the oil fields of Iraq. We turned them over to the Iraqi government, which in turn auctioned them off, and the winner was the Chinese! So it is certainly possible to criticize American decision making, but not for an excess of self-interest. Quite the opposite, we have been a model of generosity. Following World War II, we gave $13 billion to Europe under the Marshall Plan to assist in rebuilding.[7] That was about 5 percent of our total GDP at the time, equivalent to giving away $850 billion today.

The rationale for this behavior can also be found in our belief in liberty. As noted early on, one cannot live in a world claiming one's own liberty when others are denied that same right. Even after the Civil War tore apart the nation and threatened the very fabric of our political existence, President Lincoln proclaimed, "With malice toward none, with charity for all."[8]

The progressive Ruling Class do their best to denigrate the history of America and our belief in liberty. But the facts tell a radically different story. No nation on earth has ever been as much of a force for good as America. No governing political philosophy has ever been more generous toward others and more crucial in the advancement of humankind than the liberty proclaimed by our Founding Fathers.

We have no reason to be shy about the cause we believe in. And we must not be. We are a beacon for others, a crucible of prosperity, and a force for peace and the betterment of mankind. No other philosophy, not Socialism, or Progressivism, or any others built on Ruling Class empowerment, can claim the same. They have nothing to offer but empty promises built on the quicksand of ever-increasing demands on the resources, energy, and freedom of the rest of us. Theirs is a story of failure. Ours is a story that can inspire. It is the model of a win-win society and world, not the zero-sum game of endless redistribution that progressives believe in. Liberty is about the advancement of mankind—all of the humans on this planet. We, not the Ruling Class, have the moral high ground. We need to go forth believing in ourselves and our cause because we have truth on our side. Reminding the world of that fact is going to be the key to permanently breaking the grip of the Ruling Class on the levers of power.

ACKNOWLEDGMENTS

I am deeply grateful to all who contributed their diverse sets of talents toward helping me to write *Conspiracies of the Ruling Class*. I would like to thank Joe Ricketts for all of the many things he has done to make this book possible. His commitment to liberty and to America is second to none.

Nathan Zimnik has shown an amazing set of talents—one so wide that it has rekindled my faith in millennials and my hope for our nation's future.

Elizabeth Rennolds toiled through the production stage with her classically British stiff upper lip despite the travails of pregnancy.

Paul Zimnik and Christine Frates provided many timely insights as they read iterations of the book.

My colleagues at the Lindsey Group helped keep the company moving forward despite the demands of the book. Karolin Junnila did her usual brilliant organizing of the troops. Barry Jackson contributed numerous political insights. Peter Boockvar offered his market thoughts. Mica DeShields kept us supplied continuously with whatever we needed to persevere.

There are many people on the production side to thank, especially at Simon & Schuster for its rapid turnaround and immense improvements.

Any errors and omissions that remained after their many fine efforts are my responsibility.

NOTES

Chapter 1: A History of Ruling in the Absence of Liberty

1. Carl Haub, "How Many People Have Ever Lived on Earth?," Population Reference Bureau, October 2011, www.prb.org/Publications/Articles /2002/HowManyPeopleHaveEverLivedonEarth.aspx.

2. See for example: Gunther Garbrecht, "Ancient Water Works—Lessons from History," in "Managing Our Fresh-Water Resources," Jacques Richardson, ed., special issue, *Impact of Science on Society*, no. 1 (1983): 5–16, http://unesdoc.unesco.org/images/0008/000851/085175eo.pdf. See also: Robert A. Fernea, *Shaykh and Effendi: Changing Patterns of Authority Among the El Shabana of Southern Iraq* (Cambridge, MA: Harvard University Press, 1970), for a sociological discussion of how these impacted political organization.

3. Karl A. Wittfogel, *Oriental Despotism: A Comparative Study of Total Power* (New Haven, CT: Yale University Press, 1957).

4. The Editors of *Encyclopaedia Britannica*, "Grand Canal," *Encyclopaedia Britannica*, March 19, 2014, www.britannica.com/topic/Grand-Canal -China.

5. "Great Wall of China," History Channel Online, A+E Networks 2010, www.history.com/topics/great-wall-of-china.

6. Janey Levy, *The Great Pyramid of Giza: Measuring Length, Area, Volume, and Angles* (New York: Rosen, 2005).

7. Zhixin Jason Sun, "Life and Afterlife in Early Imperial China," *American Journal of Archaeology* Online Museum Review, issue 113.3 (July 2009): www.ajaonline.org/sites/default/files/AJA1133_Sun.pdf. See also: "Mausoleum of the First Qin Emperor," United Nations Educational,

Scientific and Cultural Organization, World Heritage Convention, http://
whc.unesco.org/en/list/441.

8. John Roach, "Terra-Cotta Army Protects First Emperor's Tomb," *National
Geographic,*   http://science.nationalgeographic.com/science/archaeology
/emperor-qin.

9. Marcus Aurelius, *Meditations,* trans. Robin Hard, intro. and notes by
Christopher Gill (Ware, UK: Wordsworth Editions Limited, 1997),
170.

10. Niccolò Machiavelli, *Discourses on Livy,* trans. Harvey C. Mansfield and
Nathan Tarcov (Chicago: The University of Chicago Press, 1996).

11. Edward Gibbon, *The History of the Decline and Fall of the Roman Empire,*
vol. 1 (London: J.O. Robinson, 1830).

12. See for example Eric Hines, *A Conservative's Treatise on American Government: A Brief Discussion of What a Government, Subordinate to the Sovereign People, Must Do* (Bloomington, IN: Xlibris, 2012), 110 n. 28.

Chapter 2: Liberty: The Real Meaning of 1776

1. Howard Zinn, "A Kind of Revolution," chap. 5 in *A People's History of the
United States* (New York: Harper & Row, 1980).

2. Mary Beth Norton, et al., "Forging a National Republic, 1776–1789,"
chap. 7 in *A People and a Nation: A History of the United States,* brief
9th ed. (Boston: Cengage Learning, 2012). See also: "Pop Culture: 1790,"
US Census Bureau, www.census.gov/history/www/through_the_decades
/fast_facts/1790_fast_facts.html.

3. Adam Smith, *An Inquiry into the Nature and Causes of the Wealth of Nations,* bk. 4, chap. 2 (London: W. Strahan and T. Cadell, 1776).

4. John Locke, "Of Paternal Power," chap. 6 in bk. 2 of *Two Treatises of Government* (London: Awnsham Churchill, 1690).

5. Ibid., "Of the State of Nature," chap. 2, sec. 6, bk. 2.

6. Sheila L. Skemp, *The Making of a Patriot: Benjamin Franklin at the Cock-
pit* (New York: Oxford University Press, 2012).

7. Carl Van Doren, *Benjamin Franklin* (New York: Viking Press, 1938).

8. J. A. Leo Lemay, *Soldier, Scientist, and Politician, 1748–1757,* vol. 3 of *The
Life of Benjamin Franklin* (Philadelphia: University of Pennsylvania Press,
2008), 245.

9. Hugh P. Williamson, "John Adams: Counsellor of Courage," *American
Bar Association Journal* vol. 54, no. 2 (February 1968): 148–51.

10. See for example: William Wemms and John Hodgson, *Trial of the British Soldiers of the 29th Regiment of Foot: For the Murder of Crispus Attucks [etc.]* (Boston: W. Emmons, 1824).

11. John Patrick Diggins, ed., *The Portable John Adams* (New York: Penguin Books, 2004).

12. Peter Andreas, *Smuggler Nation: How Illicit Trade Made America* (New York: Oxford University Press, 2013).

13. O. M. Dickerson, "John Hancock: Notorious Smuggler or Near Victim of British Revenue Racketeers?," *Mississippi Valley Historical Review* vol. 32, no. 4 (March 1946): 517–40.

14. John Hancock, "Boston Massacre Oration," March 5, 1774, ThisNation .com, www.thisnation.com/library/bostonmassacre.html.

15. Rush Limbaugh, "My Father's Speech—The Americans Who Risked Everything," *The Rush Limbaugh Show*, www.rushlimbaugh.com/pages /static/my_father_s_speech.

Chapter 3: Locking Down Liberty with a Constitution

1. James Madison to George Washington, December 5, 1789. Transcription: *The Writings of James Madison*, Gaillard Hunt, ed. (New York: G.P. Putnam's Sons, 1900–1910); Library of Congress, www.loc.gov/resource/mjm .04_0296_0298. See also: Neil H. Cogan, ed., "Amendment IX: Unenumerated Rights Clause," chap. 15. in *The Complete Bill of Rights: The Drafts, Debates, Sources, and Origins*, 2nd ed. (New York: Oxford University Press, 2015), 1065.

Chapter 4: The Ruling Class Rethink and Rebrand

1. Thomas Hobbes, *Leviathan or the Matter, Forme and Power of a Common Wealth Ecclesiasticall and Civil* (London: Andrew Crooke, 1651).

2. Margaret Sanger, "The Morality of Birth Control," speech first delivered November 18, 1921, at the Park Theatre in New York City, www.nyu.edu /projects/sanger/webedition/app/documents/show.php?sangerDoc=238 254.xml.

3. See for example Linda Gordon, "Depression," chap. 10 in *The Moral Property of Women. A History of Birth Control Politics in America* (Chicago: University of Illinois Press, 2002), 235.

4. George Orwell, *Nineteen Eighty-Four: A Novel* (London: Secker and Warburg, 1949).

5. George Orwell, chap. 10 in *Animal Farm: A Fairy Story* (London: Secker and Warburg, 1945).

6. Thomas Jefferson to Thomas Cooper, November 29, 1802, in *The Thomas Jefferson Papers, Series 1: General Correspondence, 1651–1827*, Library of Congress, http://memory.loc.gov/cgi-bin/ampage?collId=mtj1&fileName =mtj1page027.db&recNum=500. See also: "Wasting the labours of the people," quotation, Thomas Jefferson Foundation, www.monticello.org /site/jefferson/wasting-labours-people-quotation.

7. Bertrand Russell, "What Desires are Politically Important?" (Nobel lecture, delivered December 11, 1950), www.nobelprize.org/nobel_prizes/literature /laureates/1950/russell-lecture.html. See also: Horst Frenz, ed., *Nobel Lectures, Literature 1901–1967* (Amsterdam: Elsevier Publishing Company, 1969).

Chapter 5: The Progressive Superiority Complex

1. Satoshi Kanazawa, "Why Liberals Are More Intelligent Than Conservatives," *Psychology Today*, March 22, 2010.

2. Scott Jaschik, "Moving Further to the Left," Inside Higher Ed, October 24, 2012, www.insidehighered.com/news/2012/10/24/survey-finds-professors -already-liberal-have-moved-further-left.

3. Arthur C. Brooks, *Who Really Cares—America's Charity Divide: Who Gives, Who Doesn't, and Why It Matters* (New York: Basic Books, 2006).

4. George Will, "Conservatives More Liberal Givers," RealClearPolitics, March 27, 2008, www.realclearpolitics.com/articles/2008/03/conservatives _more_liberal_giv.html.

5. Noah Carl, "Verbal Intelligence Is Correlated with Socially and Economically Liberal Beliefs," *Intelligence* vol. 44 (May/June 2014): 142–48, www.gwern.net/docs/iq/2014-carl.pdf.

6. Jagadish Shukla, et al., "Letter to President Obama, Attorney General Lynch, and OSTP Director Holdren," September 1, 2015, web.archive .org/web/20150920110942/http://www.iges.org/letter/LetterPresidentAG .pdf. See also: Anthony Watts, "The 'RICO 20 letter' to Obama asking for prosecution of climate skeptics disappears [etc.]," Watts Up With That?, September 29, 2015, wattsupwiththat.com/2015/09/29/the-rico-20-letter -to-obama-asking-for-prosecution-of-climate-skeptics-disappears-from -shuklas-iges-website-amid-financial-concerns/.

Chapter 6: The Progressive Attack on the Constitution

1. *Federal Register: The Daily Journal of the United States Government,* "Federal Register Pages Published 1936–2014," www.federalregister.gov/uploads /2015/05/Federal-Register-Pages-Published-1936-2014.pdf.

2. Woodrow Wilson, *Constitutional Government in the United States,* intro. by Sidney A. Pearson, Jr. (New Brunswick, NJ: Transaction Publishers, 2006), 57. Originally published in 1908 by Columbia University Press.

3. Ronald J. Pestritto, ed., *Woodrow Wilson: The Essential Political Writings* (Lanham, MD: Lexington Books, 2005), 121.

4. Anne Marie Cammisa and Paul Christopher Manuel, "Of Ideas and Institutions: The Foundational Tension of American Democracy," chap. 1 in *The Path of American Public Policy: Comparative Perspectives* (Lanham, MD: Lexington Books, 2014), 15.

5. Woodrow Wilson, "Democracy and Efficiency," *Atlantic Monthly* vol. 87, no. 521 (March 1901), http://ebooks.library.cornell.edu/cgi/t/text/page viewer-idx?c=atla;cc=atla;rgn=full%20text;idno=atla0087-3;didno =atla0087-3;view=image;seq=297;node=atla0087-3%3A1;page=root ;size=100).

6. See for example: Catherine M. Lewis and J. Richard Lewis, ed., *Jim Crow America: A Documentary History* (Fayetteville, AR: University of Arkansas Press, 2009), xxi.

7. John Locke, "Of the Extent of the Legislative Power," chap. 11, sec. 141 in bk. 2 of *Two Treatises of Government* (London: Awnsham Churchill, 1690).

8. Lawrence B. Lindsey, *The Growth Experiment: How the New Tax Policy Is Transforming the U.S. Economy* (New York: Basic Books, 1990), 21–23.

9. See for example: Peter Collier and David Horowitz, *The Roosevelts: An American Saga* (New York: Simon & Schuster, 1994).

10. See for example: Conrad Black, *Franklin Delano Roosevelt: Champion of Freedom* (New York: PublicAffairs, 2003), and also, "Franklin D. Roosevelt Biography," Franklin D. Roosevelt Presidential Library and Museum, www.fdrlibrary.marist.edu/education/resources/pdfs/fdr_biography.pdf.

11. Jonathan Alter, *The Defining Moment: FDR's Hundred Days and the Triumph of Hope* (New York: Simon & Schuster, 2007), 143.

12. James M. Landis, *The Administration Process* (New Haven, CT: Yale University Press, 1938), 1–2.

13. "Obama on Super Tuesday: 'Our Time Has Come,'" *CQ Transcripts Wire, Washington Post,* February 6, 2008, www.washingtonpost.com/wp-dyn /content/article/2008/02/06/AR2008020600199.html.

14. Robert Barnes, "Supreme Court Rebukes Obama on Recess Appointments," *Washington Post*, June 26, 2014, www.washingtonpost.com /politics/supreme-court-rebukes-obama-on-recess-appointments/2014 /06/26/e5e4fefa-e831-11e3-a86b-362fd5443d19_story.html.

15. "President Barack Obama's State of the Union Address," White House– Office of the Press Secretary, January 28, 2014, www.whitehouse.gov/the -press-office/2014/01/28/president-barack-obamas-state-union-address.

16. Louise M. Slaughter, "A Democrat's View from the House: Senate Bill Isn't Health Reform," CNN, December 23, 2009, www.cnn.com/2009 /OPINION/12/23/slaughter.oppose.senate.bill.

Chapter 7: The Ruling Class Have Failed in Reducing Inequality

1. Carmen DeNavas-Walt and Bernadette D. Proctor, *Income and Poverty in the United States: 2014—Current Population Reports* (Washington, DC: US Census Bureau, 2015), www.census.gov/content/dam/Census/library /publications/2015/demo/p60-252.pdf.

2. "Supplemental Nutrition Assistance Program (SNAP)," United States Department of Agriculture Food and Nutrition Service, www.fns.usda.gov /snap/short-history-snap.

3. U.S. Department of Commerce, Bureau of Economic Analysis, "Table 2.1. Personal Income and Its Disposition," National Income and Product Accounts Tables, www.bea.gov/iTable/iTable.cfm?ReqID=9&step= 1#reqid=9&step=3&isuri=1&903=58. Historical series can be found at www.bea.gov/iTable/iTable.cfm?ReqID=9&step=1#reqid=9&step=3&is uri=1&903=58.

4. Kate Pinard, "Undistributed profits with inventory valuation and capital consumption adjustments," Table 11. Corporate Profits: Level and Percent Change, Bureau of Economic Analysis, U.S. Department of Commerce, www.bea.gov/newsreleases/national/gdp/2015/pdf/gdp3q15_2nd.pdf.

5. Data prepared by Food Research & Action Center, "Supplemental Nutrition Assistance Program: Number of Persons Participating—One Month Change," data as of September 4, 2015, http://frac.org/wp-content/uploads /2011/01/snapdata2015_jun.pdf. See also: http://frac.org/reports-and -resources/snapfood-stamp-monthly-participation-data.

6. Data collected by the Centers for Medicare & Medicaid Services of the Department of Health and Human Services, "Medicaid & CHIP: September 2015 Monthly Applications, Eligibility Determinations and Enrollment Report," released November 30, 2015, www.medicaid.gov/medicaid

-chip-program-information/program-information/downloads/september
-2015-enrollment-report.pdf.

7. Regular survey conducted by the US Census Bureau, "Survey of Income
   and Program Participation," Economic Characteristics of Households in
   the United States, Table 2: People By Receipt of Benefits from Selected
   Programs: Monthly Averages, www.census.gov/programs-surveys/sipp/pub
   lications/tables/hsehld-char.html.

8. Regular survey conducted by the US Census Bureau, "Historical Income
   Tables: Households," Table H-12: Household by Number of Earners by
   Median and Mean Income, www.census.gov/hhes/www/income/data/his
   torical/household/?cssp=SERP.

9. Elaine Maag, C. Eugene Steuerle, Ritadhi Chakravarti, and Caleb
   Quakenbush, "How Marginal Tax Rates Affect Families at Various Levels
   of Poverty," *National Tax Journal* vol. 65, no. 4 (December 2012): 759–82,
   www.ntanet.org/NTJ/65/4/ntj-v65n04p759-82-how-marginal-tax-rates.pdf.

10. Melissa S. Kearney and Lesley J. Turner, "Giving Secondary Earners a
    Tax Break: A Proposal to Help Low- and Middle-Income Families," discus-
    sion paper 2013-07, The Hamilton Project, December 2013, http://www
    .hamiltonproject.org/papers/giving_secondary_earners_a_tax_break.

11. William G. Gale, Melissa S. Kearney, and Peter R. Orszag, "Would a Sig-
    nificant Increase in the Top Tax Rate Substantially Alter Income Inequal-
    ity?," Brookings Institution, September 28, 2015.

Chapter 8: The Ruling Class Have Mismanaged America's Finances

1. "The Debt to the Penny and Who Holds It," TreasuryDirect, accessed December 26, 2015, www.treasurydirect.gov/NP/debt/current.

2. *Quarterly Report on Federal Reserve Balance Sheet Developments* (Washington, DC: Board of Governors of the Federal Reserve, November 2015),
   www.federalreserve.gov/monetarypolicy/files/quarterly_balance_sheet
   _developments_report_201511.pdf.

3. *Treasury Bulletin* (Washington, DC: Department of the Treasury, Bureau
   of the Fiscal Service, December 2015), www.fiscal.treasury.gov/fsreports
   /rpt/treasBulletin/b2015_4.pdf.

4. Compiled by Christopher Chantrill, "US Government Revenue in Recent
   Decades," www.usgovernmentrevenue.com/recent_revenue.

5. *The Budget and Economic Outlook: 2015 to 2025* (Washington, DC: Congress of the United States Congressional Budget Office, January 2015),
   www.cbo.gov/publication/49892.

6. *The 2015 Long-Term Budget Outlook* (Washington, DC: Congress of the United States Congressional Budget Office, June 2015), www.cbo.gov/pub lication/50250.

7. "Federal Unfunded Liabilities," USDebtClock, a continuously updated site, www.usdebtclock.org. See also: Liquin Liu, Andrew J. Rettenma-ier, and Thomas R. Saving, "How Much Does the Federal Government Owe?," National Center for Policy Analysis, Policy Report no. 338, June 2012, http://www.ncpa.org/pdfs/st338.pdf.

8. Michael D. Tanner, "Medicare Social Security Tabs Coming Due," re-print from March 2015 issue of *Reason*, CATO Institute, www.cato.org /publications/commentary/medicare-social-security-tabs-coming-due.

9. Bradford Richardson, "Ex-GAO Head: US Debt Is Three Times More Than You Think," *Briefing Room* (blog), TheHill.com, November 7, 2015, http://thehill.com/blogs/blog-briefing-room/news/259476-ex-gao-head-us -debt-is-three-times-more-than-you-think.

10. Data compiled by the Federal Reserve Bank of St. Louis, "Federal Surplus or Deficit as Percent of Gross Domestic Product," FRED Economic Data, https://research.stlouisfed.org/fred2/series/FYFSGDA188S.

11. *A New Era of Responsibility: Renewing America's Promise* (Washington, DC: Office of Management and Budget, 2009), www.whitehouse.gov/sites /default/files/omb/assets/fy2010_new_era/A_New_Era_of_Responsibil ity2.pdf.

12. *Budget of the US Government: Fiscal Year 2011* (Washington, DC: Of-fice of Management and Budget, 2010), www.whitehouse.gov/sites/default /files/omb/budget/fy2011/assets/budget.pdf.

13. *Budget of the US Government: Fiscal Year 2012* (Washington, DC: Office of Management and Budget, 2011), www.whitehouse.gov/files/documents /budget_2012.pdf.

14. Lisa Mataloni, "Gross Domestic Product: Third Quarter 2015," Bureau of Economic Analysis, U.S. Department of Commerce, November 24, 2015, www.bea.gov/newsreleases/national/gdp/2015/pdf/gdp3q15_2nd.pdf.

Chapter 9: The Ruling Class Have Earned an F in Education

1. Marie C. Stetser and Robert Stillwell, "Public High School Four-Year On-Time Graduation Rates and Event Dropout Rates. School Years 2010–11 and 2011–12," National Center for Education Statistics, U.S. Department of Education, April 2014, http://nces.ed.gov/pubs2014/2014391.pdf.

2. "Programme for International Student Assessment (PISA)," Organization for Economic Cooperation and Development (OECD), Results from PISA 2012, http://www.oecd.org/pisa/keyfindings/pisa-2012-results-overview.pdf, and also, www.oecd.org/unitedstates/PISA-2012-results-US.pdf.

3. "Paying for Education," chap. 4 in *Education at a Glance 2014*, Organization for Economic Cooperation and Development (OECD), November 2014, www.oecd-ilibrary.org/docserver/download/9614031ec017.pdf?expir es=1451517826&id=id&accname=guest&checksum=9B6C06879074FB 0C08A84FF584891C54, and also, http://www.oecd-ilibrary.org/docserver /download/9614031e.pdf?expires=1451518047&id=id&accname=guest& checksum=BF79634854A43862963A6E39948DE8E8.

4. Ellwood P. Cubberley, *The History of Education: Educational Practice and Progress Considered as a Phase of the Development and Spread of Western Civilization* (Boston: Houghton Mifflin, 1920), 690.

5. Bill Chappell, "Recent Teacher of the Year Resigns in Alabama over Certification Issues," NPR.org, October 31, 2015, www.npr.org/sections/the two-way/2015/10/31/453447309/recent-teacher-of-the-year-resigns-in-ala bama-over-certification-issues.

6. Originally credited to George Bernard Shaw, "He who can, does. He who cannot, teaches," George Bernard Shaw, *Man and Superman: A Comedy and a Philosophy* (Cambridge, MA: The University Press, 1903).

7. Carol Schwartz (Commission Chairman), "Prisoners of Time." The Education Commission of the States Education Reform Reprint Series, October 2005, reprint of the April 1994 report of the National Education Commission on Time and Learning, http://files.eric.ed.gov/fulltext /ED489343.pdf.

8. Data compiled by the Center for Responsive Politics, "Teachers Unions: Top Contributors," OpenSecrets.org, www.opensecrets.org/industries /indus.php?ind=l1300.

9. Data compiled by the Center for Responsive Politics, "Teachers Unions: Background," OpenSecrets.org, www.opensecrets.org/industries/back ground.php?ind=L1300.

10. MacIver News Service, "WEAC Membership Down More Than Half to Below 40,000," MacIver Institute, July 20, 2015, www.maciverinstitute .com/2015/07/weac-membership-continues-decline-blogger-says.

11. "Pay-to-Play Repeat for AFT and Hillary Clinton?," The Truth Campaign, compilation of data from the Clinton Foundation and the

American Federation of Teachers, July 31, 2015, http://edtruthcampaign.org/2015/07/31/pay-to-play-repeat-for-aft-and-hillary-clinton/.

12. Patrick Wolf, et al., "Evaluation of the DC Opportunity Scholarship Program: Impacts After Three Years," US Department of Education, March 2009, http://ies.ed.gov/ncee/pubs/20094050/pdf/20094050.pdf.

13. Rachel Mullen, "You Will Want to Watch What This Superintendent Says About Black Parents," The Political Insider, www.thepoliticalinsider.com/you-will-want-to-watch-what-this-superintendent-says-about-black-parents.

14. James P. Kelly and Benjamin Scafidi, "More Than Scores—An Analysis of Why and How Parents Choose Private School," The Friedman Foundation, November 2013, www.edchoice.org/wp-content/uploads/2015/07/More-Than-Scores.pdf#page=1.

15. "Education Spending Per Student by State," *Governing*, www.governing.com/gov-data/education-data/state-education-spending-per-pupil-data.html, compilation of US Census Bureau data available on http://factfinder.census.gov/faces/nav/jsf/pages/searchresults.xhtml?refresh=.

Chapter 10: America's Infrastructure Is Crumbling Under the Ruling Class

1. "Testimony of Secretary Jacob J. Lew before the Senate Finance Committee on the President's Budget for Fiscal Year 2015," U.S. Department of the Treasury, March 5, 2014, www.treasury.gov/press-center/press-releases/Pages/jl2309.aspx.

2. Hari Sreenivasan, "House Approves $325 Billion Transportation Bill, but Where Will Funding Come From?," PBS *Newshour*, November 7, 2015, www.pbs.org/newshour/bb/heres-325-billion-transportation-bill-fund.

3. Organization for Economic Cooperation and Development, "Transport—Infrastructure Investment," OECD Data, 2013, https://data.oecd.org/transport/infrastructure-investment.htm.

4. Ciara Browne, Attilio Di Battista, Thierry Geiger, Tania Gutknecht, "The Executive Opinion Survey: Capturing the Voice of the Business Community," survey conducted February—June 2014, World Economic Forum, http://reports.weforum.org/global-competitiveness-report-2014-2015/introduction-2/. See also: http://reports.weforum.org/global-competitiveness-report-2014-2015/rankings.

5. Gabriel Roth, "Liberating the Roads: Reforming US Highway Policy," Policy Analysis no. 538, CATO Institute, March 17, 2005, www.cato.org/publications/policy-analysis/liberating-roads-reforming-us-highway-policy.

6. Sarah Glassman, Michael Head, David G. Tuerck, and Paul Bachman, "The Federal Davis-Bacon Act: The Prevailing Mismeasure of Wages," The Heartland Institute, February 1, 2008, www.heartland.org/policy -documents/federal-davis-bacon-act-prevailing-mismeasure-wages.

7. Vince Vasquez, Dale Glaser, and W. Erik Bruvold, "Measuring the Cost of Project Labor Agreements on School Construction in California," National University System Institute for Policy Research, January 1, 2010, www.nusinstitute.org/assets/resources/pageResources/Measuring-the-Cost -of-Project-Labor-Agreements-on-School-Construction-in-California.pdf.

8. Benjamin Kabak, "Off the cuff, Horodniceanu quotes a high price for future SAS phases," 2nd Ave. Sagas, November 6, 2015, http://second avenuesagas.com/2015/11/06/off-the-cuff-horodniceanu-quotes-a-high-price -for-future-sas-phases.

9. Tanya Snyder, "Are Environmental Reviews to Blame for Infrastructure Project Delays?," StreetsBlog USA, February 15, 2011, http://usa.streetsblog .org/2011/02/15/are-environmental-reviews-to-blame-for-infrastructure -project-delays.

10. Petra Todorovich and Daniel Schned, *Getting Infrastructure Going: Expediting the Environmental Review Process* (New York: NY-NJ-CT Regional Plan Association, June 2012), www.rpa.org/library/pdf/RPA-Getting- Infrastructure-Going.pdf.

11. *Presidential Documents: Executive Order 13563 of January 18, 2011: Improving Regulation and Regulatory Review* (Washington, DC: Federal Register vol. 76, no. 14, January 21, 2011), www.gpo.gov/fdsys/pkg/FR-2011 -01-21/pdf/2011-1385.pdf.

12. "The Big Dig," Massachusetts Department of Transportation—Highway Division, www.massdot.state.ma.us/highway/TheBigDig/ProjectBack ground.aspx.

13. Ronald D. Utt, "The Bridge to Nowhere: A National Embarrassment" Web- Memo #889 on Federal Budget, The Heritage Foundation, October 20, 2005, www.heritage.org/research/reports/2005/10/the-bridge-to-nowhere -a-national-embarrassment.

Chapter 11: The Threat of the Second Amendment to the Ruling Class

1. Brakkton Booker, "After Planned Parenthood Shooting, Obama Again Calls for Action on Guns," NPR.org, December 1, 2015, www.npr.org /2015/12/01/457920110/after-planned-parenthood-shooting-obama-again -calls-for-action-on-guns.

2. Hina Shamsi, "The U.S. Government Is Putting Americans on Its No-Fly List on a Hunch," *Slate*, August 12, 2015, www.slate.com/articles/news_and _politics/politics/2015/08/the_u_s_government_is_putting_americans_on _its_no_fly_list_on_a_hunch_and.html.

3. Brian A. Reaves, *Special Report: Violent Felons in Large Urban Counties* (Washington, DC: US Department of Justice, Office of Justice Programs, July 2006), www.bjs.gov/content/pub/pdf/vfluc.pdf.

4. Marianne W. Zawitz, *Selected Findings: Guns Used in Crime* (Washington, DC: US Department of Justice, Office of Justice Programs, July 1995), http://www.bjs.gov/content/pub/pdf/GUIC.PDF.

5. "2013 Data Report: Homicide and Non-Fatal Shootings," Milwaukee Homicide Review Commission, March 18, 2014, http://city.milwaukee .gov/ImageLibrary/Groups/cityHRC/reports/2013AnnualReport-latest.pdf.

6. Katy Reckdahl, "NOPD Release of Murder Victims' Criminal Records Is Challenged," *Times-Picayune*, January 1, 2012, www.nola.com/crime /index.ssf/2012/01/nopd_release_of_murder_victims.html.

7. Kevin Johnson, "Criminals Target Each Other, Trend Shows," *USA Today*, August 31, 2007, http://usatoday30.usatoday.com/news/nation/2007-08-31 -criminal-target_N.htm.

8. Jo Craven McGinty, "New York Killers, and Those Killed, by Numbers," *New York Times*, April 28, 2006, www.nytimes.com/2006/04/28/ny region/28homicide.html?pagewanted=print.

9. *Deaths: Final Data for 2013* (Atlanta, GA: National Vital Statistics Report, Centers for Disease Control and Prevention, 2013), http://www.cdc.gov /nchs/data/nvsr/nvsr64/nvsr64_02.pdf. See also: CDC FastStats—All Injuries, http://www.cdc.gov/nchs/fastats/injury.htm.

10. Alexia Cooper and Erica L. Smith, "Homicide Trends in the United States, 1980–2008," U.S. Department of Justice, November 2011, www.bjs .gov/content/pub/pdf/htus8008.pdf.

11. Gary Kleck and Don B. Kates, "The Frequency of Defensive Gun Use: Evidence and Disinformation," chap. 6 in *Armed: New Perspectives on Gun Control* (Amherst, NY: Prometheus Books, 2001), 244–46.

12. "States with Weak Gun Laws and Higher Gun Ownership Lead Nation in Gun Deaths, New Data for 2013 Confirms," Violence Policy Center, January 29, 2015, www.vpc.org/press/states-with-weak-gun-laws-and-higher -gun-ownership-lead-nation-in-gun-deaths-new-data-for-2013-confirms.

13. Rahul Tandon, "In India, Gun Control Is Tight—but the Black Market Thrives," BBC Marketplace, February 18, 2013, www.marketplace.org

/2013/02/18/world/bbc-world-service/india-gun-control-tight-black-market
-thrives.

14. Nicholas Johnson, "The Progressive Gun-Control Charade: After Tragedy,
Politicians Glibly Call for Unworkable Reforms—Then Blame the 'Gun
Lobby' When They Fail," *Wall Street Journal*, October 25, 2015, www.wsj
.com/articles/the-progressive-gun-control-charade-1445806103.

15. Michael Planty and Jennifer L. Truman, *Special Report: Firearm Violence,
1993–2011* (Washington, DC: US Department of Justice, Office of Justice
Programs, May 2013), http://www.bjs.gov/content/pub/pdf/fv9311.pdf.

16. Samantha Lachman, "Hillary Clinton Says a National Gun Buyback Program Is 'Worth Considering,' " *Huffington Post*, October 16, 2015, www
.huffingtonpost.com/entry/hillary-clinton-gun-buybacks_56216331e4b02f
6a900c5d67.

17. Mark Antonio Wright, "Australia's 1996 Gun Confiscation Didn't Work—
and It Wouldn't Work in America," *National Review*, October 2, 2015,
www.nationalreview.com/article/425021/australia-gun-control-obama
-america.

Chapter 12: The Ruling Class and Your Property—Or Theirs?

1. "The Next Attorney General: One Area to Question Loretta Lynch Is Civil
Asset Forfeiture," *Wall Street Journal*, November 10, 2014, www.wsj.com
/articles/the-next-attorney-general-1415577638.

2. George Leef, "Loretta Lynch Has No Problem With Civil Asset
Forfeiture—And That's A Problem," *Forbes*, November 25, 2014, www
.forbes.com/sites/georgeleef/2014/11/25/loretta-lynch-has-no-problem
-with-civil-asset-forfeiture-and-thats-a-problem/. See also: "Long Island Forfeiture," Institute for Justice, http://ij.org/case/long-island-forfeiture/#en1a.

3. Gary Fields and John R. Emshwiller, "Court Rejects Justice Department
Seizure of Motel," *The Wall Street Journal*, January 25, 2013, www.wsj.com
/articles/SB10001424127887323539804578264242356172154.

4. Melissa Quinn, "After Having His Motel Seized by the Government, Victim
of Civil Asset Forfeiture Reflects on His Fight," The Daily Signal, May 7,
2015, http://dailysignal.com/2015/05/07/after-having-his-motel-seized-by
-the-government-victim-of-civil-asset-forfeiture-reflects-on-his-fight.

5. Jeff German, "Judge Cites Government 'Lack of Candor' in Returning
$167,000 Seized in Nevada," *Las Vegas Review-Journal*, June 24, 2015,
www.reviewjournal.com/news/las-vegas/judge-cites-government-lack
-candor-returning-167000-seized-nevada.

6. Pamela Brown, "Parents' House Seized After Son's Drug Bust," CNN, September 8, 2014, www.cnn.com/2014/09/03/us/philadelphia-drug-bust -house-seizure.

7. Nick Sibilla, "A Driver Had $50,000 Seized By A Nevada Cop [etc.]," *Forbes*, March 18, 2014, www.forbes.com/sites/instituteforjustice/2014/03/18/a -driver-had-50000-seized-by-a-nevada-cop-but-wasnt-charged-with-a -crime-now-hes-getting-his-money-back/. See also: *Tan Nguyen v. Humboldt County*, United States District Court for the District of Nevada, case no.: 3:14-cv-00039, February 12, 2014, http://d3n8a8pro7vhmx.cloud front.net/forfeiturereform/pages/81/attachments/original/1394247500 /Nguyen_Complaint.pdf?1394247500.

8. Steve Schultze, "Clarke Spent Asset Forfeitures on Workout Equipment, Horse Patrol," *Milwaukee Journal Sentinel*, September 28, 2012, www .jsonline.com/news/milwaukee/clarke-spent-asset-forfeitures-on-workout -equipment-horse-patrol-5j71hn1-171816481.html.

9. Nick Sibilla, "Cops Use Traffic Stops to Seize Millions from Drivers Never Charged with a Crime," *Forbes*, March 12, 2014, www.forbes.com/sites /instituteforjustice/2014/03/12/cops-use-traffic-stops-to-seize-millions -from-drivers-never-charged-with-a-crime.

10. John Burnett, "Sheriff Under Scrutiny over Drug Money Spending," NPR.org, June 18, 2008, www.npr.org/templates/story/story.php?story Id=91638378.

11. "The Sheriff's Stash: What Happens to All That Seized Money and Stuff?," *Economist*, July 10, 2008, www.economist.com/node/11707305?story_id =11707305.

12. Melissa Quinn, "The IRS Seized $107,000 from This North Carolina Man's Bank Account," The Daily Signal, May 11, 2015, http:// dailysignal.com/2015/05/11/the-irs-seized-107000-from-this-north -carolina-mans-bank-account-now-hes-fighting-to-get-it-back.

13. Dick M. Carpenter II and Larry Salzman, "Seize First, Question Later: The IRS and Civil Forfeiture," Institute for Justice, February 2015, http:// ij.org/images/pdf_folder/private_property/seize-first-question-later.pdf.

14. *Ratzlaf v. United States*, no. 92-1196, 510 US 135, Supreme Court of the United States, January 11, 1994, Legal Information Institute, Cornell University Law School, https://www.law.cornell.edu/supct/html/92-1196.ZO.html.

15. Larry Salzman and Robert Everett Johnson, "IRS Seizes First, Asks Questions Later, *Politico*, February 10, 2015, www.politico.com/magazine/story /2015/02/irs-civil-forfeiture-115089.

16. Ed O'Keefe and William Branigin, "Lois Lerner: 'I Have Not Done Anything Wrong,'" *Washington Post*, May 22, 2013, www.washingtonpost .com/politics/lois-lerner-invokes-fifth-amendment-in-house-hearing-on -irs-targeting/2013/05/22/03539900-c2e6-11e2-8c3b-0b5e9247e8ca_story .html.

17. Evan Perez, "DOJ Closes IRS Investigation with No Charges," CNN, October 23, 2015, www.cnn.com/2015/10/23/politics/lois-lerner-no-charges -doj-tea-party.

Chapter 13: The Pro-Liberty Majority

1. "Right Direction or Wrong Track?," Rasmussen Reports, December 7, 2015, www.rasmussenreports.com/public_content/politics/top_stories/right _direction_or_wrong_track.

2. "Voters Think Tax, Spending Cuts Work Best for Economy," Rasmussen Reports, March 19, 2015, www.rasmussenreports.com/public_content /business/taxes/march_2015/voters_think_tax_spending_cuts_work_best _for_economy.

3. "34% Prefer a Government With More Services, Higher Taxes," Rasmussen Reports, December 13, 2012, http://rasmussen.mugo.ca/public _content/archive/mood_of_america_archive/benchmarks/34_prefer_a _government_with_more_services_higher_taxes.

4. "50% Think More Government Regulation Means Less Fairness," Rasmussen Reports, April 25, 2012, www.rasmussenreports.com/public_content /politics/general_politics/april_2012/50_think_more_government_regula tion_means_less_fairness.

5. "Dave Leip's Atlas of U.S. Presidential Elections," http://uselectionatlas.org.

6. *National Election Pool*; Surveys conducted by Edison Research. See also: CNN Politics ElectionCenter, http://www.cnn.com/election/2012/results /race/president/.

7. Jeffrey M. Jones, "Americans Divided on Repeal of 2010 Healthcare Law," Gallup, February 27, 2012, www.gallup.com/poll/152969/americans -divided-repeal-2010-healthcare-law.aspx.

Chapter 14: Policy: Philosophically Populist, Operationally Libertarian

1. William McBride, "Fact Checking the Fact Checkers: Missing the Point on Tax Compliance," *The Tax Policy Blog*, Tax Foundation, December 14, 2011, http://taxfoundation.org/blog/fact-checking-fact-checkers-missing -point-tax-compliance.

2. Lawrence B. Lindsey, *The Growth Experiment Revisited: Why Lower, Simpler Taxes Really Are America's Best Hope for Recovery* (New York: Basic Books, 2013), 261.

3. "2010 Health Care Law Should Be . . . ," Races & Results: Exit Polls, CNN Politics ElectionCenter, http://www.cnn.com/election/2012/results/race /president/.

4. "Healthcare Law: Voters Still Want Changes to Obamacare," Rasmussen Reports, December 1, 2015, http://www.rasmussenreports.com/public _content/politics/current_events/healthcare/health_care_law.

5. Mary Lu Carnevale, "Obama: 'If You Like Your Doctor, You Can Keep Your Doctor,' " *Washington Wire* (blog), *Wall Street Journal*, June 15, 2009, http://blogs.wsj.com/washwire/2009/06/15/obama-if-you-like-your -doctor-you-can-keep-your-doctor.

6. Louis Jacobson, "Barack Obama Says That What He'd Said Was You Could Keep Your Plan 'If It Hasn't Changed Since the Law Passed,' " Politifact, November 6, 2013, www.politifact.com/truth-o-meter/statements/2013/ nov/06/barack-obama/barack-obama-says-what-hed-said-was-you-could -keep.

Chapter 15: Cementing the Restoration of Liberty and Democracy

1. *North Dakota v. US Environmental Protection Agency*, case no. 3:15-cv-00059-RRE-ARS document 70 (1-18), US District Court for the District of North Dakota, Southeastern Division, August 27, 2015, https://ago .mo.gov/docs/default-source/press-releases/2015/nd-district-court—grant -pi-motion.pdf?sfvrsn=2. See also: James M. Taylor, "EPA Defies Supreme Court, Proposes Unprecedented Water Regulations," The Heartland Institute, July 5, 2014, http://news.heartland.org/newspaper-article/2014/07/05/ epa-defies-supreme-court-proposes-unprecedented-water-regulations.

2. *Solid Waste Agency of Northern Cook County v. US Army Corp of Engineers*, no. 99-1178, 531 US 159, Supreme Court of the United States, January 9, 2001, Legal Information Institute, Cornell University Law School, https://www.law.cornell.edu/supct/html/99-1178.ZS.html. See also: Oyez–IIT Chicago-Kent College of Law for summary, https://www .oyez.org/cases/2000/99-1178.

3. FCC Chairman Tom Wheeler, et al., *In the Matter of Protecting and Promoting the Open Internet* (Washington, DC: Federal Communications Commission, March 12, 2015), https://apps.fcc.gov/edocs_public/attach match/FCC-15-24A1.pdf.

4. "Senate and House Seniority List—114th Congress," *Roll Call*, www.roll
   call.com/politics/houseseniority.html.

5. "Party Divisions of the House of Representatives, 1789–Present," History,
   Art & Archives, United States House of Representatives, http://history
   .house.gov/Institution/Party-Divisions/Party-Divisions/.

6. "Party Divisions in the Senate, 1789–Present," Senate History, United
   States Senate, www.senate.gov/history/partydiv.htm.

7. *Federal Workforce: Improved Supervision and Better Use of Probationary
   Periods Are Needed to Address Substandard Employee Performance*, Report
   to Chairman, Committee on Homeland Security and Governmental Affairs, US Senate (Washington, DC: US Government Accountability Office, February 6, 2015), http://www.gao.gov/assets/670/668339.pdf.

8. Sheryl Gay Stolberg, "Future of an Aging Court Raises Stakes of Presidential Vote," *New York Times*, June 27, 2012., www.nytimes.com/2012/06/28/us
   /presidential-election-could-reshape-an-aging-supreme-court.html?_r=0.

9. Avik Roy, "CBO: Obamacare Will Spend More, Tax More, and Reduce
   the Deficit Less Than We Previously Thought," *Forbes*, July 27, 2012, www
   .forbes.com/sites/theapothecary/2012/07/27/cbo-obamacare-will-spend
   -more-tax-more-and-reduce-the-deficit-less-than-we-previously-thought.

10. Senator Sam Brownback, *Are Health Care Reform Costs Reliable?* (Wash-
    ington, DC: Joint Economic Committee, July 31, 2009), http://www.jec
    .senate.gov/public/_cache/files/5802c84c-e821-4ab3-baeb-793f3ae2e036
    /are-health-care-reform-cost-estimates-reliable-july-31-2009.pdf.

11. "Summary of P.L. 98-21 (H.R. 1900) Social Security Amendments of
    1983," Social Security Administration—Office of Legislation & Congres-
    sional Affairs, signed on April 20, 1983, originally prepared November 26,
    1984, https://www.ssa.gov/history/1983amend.html.

12. Bruce Bartlett, "The 81% Tax Increase," *Forbes*, May 15, 2009, www.forbes
    .com/2009/05/14/taxes-social-security-opinions-columnists-medicare.html.

Chapter 16: Reforming the Fed:
The Right Way to Take Back Control of Our Money

1. "74% Want to Audit the Federal Reserve," Rasmussen Reports, November 8, 2013, www.rasmussenreports.com/public_content/business/general
   _business/november_2013/74_want_to_audit_the_federal_reserve.

2. Ellen Brown, "Revive Lincoln's Monetary Policy: An Open Letter to President Obama," *The Web of Debt*, April 8, 2009, http://www.webofdebt.com
   /articles/lincoln_obama.php.

3. Robert F. Bruner and Sean D. Carr, *The Panic of 1907: Lessons Learned from the Market's Perfect Storm* (Hoboken, NJ: John Wiley & Sons, 2007).

4. "Federal Reserve System, The First 100 Years: A Chapter in the History of Central Banking," Federal Reserve Bank of Philadelphia, October 2014, https://www.philadelphiafed.org/-/media/publications/economic-education/first-100-years.pdf?la=en. See also: Tyler E. Bagwell, "The Jekyll Island duck hunt that created the Federal Reserve," Jekyll Island History, www.jekyllislandhistory.com/federalreserve.shtml.

5. *Presidential Documents: Executive Order 6102 — Requiring Gold Coin, Gold Bullion, and Gold Certificates to Be Delivered to the Government* (Washington, DC: US Government Publishing Office, April 5, 1933), https://www.goldline.com/images/conf-order.pdf. See also: Gerhard Peters and John T. Woolley, The American Presidency Project, http://www.presidency.ucsb.edu/ws/?pid=14611.

6. Barry Eichengreen, *Exorbitant Privilege: The Rise and Fall of the Dollar and the Future of the International Monetary System* (New York: Oxford University Press, 2011).

7. *S.2665—An Act . . . to permit United States citizens to purchase, hold, sell, or otherwise deal with gold in the United States or abroad,* Public Law 93-373, 93rd Cong. (August 14, 1974), https://www.congress.gov/bill/93rd-congress/senate-bill/2665. See also: US Government Publishing Office, https://www.gpo.gov/fdsys/pkg/STATUTE-88/pdf/STATUTE-88-Pg445.pdf.

8. Z.1 *Financial Accounts of the United States,* Historical Data (Washington, DC: Federal Reserve Statistical Release, updated December 10, 2015), http://www.federalreserve.gov/releases/z1/current/data.htm.

9. *Minutes of the Federal Open Market Committee* (Washington, DC: Federal Reserve Board, September 24, 1996), http://www.federalreserve.gov/fomc/minutes/19960924.htm.

Chapter 17: America Is a Cause, Not Just a Country

1. Alexis de Tocqueville, *Democracy in America and Two Essays on America,* trans. Gerald E. Bevan, intro and notes by Isaac Kramnick (London: Penguin Books, 2003).

2. "Most Voters Expect Biased News Coverage of 2016 Presidential Race," Rasmussen Reports, May 21, 2015, www.rasmussenreports.com/public_content/politics/general_politics/may_2015/most_voters_expect_biased_news_coverage_of_2016_presidential_race.

3. Jon Clifton, "150 Million Adults Worldwide Would Migrate to the U.S.," Gallup, April 20, 2012, www.gallup.com/poll/153992/150-million-adults -worldwide-migrate.aspx. See also: Jose A. DelReal, "GOP candidates condemn Planned Parenthood shooting but dismiss link to antiabortion rhetoric," *Washington Post*, November 29, 2015, https://www.washingtonpost .com/news/post-politics/wp/2015/11/29/gop-candidates-condemn-planned -parenthood-shooting-but-dismiss-link-to-antiabortion-rhetoric.

4. *CAF World Giving Index 2015*, Charities Aid Foundation, November 2015, http://www.cafamerica.org/wp-content/uploads/1755A_WGI2015 _Report_WEB_V2_FINAL.pdf.

5. *2013 Survey of Consumer Finances (SCF) Chartbook*, Federal Reserve, September 2, 2014, http://www.federalreserve.gov/econresdata/scf/files/ BulletinCharts.pdf.

6. Joyce Dargay, Dermot Gately, and Martin Sommer, "Vehicle Ownership and Income Growth, Worldwide: 1960–2030," January 2007, Dept. of Economics, New York University, http://www.econ.nyu.edu/dept/courses /gately/DGS_Vehicle%20Ownership_2007.pdf.

7. The Editors of *Encyclopaedia Britannica*, "Marshall Plan," *Encyclopaedia Britannica*, June 9, 2015, http://www.britannica.com/event/Marshall-Plan.

8. *Inaugural Addresses of the Presidents of the United States* (Washington, DC: US Government Publishing Office, October 1993), http://www .bartleby.com/124/pres32.html.

ABOUT THE AUTHOR

LAWRENCE B. LINDSEY'S career has spanned government, business, and academia. He served three presidents: Ronald Reagan, as senior staff economist for tax policy at the Council of Economic Advisers; George H. W. Bush, as special assistant for domestic economic policy; and George W. Bush, as director of the National Economic Council. He was a governor of the Federal Reserve System from 1991 to 1997; managing director of consulting group Economic Strategies from 1997 to 2001; and has been CEO of the Lindsey Group, a global consulting firm, since 2003. Lindsey received his AB magna cum laude from Bowdoin College and his master's and PhD from Harvard University, where he became a professor. He received the National Tax Association Outstanding Doctoral Dissertation Award in 1985, was named Citicorp/Wriston Fellow at the Manhattan Institute, and is a scholar at the American Enterprise Institute.